EFFECTIVE LEARNING AND MENTAL WELLBEING

Research shows that by improving the wellbeing of learners, we also improve their learning. *Effective Learning and Mental Wellbeing* is a crucial resource, filled with ready-to-use and thought-provoking activities that support wellbeing within your school, college, organisation, community group or on your own. Woven throughout are ideas and activities that support learning and wellbeing for many different kinds of learner.

Supported by well-researched content, this essential book will enrich and improve both the wellbeing and the learning of all who use it. Areas covered include but are not limited to:

- How we learn and blocks to learning
- Mental health and self-efficacy
- Positive steps to mental wellbeing
- Wellbeing in the connected learning community
- The future of wellbeing and learning

This book is an essential resource for teachers, therapists, health professionals, parents or carers and those in the community who work to improve learning through improving wellbeing.

Sarah Philo is a cognitive behavioural therapist working with people experiencing difficulties including depression, anxiety and post-traumatic stress disorder (PTSD). She is especially interested in the role of compassion both in supporting positive wellbeing and in creating supportive and safe places to learn. She is undergoing training to also practice as an eye movement desensitisation and reprocessing (EMDR) therapist.

John Senior is a visiting researcher at the Institute for Cognitive Neuroscience and Psychology of the Hungarian Academy. His research concerns the impact of mental health issues affecting Human Intelligence (HI) and the potential psychodynamic mental health issues of Gifted Artificial Intelligent Machines (GAIM).

EFFECTIVE LEARNING AND MENTAL WELLBEING

Improving the Mental Health and Trauma-Resilience of Learners in a Trauma-Impacted World

Sarah Philo and John Senior

Taylor & Francis Group
LONDON AND NEW YORK

Designed cover image: © Getty Images

First published 2024
by Routledge
4 Park Square, Milton Park, Abingdon, Oxon OX14 4RN

and by Routledge
605 Third Avenue, New York, NY 10158

Routledge is an imprint of the Taylor & Francis Group, an informa business

© 2024 Sarah Philo and John Senior

The right of Sarah Philo and John Senior to be identified as authors of this work has been asserted in accordance with sections 77 and 78 of the Copyright, Designs and Patents Act 1988.

All rights reserved. No part of this book may be reprinted or reproduced or utilised in any form or by any electronic, mechanical, or other means, now known or hereafter invented, including photocopying and recording, or in any information storage or retrieval system, without permission in writing from the publishers.

Trademark notice: Product or corporate names may be trademarks or registered trademarks, and are used only for identification and explanation without intent to infringe.

British Library Cataloguing-in-Publication Data
A catalogue record for this book is available from the British Library

ISBN: 978-1-032-35413-2 (hbk)
ISBN: 978-1-032-35414-9 (pbk)
ISBN: 978-1-003-32678-6 (ebk)

DOI: 10.4324/9781003326786

Typeset in Sabon
by KnowledgeWorks Global Ltd.

To our families and to all those who walk the same path as, and draw on the inspiration of, John Holt (1923–1985).

CONTENTS

List of figures   *xiii*
List of tables   *xiv*
Foreword   *xv*
Acknowledgements   *xvii*
Disclaimer   *xviii*
About the authors   *xix*
Preface   *xx*

    Introduction   1

    Going further 6
    References 7
    Further reading 7

1 Everybody is a learner   8

    How do learners learn? 10
      Exploring their senses 12
      Learning about patterns 12
      Understanding cause and effect 12
      Imitation 12
    Types of learners 16
    Learning styles 17
    "VARK" 18

*Thinking about learning, wellbeing and
   self-actualisation 18
   Socrates 18
   Freud 19
   B.F. Skinner 19
   Abraham Maslow 19
   Benjamin Bloom 21
   Carl Rogers and the path to personal growth 21
   Fritz Perls's Gestalt approach to individual and
      organisational change 24
Stages of cognitive development 25
Lev Vygotsky 26
Applied skills for twenty-first century living, working
   and learning: a proposed menu 29
Where do people learn? 30
What prevents learners learning? 30
Going further – extended learning 34
Notes 34
References 35
Further reading 36*

2 Mental health and self-efficacy   38

 Activities
  1. *Maximise your memory 40
    Going further 41*
  2. *Managing anxiety to boost your self-efficacy 42
    Going further 45*
  3. *Perfectionism and procrastination 46
    Going further 48*
  4. *Visualisation: your ideal learning supporter 50
    Going further 51*
  5. *Distress tolerance and emotional regulation
    skills 53
    Going further 59*
  6. *How to value you for you and not just for what
    you achieve: human beings not human doings 60
    Going further 64*
  7. *Assertiveness 65
    Going further 68*
  8. *Approach/avoid awareness: goal orientation theory
    and your learning 69
    Going further 72*

9. Thinking styles 75
   Going further 77
10. Self-esteem and self-efficacy 79
    Going further 81

3 Steps to mental wellbeing   82
   Activities
   1. Sleep 84
      Going further 88
   2. Exercise 89
      Going further 91
   3. Eat 92
      Going further 93
   4. Relax 95
      Going further 102
   5. Managing anxiety 103
      Going further 108
   6. Keeping perspective 110
      Going further 112
   7. Rest 113
      Going further 115
   8. Connect with others and give to others 117
      Going further 119
   9. Building a positive self-image 121
      Going further 122
   10. Meditation and mindfulness 123
       Going further 124

4 Wellbeing in the connected learning community   127
   Activities
   1. Emergent properties of connected learning communities: what will we create by learning together? 130
      Going further 131
   2. Distress tolerance and emotional regulation skills in groups 132
      Going further 134
   3. Making a safe place to learn 135
      Going further 135
   4. Active listening 137
      Going further 139

5. Take a wellbeing walk together 140
   Going further 142
6. Thinking together: TASC 144
   Going further 144
7. Getting through, together: depersonalising resilience 146
   Going further 147
8. Empathy and compassion 148
   Going further 149
9. Combatting dark learning 150
   Going further 153
10. Values based living and learning in the connected learning community 155
    Going further 155

5 Wellbeing and learning in a COVID-impacted world   157
   Activities
   1. What have we learned from remote learning? 160
      Going further 161
   2. Grief and loss: what was and what is 162
      Going further: post-traumatic growth 163
   3. Anxiety management in a COVID-aware world 166
      Going further 168
   4. Brain fog and Long COVID: strategies for learning 170
      Going further 173
   5. Motivation: finding it, reviving it 174
      Going further 178
   6. Spoons theory: a way of understanding the impact of low energy levels with Long COVID 179
      Going further 179
   7. Building new ways of learning 181
      Going further 182
   8. Where do you want to go? Where do we want to go? 184
      Going further 185
   9. Coping with and managing change 186
      Going further 189
   10. Letter (or time capsule) to the future 190
       Going further 191

Contents **xi**

6 Wellbeing and learning on your own 192
   Activities
   1. *Choosing your learning path 193*
      Going further 194
   2. *Self-directed learning – where (and how) do I start? 195*
      Going further 202
   3. *Information overload – finding your focus in an information-rich world 203*
      Going further 206
   4. *Looking after you: from self-criticism to being your own supportive learning coach 207*
      Going further 208
   5. *Your health and wellbeing wheel 209*
      Going further 209
   6. *Who is on your learning and wellbeing support team? 211*
      Going further 212
   7. *Self-compassion to support your learning and wellbeing 213*
      Going further 213
   8. *Positive learner data log 215*
      Going further 216
   9. *Values based living – and values based learning 217*
      Going further 218
   10. *… and breathe 219*
       Going further 220

7 The future of wellbeing and learning – your impact on the world 222
   Activities
   1. *Time for a learning-wellbeing rethink? 232*
      Going further 236
   2. *Modelling and passing it on 238*
      Going further 239
   3. *Making a friend of uncertainty 241*
      Going further 243
   4. *Going beyond problem-solving 245*
      Going further with the yes, no or mu game: wellbeing 247

5. Wellbeing and learning online: from trauma machine to a more wellbeing-supportive social media environment? 250
  Going further 251
6. How can we manage eco-grief and eco-anxiety? 252
  Going further 253
7. Your future mental health and wellbeing: what would you like the future to hold for you? 254
  Going further 255
8. The wellbeing of the natural world 256
  Going further 257
9. Measuring progress – and taking the pressure off 259
  Going further 260
10. Reflections of impact: making sense of ripples 261
  Going further 263

8 Learning to be well   265

The complete learner 265
Mental competency 267
  Medical definition of mental capacity 267
Gillick competency and Fraser guidelines 268
  Child protection concerns 268
  Personal and institutional liability 269
  Collective responsibility for well learning 269
  Additional factors to consider 270
Going further 270
  Remember 271
References 271
Note 272
Further reading 272
Further viewing 272

Appendix: A guide to online mental health, wellbeing and learning provision   273
Afterword   277
Glossary   280
Index   283

FIGURES

1.1	Baby learners	12
1.2	Piaget's four stages of development	25
1.3	Anxiety disorders in children (NHS, 2022, www.nhs.uk)	32
2.1	Assertiveness communication style	65
5.1	Long COVID	173
5.2	My learning map	177
5.3	Capture COVID thoughts	184

TABLES

1.1	Schein: approaches to learning	14
1.2	Learning styles: summary	17
1.3	VARK learning styles	18
1.4	Physical, psychological and emotional barriers to learning	30
2.1	Anxiety and self-efficacy	44
2.2	Perfectionist beliefs	48
2.3	Perfectionistic behaviours	48
2.4	Communication continuum	66
2.5	Learning and avoidance behaviours	71
2.6	Learning behaviours	72
2.7	Diary reflection	73
2.8	Thinking styles	75
2.9	Thinking styles activity	78
3.1	Sleep and dream diary	85
3.2	Impacts of anxiety on learning and wellbeing	104
3.3	Three threat model	115
3.4	Current life	118
3.5	Positive data log: reflect on the evidence and information	122
4.1	Learning setting	133
5.1	Changes	163
6.1	Tasks (i)	199
6.2	Tasks (ii)	200
6.3	Positive learner data log: reflect on the evidence and information	215
7.1	How to solve it	248

FOREWORD

Improve wellbeing and you improve learning.

This book is, we hope, a mixture of ideas, activities and content with the central belief that good wellbeing supports good learning and vice versa. We hope this is a book you will enjoy and find useful as a resource, whether you are working to support others with their learning and wellbeing, or seeking ways to support your own learning and wellbeing, or, of course, both of these! Presenting ready-to-use thought-provoking wellbeing activities, and content supported by research, this book will, we hope, support and enrich both the wellbeing and the learning of all who use it. We hope this book will have relevance to you whether you are new to the world and possibilities of learning and wellbeing, or you have been working on supporting others with their learning and wellbeing for some time.

We also hope this book offers some practical and thought-provoking activities that are relevant to the learning and wellbeing needs of a range of learners: children, young people and adults and both learners and those who support learners (whilst also of course being learners themselves).

Good mental health is important for everyone, everywhere, and goes beyond the absence of a mental health condition. Good mental health is integral to our physical as well as our emotional wellbeing, enabling us to realise our full potential, to show resilience in adversity, to be productive across the various situations and activities of daily life, to form meaningful relationships and to contribute to our communities and our world. Promoting and protecting mental health is critical to a well-functioning society. It fosters social capital and solidarity, which are essential during times of crisis (World Health Organization, 2022). We acknowledge that whilst the activities within this book often take an individual focus, there are physical, psychological, social, cultural, spiritual and other interrelated factors that contribute to mental health, that there are inseparable links between mental and physical health and that the importance of the communities and the society around us to the individual wellbeing of us all is inestimable. We are not alone in our striving for good wellbeing, nor should we be; we need to make a collective effort. We hope this book, along with the way you make use of it, can be a part of that.

Reference

World Health Organization. (2022). Mental health. https://www.who.int/westernpacific/health-topics/mental-health#tab=tab_1

ACKNOWLEDGEMENTS

Our sincere thanks to Bruce Roberts, Senior Commissioning Editor at Routledge – Taylor & Francis. Our thanks also to Lauren Redhead and Molly Selby, Editorial Assistants at Routledge – Taylor & Francis for their generous, professional, thoughtful and patient support.

DISCLAIMER

Please note that we cannot make any guarantees about the results of the application of the information, ideas and concepts within this book. We happily share ideas, further reading, educational and informational resources here that are intended to help you succeed in meeting the needs of the learners you seek to support and guide, including yourself, the active, participant learner-reader. The outcomes of your and others' interaction with and application of the materials in this book will be affected by many variables, not limited to the situation you are working in, the support around you, the time available and many other contextual factors. As Leonardo da Vinci, as quoted by Richter (2018), observes, we should always keep in mind that everything connects to everything else. We would encourage engaging with the following with a curious, open mind, with the willingness to try out ideas and with compassion for yourself – and others.

Reference

Richter, J.P. (2018). The Literary Works of Leonardo da Vinci; Volume 1. Franklin Classics Trade Press.

ABOUT THE AUTHORS

Sarah Philo is a cognitive behavioural therapist working with people who are experiencing difficulties including depression, anxiety and PTSD. She is especially interested in the value of compassion towards others and self, both in supporting positive wellbeing and in creating supportive and safe places to learn. She is currently undergoing training to also practice as an eye movement desensitisation and reprocessing (EMDR) therapist.

John Senior is a visiting researcher at the Institute for Cognitive Neuroscience and Psychology of the Hungarian Academy. Lecturer and Creative. Publications include "AI and Developing Human Intelligence" (Senior & Gyarmathy, 2022) and enrichment activities that stimulate independent thinking. His research concerns the impact of mental health issues affecting Human Intelligence (HI) and potential psychodynamic mental health issues of Gifted Artificial Intelligent Machines (GAIM).

Reference

Senior, J., & Gyarmathy, É. (2022). *AI and developing human intelligence: Future learning and educational innovation*. Routledge.

PREFACE

It has never been more important to support learners and learning than it is now. There can rarely have been such a range of challenges and pressures facing us whereby we need to have well informed and active learners in respect to the challenges our world community faces. The effects of the COVID pandemic, both social and economic, and conflicts in recent years have created sudden and profound disruptions to the process of learning for many, as well as having profound impacts on collective wellbeing. Both learning and wellbeing were already under pressure from a range of situations including social and demographic pressures, political developments and the escalating climate crisis. There is therefore a pressing need to provide support to learning institutions and organisations including schools and colleges and to individual learners in a range of settings both formal and informal. This support needs to be both novel and accessible, rather than simply a reiteration of existing approaches, to reflect the ruptures to business-as-usual that recent years have brought and the immediate future will continue to create. Without a novel approach, we as learners, and as those who support learners, will struggle to address the many challenges we are facing now and will face in the years to come.

This book takes an interconnected and comprehensive approach to understanding wellbeing and learning; considering learning and wellbeing to be interlinked, symbiotic and interdependent processes, where each supports the other. It will consider how an understanding of the importance of emotional safety, the impact of trauma, living a valued life and compassion for self and for others is vital for beneficial learning, both as individuals and as interconnected learning networks, whether formal or informal. It will present these understandings as also vital for the support and well-functioning of those who support learners, as teachers, lecturers, therapists or other learning facilitators.

We are living through a mental health and wellbeing crisis. A range of concurrent and intersecting events, including the escalating climate crisis, the pandemic, international conflict and their associated developing pressures on resources and health and social structures, and significant social, technological and political changes are together creating a developing crisis on multiple fronts. This crisis is impacting civil society and the public sphere, education, employment and all of us on an individual basis. It is not surprising that, as a result, the mental health and wellbeing of so many people is suffering; indeed, it would be more surprising were these interlinked crises not making a significant negative impact.

The need to understand the severity of the wellbeing crisis and to provide ways of addressing it is acute and will become more so in the future. A society needs good mental health as an absolute foundation for everything it does; without this, everything falters. This book supports the idea that the ability of a society to learn and develop is deeply reliant on the wellbeing of its members. It provides both an exploration of what wellbeing is and requires and what learning is and requires. The book explores the research and theoretical background to our current understanding of both wellbeing and learning to set these concepts in context. It offers the chance for educators, researchers, individual learners and groups or networks of learners both informal and formal, institutional and organisational to consider how we best learn and what we need to do to support our own and others' wellbeing. It also provides tools for improving and maintaining wellbeing as part of becoming a successful and thriving learner, even in the challenging times that are around and ahead of us all; if the only way out is through, then this book offers a map and guide for making the journey.

Not every aspect of learning is discussed in this book. We as both researchers and practitioners have chosen to present ideas and information, making decisions as to what will help you as a practitioner in your own field of specialism. We also hope to promote your curiosity to extend your own skills and knowledge through pursuing ideas within the text and through the recommended reading offered related to each activity.

Woven into this book are theories, stories and good practice activities for use by professionals working in the field of wellbeing in schools, tertiary education, training, talking therapies (Psychological Wellbeing Practitioners, CBT therapists and counsellors); those working with parents and carers at home; and others in therapeutic settings and the wider community. Learners can enjoy and be stimulated by a wide range of activities which reflect excellent wellbeing professional practice.

INTRODUCTION

The nature of learning is changing. What it means to be a learner has changed. What it means to be a teacher has also changed, and this is impacting those who make up learning communities including educationalists, psychologists and therapists. The rapid developments in the field of artificial intelligence (AI) are integral components of continuous accelerated change; we swim in this new sea of change.

Understanding the future of learning is in part having a recognition of the reality that we are all now potentially learner and teacher, client and therapist, and co-creators of what we know and what we need to learn. These changes are with us now and will continue without a pause or interruption, continuing to shape the age of new learning.

This book is part of this changing learning environment: a book for educationalists to enable, support and reflect on their own needs as learners and the needs of other learners within the learning community; this book also addresses the needs of therapists and counsellors as we all, together, seek and explore ways to assist the learner-client. "Wellbeing improves students' academic performance, behaviour, social integration, and satisfaction. Wellbeing improves teachers' ability to interact with students, teach concepts, face challenges, and avoid burnout" (Teacher Wellbeing, 2022)."Education doesn't make us smarter. It makes us whole" (Biden, 2018).

Each chapter of this book opens with an introduction to the content of the chapter, suggestions as to how to use the content and factors to consider related to the chapter theme. Each chapter then offers ten activities which can be used independently or in the order presented, as you feel appropriate for the age of learner or learners you are working with and their specific needs. We have taken the view that the ideas, activities and thinking in this book can travel across from the adult learner-client to a much younger learner-client. We have aimed to produce a resource that is not necessarily age specific but more a book of ideas and experiences which can be used directly or be the seed for adapted thinking and use in different learning settings.

We have not aimed the activities at a particular subject area or teacher area of responsibility normally found in schools. This book is a book of things to think about and things to do to promote learning and wellbeing.

Each activity is designed to be free-standing and to fit in with the needs of an educationalist-therapist programme or to fit in with the needs of an individual self-directed learner.

Resources required for presenting and running a particular activity are provided or suggested as an integral part of the activities. The resources required for many of the activities will be entirely dependent on the direction the user of the activity wishes to take it in.

Each activity includes a "going further" section which are intended to offer the reader ideas for taking activities and projects further. These extended activities and ideas are also designed to help embed and empower the reader's knowledge, skill and ambition to further study a particular area of study and/or to create activities of their own. Learning is not a straight track railway line but an infinitely branching series of possibilities!

Now we can begin. First let's look at the essentials. The following are key concepts to keep in mind in relation to the approach and ideas found throughout this book.

Cognitive behavioural therapy (CBT) is a talking therapy that can help you manage your problems by changing the way you think and behave. It is most used to treat anxiety and depression but can be useful for other mental and physical health problems, which can be experienced by many learners. CBT is at the heart of this book. CBT developed during the twentieth century from behaviour therapy and cognitive therapy and has combined elements of both approaches into a therapy taking a psycho-social approach to wellbeing and to understanding the difficulties we can experience with our wellbeing.

- **Learning and wellbeing**: what it is:
  Learning, n. the act of gaining knowledge (Collins, 2022).

Wellbeing, n. healthy, contended, or prosperous condition; moral or physical welfare (Oxford English Dictionary, 1993).

Without a secure sense of wellbeing, learning how to be a successful, whole, self-managing person will not take place in a free and positive way.

- The wellbeing prime directive
  To recognise the importance of beginning with the assumption that the individual is best placed to judge the individual's wellbeing (GOV.UK, 2022).
- How to embrace this book and apply it to improving learning wellbeing

Many readers will be familiar with some of the material in this book relating to learning styles and learning pedagogic thought. Other readers in the therapist community will be able to reference the content to inform their judgement and professional expertise when working with learners. This book is a reference and a guide to action for supporting learners develop and secure their learning wellbeing. We have chosen to include the essentials of educational mainstream thinking and the occasional eccentric bonus glimpse of otherwise thinking.

- Technical – the CBT model, wellbeing and learning

The CBT model is grounded in the idea that our cognitions are central to how we feel and act. It considers that some ways of thinking can lead to responses that contribute to good wellbeing and others to poor wellbeing. It explores the sense we make of situations through our thoughts (cognitions), our linked emotions and somatic experiences and how we then respond and behave in response.

For example:

Situation: something happens to us: a situation, an event, an occurrence
Thoughts: we interpret the situation in a particular way (positive/negative/neutral) via thoughts and sense-making/meaning making processes
Feelings: our cognitive responses lead to us experiencing emotions (positive/negative/neutral)
Physical sensations: the above thoughts and feelings can be accompanied by a physical sensation or sensations
Behaviours: we then act, respond and behave in response to the above interconnected factors, in different ways: helpful, unhelpful, harmful, positive and negative, depending on what sense we've made of the situation.

The Beck Institute, founded in 1994 by Dr Aaron Beck and Dr Judith Beck, describes CBT as follows:

> CBT is based on the theory that the way individuals perceive a situation is more closely connected to their reaction than the situation itself.

Individuals' perceptions are often distorted and unhelpful, particularly when they are distressed. Cognitive Behavior Therapy helps people identify their distressing thoughts and evaluate how realistic the thoughts are. Then they learn to change their distorted thinking. When they think more realistically, they feel better. The emphasis is also consistently on solving problems and initiating behavioral changes.

CBT can be regarded as a model of resolving biased or otherwise inaccurate thinking when it contributes to us feeling unhappy, distressed or otherwise emotionally discomforted. It might ask us to work towards seeing things "as they are" rather than through a prism of our assumptions, biases and other distorting factors. To be able, for example, to see the glass rather than either half full (great!) or half empty (bad!), as simply containing 300 ml of water.

The thoughts, emotions and behaviours that arise following a person's perception of a situation when it is perceived in an unhelpful way can form a vicious cycle that maintains a problematic or distressing reaction, with the interpretations of all factors within the cycle often triggering further negative thoughts, emotions, somatic experiences and responses.

CBT seeks to help us understand and make sense of the cognitive, emotional, behavioural cycles we may be unhelpfully caught up in and then to seek what options there might be for changing these unhelpful cycles into more helpful ones that promote and boost our wellbeing rather than keep us stuck in feeling bad.

- The biopsychosocial model

    The biopsychosocial model helps us understand:
    - What influences mental health?
    - Why does one person have poor mental health?
    - Why does one person have good mental health?
    - What triggers poor mental health episodes?
    - What are the core reasons for poor mental health?

- The learning-wellbeing champion

The NHS People Plan outlines an ambition to enable NHS organisations to create cultures of wellbeing across their organisations, through encouraging wellbeing conversations and the introduction of networks of health and wellbeing champions.

Health and wellbeing champions are individuals who work at all levels of the NHS, from all demographics and roles, who will promote, identify, and signpost their colleagues to local and national health and wellbeing support offers supporting colleagues with their emotional wellbeing (NHS, 2020).

Drawing on this idea, a learning-wellbeing champion could be an individual who will work at all levels where learning and wellbeing embrace each other as active forces supporting the learning and wellbeing of all learners – educationalists and therapists coming together to listen and advise. A champion promotes in an informed way the learning-wellbeing philosophy where listening comes first.

- CFT self-compassion (Gilbert model)

Compassion Focused Therapy (CFT) is a method of understanding human difficulties such as the self-to-self relationship, examining how our personal history can sensitise our threat system. CFT recognises that types of relationships such as self-critical, harsh, punishing behaviours can create vicious cycles, whereby current fears and threats are magnified to a debilitating and painful level. CFT formulation is designed to help clients to understand and adopt safety strategies used to manage their fears, and to challenge, from a place of safety, unintended consequences of certain fear management strategies.

CFT seeks to help clients and therapists come to a compassion-informed and de-shaming understanding of the client's life and experiences (CFT, 2022).

- The impact of poor wellbeing on learning potential

Poor wellbeing has a huge impact on our ability to learn. Before successful and meaningful learning can take place, we need to have a healthy diet, healthy sleep and emotional equity. We need to feel secure and have a clear view as to our place in the world and our relationship with others and our larger communities.

- Why and how wellbeing is important to boost effective learning

Poor learning conditions such as inadequate or unsafe physical infrastructure combined with a corrupted sense of wellbeing experienced by the learner is likely to have a lasting effect, whereas learning in a supportive environment blended with a co-mutual sense of mental security and continuous attention to the welfare of all learners makes effective learning more likely. Learning-wellbeing is a complimentary human state of enriching learning and mental health for an individual to become and remain an effective learner and an emotionally secure learner.

- Co-production/co-creation of wellbeing and learning

The challenge to create a learning and wellbeing partnership response needs to be met through active interventions. Educationalists-therapists and learners need to be encouraged to recognise the immense value of working together. Learning without wellbeing is a bird without wings.

- What we have learned:
  - We have learned to doubt our self-worth, seeing the validation of ourselves through means external to our sense of a strong and resilient self.
  - If the purpose of education is to turn learners into fully functional, happy and healthy adults, this aspiration is failing on numerous levels.
  - We have learned because of the enormous challenge of home-online learning during COVID lockdowns that:
    On-line learning is not a subset or analogue of face-to-face learning: it is different, can be better and, like all learning, is complex to get right. There are no "must dos" here. No "right way to do it" (Hepple, 2020).
  - Around 20% of the world's children and adolescents have a mental health condition, with suicide the second leading cause of death among an age range of 15- to 29-year-olds. Approximately one in five people in post-conflict settings have a mental health condition.

It is urgent that we find ways to address, in any way possible, the mental health crisis that is reducing learners' ability to learn through a commitment to building and supporting wellbeing communities.

- What we could learn to be through developing learner wellbeing

CBT is a well-established method of treatment for many mental health conditions. Many of the skills and strategies provided by addressing wellbeing are of use both in the short and long term. CBT therapies operate and are applicable to the experiences of client-learners. There is a pressing need to address both the needs of the learner as a learner, and the needs of the learner as a whole person seeking to become fully themselves. A whole functioning person needs good wellbeing to learn, and needs to learn to have good wellbeing. CBT strategies can support the individual learner-client to develop the confidence and skills to own their individual learning ambitions, to succeed as a learner, and to become a contributor to their learning communities.

Going further

In a similar way to the Biopsychosocial Model of Mental Health (Delphis, 2019) presenting, enriching and using the ideas covered in this introduction suggest many issues need to be addressed. To address these, it's likely you will need to work with others. Here are some questions to consider:

- Who is already working with you and thinking like you to deliver a learner-wellbeing offer? Who is already a fellow traveller on your team?
- Who do you need to add to your team to explore and deliver a learner-wellbeing offer?

References

Biden, J. (2018). Cubberley Lecture, 9th May 2018, Stanford Graduate School of Education.
CFT: Psychology Tools. (2022). CFT compassion formulation. https://www.psychologytools.com/resource/cft-compassion-formulation/
Collins. (2022). Learning. https://www.collinsdictionary.com/dictionary/english/learning
Delphis. (2019). The biopsychosocial model of mental health. https://delphis.org.uk/mental-health/the-biopsychosocial-model-of-mental-health/
GOV.UK. (2022, September 2). Care and support statutory guidance. https://www.gov.uk/government/publications/care-act-statutory-guidance/care-and-support-statutory-guidance#chapter-1
Hepple, S. (2020). http://heppell.net/lol/
New Zealand Teaching Council. https://teachingcouncil.nz/resource-centre/teacher-wellbeing/
NHS. (2020). England. https://www.england.nhs.uk/supporting-our-nhs-people/health-and-wellbeing-programmes/health-and-wellbeing-champions/
Teacher Wellbeing. (2022). Teacher Wellbeing Index 2022: www.educationsupport.org.uk/news-and-events/news/teacher-wellbeing-index-2022-record-numbers-plan-to-leave-profession-as-mental-health-suffers/

Further reading

Feltham, C., & Dryden, W. (1993). *Dictionary of counselling*. Whurr Publishers.
Gilbert, P. (2010). Training our minds in, with and for compassion: An introduction to concepts and compassion-focused exercises. https://www.getselfhelp.co.uk/docs/GILBERT-COMPASSION-HANDOUT.pdf
Greenberger, D., & Padesky, C. (1995). *Mind over mood: Changing how you feel by changing the way you think*. Guilford.
Seligman, L. (2006). *Theories of counselling and psychotherapy: Systems, strategies, and skills*. Pearson Prentice Hall.
Sousa, D. A., & Tomlinson, C. A. (2011). *Differentiation and the brain: How neuroscience supports the learner-friendly classroom*. Solution Tree Press.
Tomlinson, C. A. (2021). *So each may soar: The principles and practices of learner-centered classrooms*. ASCD.
Wills, F. (2022). *Beck's cognitive therapy: Distinctive features*. Routledge. (Original work published 2009)

1
EVERYBODY IS A LEARNER

Helping people to think and listen to their own voice is surely the aim of all educationalists and therapists. Helping people to listen and listening to what client-learners want to achieve is a perfect way for teachers to present the agenda they are tasked with delivering and for the therapist to help the learning client establish their own self-learning identity. The aim of the educationalist and therapist is clear; addressing learning and wellbeing so that the client-learner becomes empowered and can achieve free and critical thinking, then confidence as a learner; in this way, they support the client-learner to become a confident and complete person.

All problems faced by learners are not guaranteed to be resolved, they will however be better understood and become immensely more manageable by a learner who understands their own needs. These needs are likely to include removing barriers to learning and building a sense of wellbeing. By remaining secure in their ability to be curious about the lives they are living and learning about, a learner can grow and become a mature and an able learner.

We live in an all-embracing inescapable state of crisis both at an intimate level and as a collective, local and world community. A learning mind when faced with incomprehensible stupidity in the world will have many questions to ask and many fears and anxieties to address. We as teachers and therapists will just have to humbly accept certain questions; we cannot answer them ourselves. We can as teachers, therapists and learners however set the example of how we negotiate the puzzlement in our existence, past, present, future and our purpose in existing when poverty, illness, mental health issues and injustice are commonplace in the world. We can in other words, as Sternberg (2022) reminds us, keep our focus as teachers, therapists and learners on supporting those learning acquisitions in each other that are most likely to help to achieve a collective common good.

Shifts in learning are increasingly redefining what it means to be intelligent. The future focus of learning will be on developing both an understanding of technology and, importantly, the expansion of the human learner's ability to be creative, curious and conscientiously tenacious. The learner's key task will be one of synthesising a complex world in which learning is applied as breathing is to keep us alive and functioning (Senior & Gyarmathy, 2022).

Learners learn through listening – not just listening to what the teacher-therapist says but by the listening to the learner that the teacher-lecturer-therapist-counsellor does. When the voice of the learner is very quiet, just a whisper or even mute, we should strive to listen skilfully to what is being said in silence as well as at volume. Even silence speaks.

> For it seems to me a fact that, in our struggle to make sense out of life, the things we most need to learn are the things we most want to learn. To put this another way, curiosity is hardly ever idle. What we want to know, we want to know for a reason. The reason is that there is a hole, a gap, an empty space in our understanding of things, our mental model of the world. We feel that gap like a hole in a tooth and we want to fill it up. It makes us ask How? When? Why?
>
> *(Holt, 1977)*

Learners learn by being listened to. Learners learn with ease and enthusiasm when they learn about what interests them, what excites their capacity to both wonder at existence and to be curious about it. The particular focus for committed, enthusiastic learning is not important, what is important is discovering what the learner wants to learn and talk about. It could be that the learner is curious about a moth's attraction to light, bridge-building (the learner, not the moth), the invention of the semi-colon, coat hangers, molluscs[1] or string theory. Teachers and therapists should listen to their student/clients and assist with the individual learner's journey.

Many, if not most, curricula despite the heroic attempts of educationalists are hopelessly out of date, existing with a core belief, that, at the very kindest interpretation, "historic" curriculums, are necessary for the advancement and success of the individual who needs the skills appropriate for the past rather than preparing "self-educators" equipped for the demands of the world now and in the future. The world is changing at an unprecedented rate, and learning as a key component of wellbeing must adapt to a changing, increasingly complex information environment where learning clients are a part of a learning – wellbeing environment.

"As an aspect of a learner's wellbeing addressing spiritual intelligence provides opportunities for them to honor life's most meaningful questions: How can I be effective? Why am I here? Does my life have meaning?" (Sisk, 2002).

Learners want to learn because of a need to satisfy their curiosity about the world, their existence both physically and spiritually in the life they are living.

The importance of listening to a learner-client, young or old, cannot be stressed enough! It is important to listen to how they want to learn and how they would prefer to learn what they want to learn about. Listening and taking seriously the views of the individual learner-client allows for a learning partnership, a relationship of trust and mutual respect to exist. Listening is important.

Listening to the learner and learning about what motivates and excites them is a central aspect of the learner-client embracing the benefits of address their wellbeing. Only through listening will the needs of the learner be established – experiences that encourage learning through a lifetime and the removal or management of emotional issues that may prevent successful learning all need to be addressed. Learning is about change and satisfying the learners insatiable curiosity, satisfying their need to know, understand existence and thereby reducing the anxiety of existing.

Learning can be a challenge because it does involve change requiring tenacity and supportive guidance. Learning requires that a symbiotic relationship be established between the educationalist and the learner both inhabiting the same arena of need; how to find out – how best to answer questions – how to understand and know more – to prepare for all our future lives.

- Learning is tough
- Achieving wellbeing is challenging
- Learning and achieving wellbeing is a therapeutic act
- Read on

How do learners learn?

In the very beginning, baby learners learn to be infant learners who in turn learn to be young maturing learners.

Understanding how babies learn helps us understand how we learn, but it also helps us understand how learning is possible. It helps us understand how any physical system could learn, including both the computers on our desk and the ones in our skulls (Gopnik, 1999).

What Gopnik suggests is that as babies, we learnt to learn as our pre-programmed skills respond and combine with the environmental influences that bathe our early existence as a motivated, driven learner. We evolve into highly efficient learners by a combination of observation and experimentation, establishing research projects, evaluating the results of our experiments and research and then conjoining and synthesising our experiences to make us the natural learner that the human being is supposed to be.

How a baby learner achieves the sophistication of a learner to whom we should listen to is a complex question in that it addresses the disciplines of philosophy, psychology, linguistics, neuroscience, artificial intelligence, biology, medicine and environmental studies.

The growth of the baby learner's brain is influenced by their sense of security, care, new ideas and information; all helping the baby learner's new brain cells connect in ways that help the learner to learn new things.

The baby learner is at the centre of a 360° learning opportunity where the baby learner can learn and progress towards a greater understanding of the environment they learn in. Every sense will be a part of the baby learner's experience. If we listen to the baby learner as they develop into the infant learner, we will very quickly realise that they will interact and respond to others in a clear and increasingly precise way. The baby learner quickly reaches sufficient developed ability to be able to express their own increasingly sophisticated questions about their existence – they seek to understand the environment around them. Life knows what it wants to learn.

A baby is born weighing around 5% of its adult weight, the baby's brain will be around 25% of its final size. By the time a baby reaches three years, the brain will have grown to 80% of its adult size and given a safe learning environment will be a proficient learner (Baby Centre, 2022).

As educator-therapists, we listen and watch, and we learn by listening and watching what it is that the baby learner wants to know about. A baby learner will know how to learn from their directed and undirected interaction with the world they are living in. Parents, older siblings and carers are the earliest educators with a profound influence on the success or otherwise of the baby learner becoming an advanced tenacious, curious, question-driven older learner. Listening is the key to supporting a competent learner who knows what they want to know. The first things a baby learner will learn are the patterns that make up the world they find themselves in, from there they will learn to make sense of the stimulus they are surrounded by and importantly they will also learn how to ask questions. In other words, they will experience the drive to learning called curiosity. This response to patterns is one of the keys to opening the doors to understanding existence.

We know that a baby's brain learns much more quickly than an adult's brain or even an older child's brain. Encouraging the baby learner to learn new things is vital to the development of a natural learning curiosity.

Baby learners use a combination of learning approaches to make sense of the world they experience (Figure 1.1).

12 Everybody is a learner

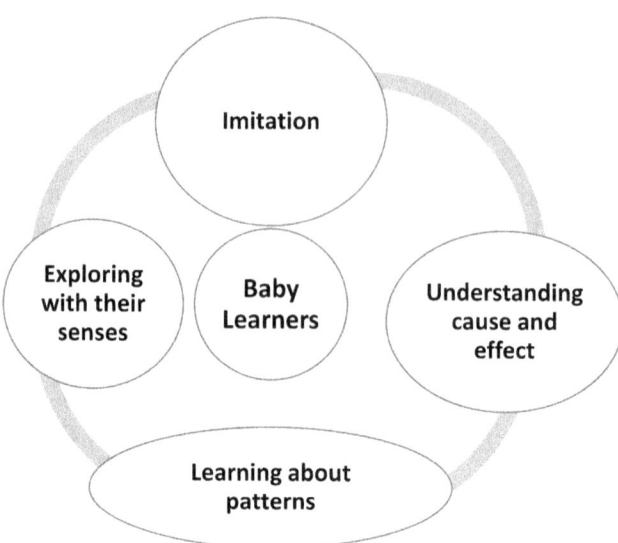

FIGURE 1.1 Baby learners.

Exploring their senses

From birth to around two years, a baby will learn through the senses of touch and taste. Once they can move about more, the baby learner will be able to choose what she/he explores by moving towards or away from certain objects and people.

Learning about patterns

The baby learner learns about patterns in the daily routine of care, remembering cues that help predict what happens next.

Understanding cause and effect

If something nice happens because of actively doing something, the baby learner (as us all) is much more likely to do it again. It can forcibly work the other way too in so much that an unpleasant learning experience can close a potential area of exploration.

Imitation

Like any professional sportsperson or musician – practice makes perfect.

The 10,000-hour rule is a popular idea that when you put 10,000 hours practising deliberately on an activity, you can master it. The psychologist

K. Anders Ericsson (Gladwell, 2009) introduced this number. The 10,000-hour rule argues that anyone can be an expert at an activity or process by committing thousands of hours to becoming highly proficient. It needs to be noted that not all psychologists necessarily support this view – this however does not detract from the general observation he makes. The baby learner has a magic learning combination of devoted and largely uninterrupted, research time and a talent for imitation – the ability to copy activities around them while increasing their understanding of the world (Healthy children, 2022).

As we move from considering the baby/infant learner, we move from the world of encouragement and exploratory growth and research activities of the learner to recognise that learning is pleasurable and rewarding. We also move into a world of pedagogy and epistemology. Before we leave the safe world of simply (mainly) enjoying learning to consider some theories concerned with suggested explanations as to how learners learn, we must not lose sight of the learning pleasure reward.

> It may seem to us that we make up theories of the world because we want explanations, just as it seems to us that we have sex because we want orgasms. From the evolutionary point of view, though, the relationship is the reverse. Orgasms guarantee that we will keep trying to have sex, and our joy in explanation guarantees that we will keep trying to construct better, truer theories of the world. Getting the world right, like having sex, gives us a long-term evolutionary advantage. Drives and emotions turn those long-term advantages into shorter-term motivations. All of us are driven by these cognitive emotions sometimes, scientists are driven by them much of the time, and babies, who have so much to learn, are in their grip practically all the time.
>
> *(Gopnik, 1999)*

In other words, learning is pleasurable, yet this important fact is seldom reflected in pedagogic and philosophical explanations regarding "how and why" learner-clients seek to achieve explanations and theories or in relation to the individual learning-wellbeing challenges a learner-client faces.

Some theory follows.

There are four key schools of thought when considering learning and effective individual learning improvement and self-change management:

- The behaviourist approach is about achieving results through changing the behaviours of learners
- The cognitive approach is about achieving results through developing new cognitive pattern and responses in learners
- When, as now, learners are going through a challenging time involving all aspects of both personal and global challenges and resulting change, the

psychodynamic approach is about understanding and relating to the inner world of change
- The humanistic psychology approach is about believing in the potential of learners to develop and to maximise their individual potential to manage healthy change

Schein (2004) identified two competing anxieties in individual change: survival anxiety versus learning anxiety. Survival anxiety must be greater than learning anxiety if a change is to happen. He advocates the need to reduce people's learning anxiety rather than increase their survival anxiety. We address the issue of anxiety later in the book.

Each of the four approaches presented by Schein led him to derive a set of guidelines for managers (Table 1.1). Each of the four approaches offer a key to open the door to our basic understanding of how different approaches to managing learning may work.

TABLE 1.1 Schein: approaches to learning

Behavioural: get your reward strategies right	Cognitive: link goals to motivation
Psychodynamic: treat people as individuals and understand their emotional states as well as your own!	Humanistic: be authentic and believe that people can change

The tendency to categorise things into dyads and simple binary choices of this or that is not the best principle when addressing the learning-wellbeing needs of a learner. The point of listening to the learner is to respond as closely as possible to their needs regarding how and what learning circumstances are best for them and best reflect their need. A complex learning mix may be needed, compromises will be needed and agreement about compromises can be reached in a learning partnership focused on a sense of wellbeing.

Just as there are different human resource management theories and teaching methods, so there are different, often complex learning styles. Since the mid-1970s, pedagogy has been concerned with the idea that learners have different learning styles.

Everyone has a unique preferred learning style or method; it would be wrong therefore to say that recommending a specific learning style is best for all learner-clients.

Ignoring or addressing the way in which the learner-client learns can be a significant feature of their academic success or failure. Understanding what kind of learning a learner-client prefers is therefore important – listening to what your learner-client has to say about their preferences and learning experiences is vital. Once you know what learning style is the learner-client's innate approach, your approach to supporting your learner-client can be adapted to fit their needs.

Understanding your own style or style mix of learning is particularly useful in focusing on your own preferences and instructional biases as an educationalist-therapist when collaborating with learner-clients. Understanding and reflecting on your learning style or preferences can help you both learn and work more effectively and become more relaxed with your learner-client.

As previously mentioned, there are many factors that influence how someone learns most effectively, including environmental, physical, psychological, cognitive and emotional pressures. Being aware of these issues is key to helping and guiding your learner-client.

Educators and therapists need to be aware of the many different learning styles they might encounter when working with their client-learners. It is easier to respond fully to one individual and understand and incorporate a specific learning style to get better results; it is not however easy for a teacher with, for example, 30 students in one classroom or, exceptionally, 200 students. Both scenarios have severe restrictions of resourcing this time-consuming work – time spent in research and development is however seldom wasted as once a start is made in understanding how somebody learns, it is a valuable tool for the educationalist-therapist faced with the huge task of enabling joint learning, that is the educationalist and the client.

A word of caution! There is an increasingly widespread view that concentrating solely on what is the learning style of a learner helps no-one learn more effectively. A part of the argument being that concentrating for example on meeting the learning needs of a learner identified as having a learning style described as Logical/Analytical can in fact be detrimental to the individual's learning because it excludes all other mixes of learning opportunities.

> The notion of "learning styles" is a persistent "neuro-mythologies" in education that just won't go away. Studies have found that 90%-97% of teachers believe that there is an optimal delivery style for each learner. While a number of different learning style models exist – ranging from 3 to 170 learning styles.
>
> *(Kaufman, 2018)*

The Kaufman perspective is one that challenges orthodoxy but in turn supports the essential theme of this book and that is for educationalists and therapists to listen to learners rather to make their own judgements as to the needs of the learner-client.

All models of learning styles can be valuable, but the only real and valuable insight will come from listening to the preferences and views of all involved in helping the learner-client to learn effectively and then forming an individualised learning approach.

But here's the thing; giving students the message that "It's OK if you're not good at <insert 'intelligence' or 'learning style' here>, you can still be good at <insert 'whatever' here>" can lead students to give up on cultivating key learning skills that can be developed, to an extent, in everyone. Believe it or not, by promoting a dominant learning styles mentality, we are limiting students with self-fulfilling prophecies despite the best intentions.

> Teachers often *think* they know what is best for the student, but this rarely matches with what the students think is the best thing for themselves. This is quite problematic, because it is possible for students to fall between the cracks because their greatest strengths are not actually being recognized.
> *(Kaufman, 2018)*

Kaufman's view does not mean that a teacher should just give up trying to understand and cater to their students' needs altogether. A solution to this dilemma might be using as many activities and exercises as possible that respond to different learning styles. This way, a teacher has a better chance of effectively reaching a larger and more diverse learning group with every student having an opportunity to encounter learning and thinking reflectively in their preferred learning model. Which returns us to the preferred approach of the learner of whatever age being supported to be independently directed as a learner with appropriate support. It is fair to say that few people, in reality, could achieve such a range of nuanced support and not fall over with sheer exhaustion.

Several models of learning effectiveness present themselves as worth considering when deciding how to approach the learner-client. Not one teaching style is "correct" or appropriate for every learner. Most people use a combination of learning styles, but more times than not, they have a predominant style of learning. A synthesis of learning approaches should be considered and evaluated to meet the needs of the individual learner. Importantly, an agreed learning model within the constraints of a national approved curriculum should not become a "set piece" style. As the learner changes (both educationalist and learner are learning!), the best learning agreed approach may well need to be reassessed and flexibility of teaching styles need to be incorporated.

Types of learners

The widely accepted concept of learners having preferred learning styles should be familiar to all educationalists. Renewing our knowledge through the lens of supporting learners through managed and improved learning resulting from wellbeing intervention offers a distinct perspective on familiar knowledge and professional practice. Table 1.2 below summarises learning styles.

Learning styles

TABLE 1.2 Learning styles: summary

Logical (mathematical/analytical) learners are analytical learners who depend on logic and analytical skills to understand a particular subject. These types of learners search for connections, causes, patterns and results in their learning. This type of learner can solve complex problems using strategic thinking and scientific principles. A teacher can engage and motivate analytical learners by posing questions that require interpretation, using material that activates problem-solving skills and stimulating students to reach conclusions based on facts or reasoning. Key words: computer programming, maths, science.

Verbal (linguistic) learner. This type of learner prefers speech and writing; learning through words as their key preference. They will be avid readers and writers. Their vocabulary will be extensive, and they will enjoy activities involving speaking and debate.

Aural (auditory) learners are individuals who learn better when they take in information in auditory form when it is heard or spoken. They are prone to sorting their ideas after speaking rather than thinking ideas through before. Since, to them, saying things aloud helps them understand the concept. Sound and music appeal to this type of learner. They are good, efficient/effective listeners. Auditory learners learn best when information is presented to them via strategies that involve talking, such as lectures and group discussions and accessing recordings of lessons, and lectures.

Nature (environmental) learners. These types of learners excel when in contact with nature. A nature learner's ideal study environment is a calm and relaxing environment. If we had to compare nature learners with another type, it would be physical/tactile learner. The complexity of this type of learner rests within the observation that a synthesis of learning styles is necessary for this type of learning style to work well for the learner. Nature learners revel in being outside rather than the library or study to learn better.

Physical (kinaesthetic) learners prefer to learn by doing. Their learning is all body and hands-focused. They enjoy a developed sense of touch being usually more in touch with reality and more connected to it, which is why they require using tactile experience to improve their understanding of whatever they are learning. They love to tinker and learn. To aid a kinaesthetic learner will be through personal experience, practice, examples or simulations or experiment they can recreate for themselves.

Social (interpersonal) linguistic learners. These learning types have a strong social style, they communicate well with people, both verbally and non-verbally. They listen well and understand other's views. These learners prefer learning in groups which they find rewarding. They will also respond well to one-on-one time with an educator-therapist. They learn by bouncing their thoughts off other people and listening to how they respond. Preferring to work through issues, ideas and problems with a group is an observable characteristic. This type of learner typically enjoys working with a compatible or synergistic group of people. They are motivated and enjoy using role-playing, group activities, asking questions, sharing stories, peer work or socialising participation.

(Continued)

18 Everybody is a learner

TABLE 1.2 (Continued)

Visual (spatial) learners are individuals who prefer to take in their information visually – be that with maps, graphs, diagrams, charts and others. They learn by observing. Visual learning is not necessarily satisfied by learners simply watching a video or looking at photographs! They prefer their information to be available using different visual aids including patterns and shapes. An example would be an explanation of a scientific principle or method via diagram or flow chart.	Solitary (intrapersonal) learners or solo learners are the opposite of social learners. Solitary learners prefer to self-study alone without having to interact with other learners. Individual work is a solo learner's strength. Teachers can help these types of learners by using activities that require individual work preferring to learn in a quiet place. They are usually very self-aware. They can be tenacious, initiative-taking and extremely focused learners.	Invisible learners are learners whose learning styles and style mix cannot be easily addressed. In figures for 2020, around 75,918 missing children were recorded in the United Kingdom. Many of the missing will be involved in unwilling-coerced criminal activities. Some of the missing children and to broaden out the number of missing learners will be involved in new – unknown – learning strategies reflecting the time of change we live in and the future we can expect to be realised.

"VARK"

It is worth being familiar with "VARK" learning styles, a relatively new perspective to the discussion focusing on learning styles and learning styles research. Learning styles or learning preferences are presented below (Table 1.3):

TABLE 1.3 VARK learning styles

"visual" (drawings and diagrams)	"acoustic" (listening, discussing)
"reading" (engaging with the written word)	"kinaesthetic" (active, movement)

Thinking about learning, wellbeing and self-actualisation

Here is a quick dip into the mixing pot of learning/wellbeing/self-actualisation theories and beliefs.

Socrates

The question Socrates sought to answer was how can we understand something when we have no direct experience of it? Socrates' answer was that we did not learn about abstract concepts from our experience of them. We must have known about it in the first place. Socrates thought we "learned," remembered the concepts from a past life. Our contemporary understanding of DNA may well support the views Socrates presented (Socrates, 2023).

Freud

Freud's greatest contribution to psychology is the idea of the subconscious mind, which he sometimes also referred to as the "unconscious mind." According to Freud, there is the conscious mind, which is what we use to do things like make decisions. There is also the subconscious mind, which we are not aware of but which influences the conscious mind (Jaehnig, 2022). The Freudian concept of personality comprised of three interacting elements of id, ego and superego is significant in the development of our understanding of the self.

B.F. Skinner

B.F. Skinner was a psychologist who made significant contributions to the development of behaviourism. Skinner's view was that children were the ultimate blank tablets waiting to be inscribed by reinforcement schedules (Harvard, 2020).

Abraham Maslow

Maslow was an American psychologist who was best known for creating Maslow's hierarchy of needs, a theory of psychological health predicated on fulfilling innate human needs in priority, culminating in self-actualization (Maslow, 2022).

Let's look at the ideas of Maslow in a little more depth.

Self-actualisation refers to the desire that everybody has "to become everything that they are capable of becoming." In other words, Maslow (1970) suggests that all individuals have an in-built need for personal development which occurs through a process called self-actualisation which refers to self-fulfilment and the need to reach full potential as a unique human being. Getting in slightly ahead of Maslow, Oscar Wilde put it as follows: "To realise one's nature perfectly—that is what each of us is here for" (Wilde, 1890).

Unlike earlier psychological studies, Maslow did not focus on ill-health and disease as indicator influences of human behaviour. Maslow researched the lives of people who had shown creativity, compassionate behaviours and tenacity during their lives, all leading to his theory of motivation, the hierarchy of needs (see Figure 1.2), recognising all individuals have the need to see themselves as competent and autonomous.

The extent to which people can develop depends on certain needs being met, and these needs form a hierarchy. Only when one level of need is satisfied can a higher one be developed. As change occurs throughout life, however, the level of need motivating someone's behaviour at any one time will also change.

Maslow's hierarchy of needs begins with the human physiological, safety, love and self-esteem needs that must be achieved before self-actualisation.

Maslow's hierarchy is as follows:

- First, the basic physiological needs for food, drink, sex and sleep, that is, the basics for survival.
- Second are the needs for safety and security in both the physical and economic sense.
- Thirdly, progression can be made to satisfy the need for love and belonging.
- The fourth level refers to meeting the need for self-esteem and self-worth. This is the level most closely related to "self-empowerment."
- The fifth level relates to the need to understand. This level includes more abstract ideas such as curiosity and the search for meaning or purpose and a deeper understanding.
- The sixth relates to aesthetic needs of beauty, symmetry and order.
- Finally, at the top of Maslow's hierarchy is the need for self-actualisation.

For Maslow, the path to self-actualisation involves being in touch with your feelings, experiencing life fully and with total concentration (Maslow, 1970).

Basic needs must be sufficiently met before you can proceed to produce your best work and feel comfortable and confident in your (student learner/therapist) environment. This does not mean that you must have every need (or importantly, want) satisfied. It simply means that there is a level of basic needs that cannot be ignored before you are able to attend to more abstract needs (Mair, 2019).

According to Maslow, only when the lower level needs were met could an individual progress to the aspirational needs higher up the pyramid. He argued that moving up the first four levels of needs was fuelled by the individual's sense of absence of needs met; then, meeting needs encouraged and motivated the individual to strive for more. In other words, it was the lack of completeness that acted as the motivator in achieving higher levels in Maslow's hierarchy.

Physiological needs are requirements such as food, water, shelter, rest and sexual needs. Without these needs being satisfied or addressed, the individual will experience physiological symptoms such as hunger, thirst, discomfort, exhaustion and frustration.

Maslow viewed safety needs as those that are concerned with the level of threat and desire for a sense of security concerned with both physical safety and psychological safety.

Love and intimacy. This involves the need for affection and affiliation, an emotionally loving state and a sense of belonging at an intimate level. It is important here to note that Maslow introduces a sense of reciprocity into the equation. Achieving a sense of belonging can rarely be achieved without reciprocity.

Self-esteem needs are met in two ways. They are met through the satisfaction individuals get when they achieve competence or proficiency in doing something. They are also met through receiving recognition for their achievement or achievements.

As discussed, Maslow proposed that the need of an individual was ultimately for self-actualisation; the desire to become increasingly what one is, to become everything that one can become (Maslow, 1970). Maslow observed that people continued to search for something else once all their other needs were being satisfied. We try to become the person we believe we are capable of becoming.

Self-actualisation can take many forms, depending on the individual. These variations may include the quest for knowledge, understanding, peace, self-fulfilment, meaning in life or beauty … but the need for beauty is neither higher nor lower than the other needs at the top of the pyramid. Self-actualisation needs are not hierarchically ordered (Griffin, 1991).

Children stuck in Maslow's lower survival level may never fully attain their educational potential. Children stuck in their lower levels are at high risk of anxiety and depression, while also having never achieving self-actualisation. During the coronavirus pandemic, child abuse calls increased, as children living in dysfunctional households, stuck at home due to school closures, found no viable outlet of escape from abuse. A worldwide pandemic is certainly responsible for why many people, both young and old, feel as if they are now stuck in "survival mode" (Kuzujanakis, 2021).

Benjamin Bloom

Bloom's taxonomy serves as the backbone of many teaching philosophies, in particular those that lean more towards skills rather than content. These educators view content as a vessel for teaching skills. The emphasis on higher order thinking inherent in such philosophies is based on the top levels of the taxonomy including application, analysis, synthesis and evaluation. Bloom's taxonomy can be used as a teaching tool to help balance evaluative and assessment-based questions in assignments, texts and class engagements to ensure that all orders of thinking are exercised in students' learning, including aspects of information searching (Janson, 2009).

Bloom's taxonomy of educational goals comprises cognitive, affective and psychomotor domains to illustrate the transitional steps from lower to higher levels of thinking.

Carl Rogers and the path to personal growth

Carl Rogers is one of the founders of the humanistic movement in psychology. He has written extensively on the stages through which people travel on their journey towards "becoming a person." He was interested in how people learn, how they exercise power and how they behave within organisations.

Rogers promoted a "client-centred approach" to growth and development. He was interested in how agents of change might bring about individual emotional growth and development.

He highlighted three core conditions for meaningful change to occur:

- Genuineness and congruence: to be aware of your own feelings, to be real and to be authentic. Rogers's research showed that the more genuine and congruent the change agent is in the relationship, the greater the probability of change in the personality of the client.
- Unconditional positive regard: a genuine willingness to allow the client's process to continue and an acceptance of whatever feelings are going on inside the client. Whatever feeling the client is experiencing, be it anger, fear, hatred, then that is all right. It is saying that underneath all this, the person is all right.
- Empathic understanding: in Rogers's words,

  it is only as I understand the feelings and thoughts which seem so horrible to you, or so weak, or so sentimental, or so bizarre – it is only as I see them as you see them, and accept them and you, that you feel really free to explore all the hidden roots and frightening crannies of your inner and often buried experience.

In trying to grasp and conceptualise the process of change ... "I gradually developed this concept of a process, discriminating seven stages in it" (Rogers, 1967).

The following are the consistently recurring qualities at each stage of the Rogers's change process:

1

- an unwillingness to communicate about self, only externals
- demonstrating no desire for change
- a sense of invalidated feelings
- problems unrecognised

2

- communication begin to flow
- feelings although shown are not integrated as sense of self
- problems perceived but remain as existing external to self
- no sense of personal accountability or responsibility for actions or consequences
- past experiences, not the present dominant in referencing experiences

3

- the self, experienced as an object
- expression of past feelings, but not the present
- non-acceptance of bad, shameful, abnormal feelings
- recognition of contradictions and ambiguity
- personal choice seen as ineffective

4

- past feelings experienced more intensely than present
- occasional demonstration and awareness of present time feelings
- anxiety of direct expression of feelings
- low acceptance or responsibility for self-generated feelings
- slight response to current experiences
- some awareness and acceptance of personal constructs
- unfamiliar but nonetheless feelings of self-responsibility in problem causation
- close relationships seen as threatening and potentially dangerous
- the acceptance and toleration of small risk-taking

5

- freely expressed feelings recognised in the present
- shock and fear as emerging feelings are recognised
- increasing ownership of feelings
- a growing sense of self-responsibility
- recognising and facing up to contradictions, incongruence and ambiguity

6

- acceptance of past feelings experienced in the here and now
- the self increasingly viewed as less of an object and more of a feeling
- recognition and appreciation of physiological release
- some psychological release – new ways of seeing a relationship between the world and a sense of self
- reduction of perceived paradox between experience and awareness

7

- new feelings experienced and accepted as contemporaneous
- emerging trust in procedures and processes
- self becomes confidently recognised in the process of being
- less rigid personal constructs
- strong feelings of self-responsibility and choice making (Rogers, 1967)

Fritz Perls's Gestalt approach to individual and organisational change

Fritz Perls was the originator of Gestalt therapy. He was interested with the here and now. Perls believed that a person's individual difficulties arise because of the way they are acting today, here and now. In his words:

> The goal ... must be to give him the means with which he can solve his present problems and any that may arise tomorrow or next year. The tool is self-support, and this he achieves by dealing with himself and his problems with all the means presently at his command, right now. If he can be truly aware at every instant of himself and his actions on whatever level – fantasy, verbal or physical – he can see how he is producing his difficulties, he can see what his present difficulties are, and he can help himself to solve them in the present, in the here and now.
>
> *(Perls, 1976)*

> The Gestalt approach has the primary aim of showing clients that they interrupt themselves in achieving what they want. Gestalt is experiential, not just based on talking.
>
> *(Perls et al., 1992)*

Jean Piaget is still exciting![2]

Piaget suggested that children sort the knowledge they acquire through their experiences and interactions into groupings known as schemas. When new information is acquired, it can either be assimilated into existing schemas or accommodated through revising an existing schema or creating an entirely new category of information. Piaget's theory had a huge influence on the emergence of developmental psychology as a distinctive subfield within psychology and contributed to the field of education. He is also credited as a pioneer of the constructivist theory, which suggests that people actively construct their knowledge of the world based on the interaction between their ideas and experiences (APA, 2022). Piaget's thinking on schemas is of high relevance to the cognitive behavioural therapy (CBT) concept of schemas about self, others and the world.

Piaget's works made a significant contribution to a reconfiguring of thinking about children's abilities and processes when learning. His work influenced both theory and practice, leading to a more "child-centred" approach. His theory of cognitive development can be used as a tool in the early childhood classroom. According to Piaget, children developed best in a classroom with interaction.

Piaget defined knowledge as the ability to modify, transform and "operate on" an object or idea such that it is understood by the operator through the process of transformation. Learning, then, occurs because of experience, both physical and logical, with the objects themselves and how they are acted upon. Thus, knowledge must be assimilated in an active process by a learner with matured mental capacity so that knowledge can build in complexity by scaffolded understanding.

Understanding is scaffolded by the learner through the process of equilibration, whereby the learner balances new knowledge with previous understanding, thereby compensating for "transformation" of knowledge (Piaget, 1964).

Learning, then, can also be supported by instructors in an educational setting. Piaget specified that knowledge cannot truly be formed until the learner has matured the mental structures to which that learning is specific, and thereby development constrains learning. Nevertheless, knowledge can also be "built" by building on simpler operations and structures that have already been formed. Basing operations of an advanced structure on those of simpler structures thus scaffolds learning to build on operational abilities as they develop. Good teaching, then, is built around the operational abilities of the students such that they can excel in their operational stage and build on pre-existing structures and abilities and thereby "build" learning.

Stages of cognitive development

Jean Piaget's theory of cognitive development (Figure 1.3) suggests that children move through four distinct stages of intellectual development which

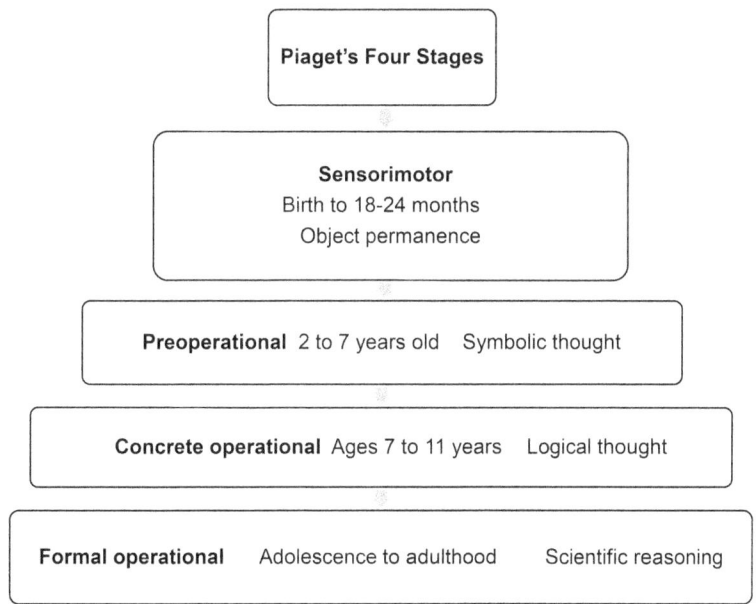

FIGURE 1.2 Piaget's four stages of development.

reflect the increasing sophistication of children's thoughts. Each child goes through the stages in the same order, and child development is determined by biological maturation and interaction with the environment. At each stage of development, the child's thinking is qualitatively different from the other stages, that is, each stage involves a different type of intelligence (Piaget, 2022).

In conversations with Jean Piaget, Bringuier says: "Education, for most people, means trying to lead the child to resemble the typical adult of his society … but for me and no one else, education means making creators … You have to make inventors, innovators—not conformists" (Bringuier, 1980)

Lev Vygotsky

Lev Vygotsky is extraordinary!

Vygotsky's sociocultural theory views human development as a socially mediated process in which children acquire their cultural values, beliefs and problem-solving strategies through collaborative dialogues with more knowledgeable members of society. Vygotsky's theory is comprised of concepts such as culture-specific tools, private speech and the Zone of Proximal Development (Mcleod, 2022).

The work of Vygotsky has proved to be very influential in the discussion and emergent pedagogic delivery. His work has become the foundation of much research and theory in cognitive development influencing the emergence of sociocultural theory.

Vygotsky's theories stress the fundamental role of social interaction in the development of cognition (Vygotsky, 1978), as he believed strongly that community plays a significant role in the process of "making meaning." In other words, social learning tends to precede development (Bringuier, 2022).

It must be noted that while all and every theory/view of how learners learn has its critics and supporters – no theory is freely accepted by everyone as totally resolving the complexities of supporting learning and how learning happens.

"The major message, however, is that rather than recommending a particular teaching method, teachers need to be evaluators of the effect of the methods that they choose" (Hattie, 2012).

Psychologist Mark Seidenberg has criticised the field of Education Studies for placing too much emphasis on the works of Jean Piaget, Lev Vygotsky and other historical psychologists while failing to keep up with the major advances in cognitive science in the decades since they were active. Meanwhile, one review of education research showed that constructivist approaches to early childhood education inspired by Piaget and Vygotsky are less effective than comprehensive approaches that incorporate direct skills teaching (Chambers et al., 2016).

The range of different theories some based on research, some based on prejudice and again some based firmly in dogmatic beliefs is vast. We must remember the choice of approach and action as to what we believe to be "correct," "appropriate" or suitable for the needs of the individual learner, and the community they are learning in and about always returns to listening to those who are making the future. Learners will only learn in a stable, well-organised environment appropriate for learning to take place. It is astonishing how strong the desire to learn is: that even in the most hostile, inappropriate settings, learners will tenaciously and persistently try to find a way to learn.

- Creativity and mental health

Creativity is as important as literacy (Robinson, 2006).

It is widely accepted that creativity is directly linked to artistic endeavours and achievements such as painting, theatre, music and multi-media creations. However, seeing creativity as only present within such activities neglects to recognise the importance of creativity to all areas of human endeavour: mathematics, business innovation, medicine, space exploration, combatting aggression, scientific research and problem-solving in our changing and often chaotic world all require significant creativity.

Creativity and its relationship with mental health remains an area of dispute with educationalists and psychologists. There may be relationships between creativity and aspects of our mental health. Types of difference or difficulty linked with creativity include attention deficit hyperactivity disorder (ADHD), anxiety disorder, bipolar disorder, major depressive disorder, obsessive-compulsive disorder (OCD) and schizophrenia.

I think I've only spent about 10% of my energies on writing. The other 90% went to keeping my head above water (Porter, 1987).

It is still a largely held popular view that acts of creativity and mental health conditions were closely associated as demonstrated, for example, by lives of highly regarded writers such as Virginia Woolf, Ezra Pound, the writer/illustrator Mervyn Peake and visual artists, for instance Hogarth and Van Gogh. Many artists of great international significance can and have been characterised as suffering from mental health issues such as bipolar disorder or depression and anxiety disorders. To paraphrase a well-known aphorism – you have to be mad to paint/sculpt/write … create here.

Nancy Andreasen's (2022) research presents us with the counter argument regarding creativity and mental health issues which is that many successful writers and artists became successful not because of their mental health but despite it. The suggestion to consider is that the activity of writing and creative expression actually serves to ameliorate mental health difficulties because of the levels of concentration and discipline involved in the creative process. Andreasen is largely responsible for development of the concept of negative symptoms in schizophrenia, having created the first widely used scales for rating the positive and negative symptoms of schizophrenia.[3]

Research by Zorana Ivezic Pringle (2022) found that those who took part in some form of creativity such as pottery, photography, wood/metal work or creative writing tended to be more actively curious, affirmative and motivated by their involvement in a creative activity. The forms of everyday creativity also led to increased feelings of wellbeing and personal happiness.

It is overwhelmingly clear that the application of creativity within the arts, economic, social and science worlds significantly contribute to helping and supporting various forms of treatable mental health difficulties and is a key component of increasing wellbeing.

Creativity has a positive impact on learning and learners in promoting wellbeing. Creativity is vital to flourish in society today, vital to the economy and vital to enrich future lives. There are a proliferation of complex problems to be addressed, new types of jobs and new ways of working, and the influence of technology is ubiquitous. Fusion[4] will be the predominant way of being and be crucial for future success and happiness. Thriving in this world will require creativity.

The relationship that exists between creativity and wellbeing needs to be all-embracing if we are to secure a positive, peaceful, healthy and innovative twenty-first century.

Channelled creativity can have an immense impact on both managing and resolving mental health and wellbeing helping people find stability, meaning and significance and an increased sense of purpose (Zhao et al., 2022).

Creativity may well be the most important skill for students to learn for the twenty-first century, as it is necessary for devising innovative solutions to the many twenty-first century challenges we face (Fadel et al., 2015).

- Developing ideas

Everyone has a strategy or strategies they use to remember information more efficiently while studying. Some learners will take notes, others may make record information visually and others may prefer to listen to information, presentations and lectures while others may build a micro-computer or write poetry.

However, despite the deeply held views of many educationalists regarding learning styles, as we have discussed, is that no one learning strategy fits all learners. Increasingly nuanced views exist, whereby the learner is increasingly regarded as a complex mass of connectivity utilising (perhaps unwittingly) all learning styles in no preference other than effectiveness in resolving curiosity.

The neuromyth of learning styles persists even though we know that the brain is massively interconnected and that common brain functions (particularly in the prefrontal cortex) cut across virtually any act of deliberate learning. Studies have consistently shown that catering to differences in students' preferred learning style does not actually result in any improvement in learning outcomes. On the contrary, there is good reason to believe that optimal learning for everyone involves the opportunity to engage in as many sensory modalities as possible (Kaufman, 2018).

We are, with relation to AI and developing intelligence in humans, experiencing a learning environment that reflects the situation of a to-be-born and born child: the first learner who is without a guidebook as to how to use their eyes, ears, senses and tactile information in a developing and growing mind (Senior & Gyarmathy, 2022).

As a new-born baby enters the world, so do we. Our distinct disadvantage in comparison with a new-born baby is that we believe we know things and that we do have ways of understanding the world. We therefore feel comfortable with applying the knowledge we consider that we have to the futures we are now growing into, especially our relationship with artificial intelligence. This of course is a mistake. Without developing, questioning and vigorously challenging our ideas as to the bedrock of new learning, we will not advance, develop or understand the world of now and the world of the near future.

The challenge of developing our strategies for learning in the present, near and distant future, is to recognise what we must forget as well as what we must embrace as a part of our learning-to-learn transitional arrangements. Living, working and learning to negotiate the future are going to require us to address old and new challenges with new thinking and creativity.

Applied skills for twenty-first century living, working and learning: a proposed menu

- Physical and mental health including fostering wellbeing
- Critical thinking: distinguishing lies from facts
- Creativity
- Collaboration
- Psychological flexibility
- Resilience
- Oral communication skills
- Written communication skills
- Information literacy
- Ethical sophistication and knowledge
- Efficacy and self-direction/motivation
- Leadership and the management of diversity
- Teamwork and collaboration
- Initiative: confidence and maturity of responsible actions
- Productivity
- Social interpersonal skills including around gender expectations and understandings
- High toleration for change

Where do people learn?

- Learning in safe places

Learners learn in an environment where basic needs are achieved. It is difficult to learn if one is hungry, cold, in fear, ill, abused or unloved. Allowing and supporting a platform for learning based on individual preferences can happen when learning is seen as an increasingly challenging state to achieve. Learners will learn quickly and in depth through what they find enjoyable; we will experience a sense of intellectual glow when we are nourished intellectually, spiritually and physically. A learner's mind is not an empty vessel. More a stranger in a strange world – an environment where the skills of research, truth, evaluation and language between the environment and other learners (human, machine, otherwise) can be explored.

What prevents learners learning?

- Barriers and blocks

"It is increasingly recognised that young learners 'doing better' is not just about improving test scores but is about providing the kind of environment which enables children and young people to thrive in the fullest sense of the word" (Carnie, 2017).

Some barriers to learning include the following factors:

TABLE 1.4 Physical, psychological and emotional barriers to learning

Poor school performance – shaming by assessment	Eating disorders	Restlessness	School phobia
Irritability	Loss of appetite	Sleeping disorders	Poverty
Physical abuse – brain injury	The amygdala (the emotional centre) a powerful role in a decline in normal serotonin (the relaxation and wellbeing hormone) during adolescence	Ethical and moral sensitivity	Hypochondria
Depression	Social isolation	Loneliness	Being a bullying target
Racial intolerance	Mental breakdown	Mental abuse	Racist attitudes and behaviours

(Continued)

TABLE 1.4 (Continued)

Perfectionism	Abuse at home with no respite during the pandemic – dysfunctional households	Toxic stress	Abusive school/home life
Neglect, physical and emotional	Mitochondrial dysfunction	Oxidative stress	Effect of free radicals
Androgyny – gender-role stereotypes – LGBTQ (lesbian, gay, bisexual, transgender, and queer [or questioning]) identification anxiety	The classroom is becoming a museum (Senior & Gyarmathy, 2022)	Domestic home abuse	Traumatised learning – an impossible achievement of tenacity and efficacy and learning willpower.

Barriers and blocks to learning are many, seemingly intangible and deeply embedded in our global community. As we have discussed earlier, Maslow offers a core for our thinking about self-realisation while Vygotsky shows us the living concept which learners are immersed in and influenced by. The problem of releasing learners from the huge range of learning challenges to be overcome is daunting. While many agencies exist to both mitigate and eradicate the barriers and blocks outlined in Table 1.4, we need to concentrate on what can be done both in raising awareness of the barriers to learning and on the reduction of suffering in the world.

With this view in mind, we can identify our key contribution to reducing the barriers and blocks to learning – in a word, we need to and must address the anxious state that we all, as social learners, learn in.

It is normal to feel anxious sometimes. It is how we respond to feeling threatened, under pressure or stressed: for example, if we have an exam, job interview or doctor's appointment.

Identifying anxiety is a particularly important matter for educationalists and therapists when working with any type of client but particularly vulnerable young learners (See Figure 1.3).

- Anxiety is not in itself a negative thing. It can make us conscious of risks and motivate us to resolve problems.
- If anxiety affects the learner-client's ability to live a balanced and effective life, then anxiety can become a problem. If anxiety is ongoing, intense, hard to control or out of proportion to the learner/client situation, it becomes problematic.

> Symptoms of anxiety in children
>
> "Toddlers, even before they begin school, can also exhibit symptom of anxiety, as well as anxiety's counterpart – depression." (Kuzujanakis, 2021)
>
> Look out for the young learner if they are:
>
> - finding it hard to concentrate
> - not sleeping, or waking in the night with bad dreams
> - not eating properly
> - quickly getting angry or irritable, and being out of control during outbursts
> - constantly worrying or having negative thoughts
> - feeling tense and fidgety, or using the toilet often
> - always crying
> - being clingy
> - complaining of tummy aches and feeling unwell

FIGURE 1.3 Anxiety disorders in children (NHS, 2022, www.nhs.uk).

Panic attacks are only one of the five major types of anxiety disorders that include generalised anxiety disorder (GAD), obsessive-compulsive disorder (OCD), social anxiety disorder (SAD), and post-traumatic stress disorder (PTSD). Phobias, childhood selective mutism, separation anxiety, and hypochondria are a few other recognized anxiety disorders. Anxiety sufferers often have more than one distinct type.

(Kuzujanakis, 2021)

Adolescent girls experience anxiety more often and may be twice as likely to experience anxiety than boys (30% vs. 20%) (Merikangas, 2010).

The speed with which our familiar world can become a threatening, alien, strange place linked to both economic and technological developments is perhaps the greatest barrier to learning is quoted as saying that in a rapidly evolving technological economy training workers to solve problems as opposed to fixating on one job might be a better alternative.

(Juskalian, 2018)

Everyone has a view of learning based on their own favoured beliefs and interpretative stance when presented with concepts, observations, facts and figures. Creative tensions can result from challenging and exploring different viewpoints. For this reason, finding a global, all-encompassing picture of what we can do to respond to the learning and wellbeing needs of the client-learner that we can all agree on is challenging.

Countries, like individuals, are complicated, wilful, contradictory and sometimes confused as to their ambitions and desires for their respective populations. Countries, like individuals, have limited resources and many pressing issues to consider and manage. They also have political, religious and social forces at play in their respective societies, which, in turn, also influence how and what they provide for their collective wellbeing.

Ideally, learners should be supported to learn and to be invested in the support of their own wellbeing and the wellbeing of others.

The educational process should be aimed not only at the development of the student's intellect but also at their whole personality, including motivation, creative activity and ethics.

There are 195 countries in the world today that are member states of the United Nations (UN). Two of these recognised countries are non-member observer states: The Holy See and the State of Palestine.[5]

In many of these countries, duplication of ideas and policies are present. In other countries, diametrically opposed views are present as to how to provide for learners and why they should consider their learning-wellbeing.

It's all extremely complicated: one choice that a country may make related to providing for their learner's wellbeing does not necessarily exclude another apparently contradictory choice; nothing in the world of learning is without a degree of ambiguity.

The challenges of scale are an important issue to consider when making judgements as to how and what policies are arrived at and are implemented when facing a population of around 1,420,062,022 (18.4% of the world population) which is the case with China as compared with a population of 8.42 million in Switzerland.

Humans may be the only creatures conscious of having a future, but all too often, we would rather not think about it. Likewise, our societies, unable to deal with radical uncertainty, do not make policies with a view to the long term. Instead, we suffer from a sense of powerlessness, collective irrationality and perennial political discontent (Innerarity, 2012).

Recognising the global challenge to supporting learner-wellbeing is the spur to action. We start with ourselves, those we can work with and in turn those who will work to help learner-clients learn. In other words, we do our informed best and look to a positive future.

We always need to remind ourselves that it all depends upon the needs of the learner-client – it's as simple as that! Ask the learner-client what is best for them and try to meet their needs. It may be for food or security, things that are difficult for us to address as individuals. Where we can help is in listening to learners and helping them hear their own voices. We can as learner-wellbeing champions help every learner-client we meet realise themselves.

The one thing we can be sure of is that all learners learn, just not in the same way. We need to ask what works for the learner and helps them in achieving their sense of wellbeing.

Going further – extended learning

What learners need

- Ask your learner-client to produce a list of things that learners need to have a happy and secure life. Here, below, are some examples indicating what might come up in this exercise:

    Safety, validation, love, play, recognition, food, fresh air, cuddles, exercise, education, mum, dad, compassion, nurture, boundaries, acceptance, fun, protection, role models, family, support, friends, care, encouragement and privacy.

    (Duffell & Basset, 2016)

- What works?
Compare, contrast and evolve your response to a range of sometimes complimentary and sometimes contradictory views regarding how learners learn. As an educationalist-therapist, what would you consider is your preferred learning style? Do you think using your preferred learning style affects learner-clients in that for some learners it is appropriate and for others it may establish a dysfunctional relationship?
- Is every learner-client's learning and wellbeing journey identical? If all journeys are different and everchanging, how will you set your criteria for action and support? Listening to yourself, what do you hear?
- Consider the implications of listening to the learner-client seeking a balanced style of learning and Maslow's hierarchy of needs informing the development of wellbeing within the learner. Where would you start in establishing a learning-wellbeing programme for your learner-client?

Notes

1. Piaget studied the development of molluscs in the lakes around Neuchâtel. He was intrigued by the way they adapted to being moved from one place to another. By age 21, he published 25 papers on molluscs and was known as one of the world's few experts on molluscs.
2. Piaget.
3. Nancy Andreasen's (2022) research offers the insight that while psychotic symptoms represent an exaggeration of normal brain/mind functions, negative symptoms represent a loss of normal functions, for example, alogia: the loss of the ability to think and speak fluently, affective blunting: the loss of the ability to express emotions, avolition: loss of the ability to initiate goal-directed activity and anhedonia: loss of the ability to experience emotions.
4. "Fusion": The role of creativity on flourishing and wellbeing.
5. Not included in the 195 recognised countries are:
    - Taiwan – the UN considers it represented by the People's Republic of China.
    - The Cook Islands and Niue, both states in free association with New Zealand which are members of several UN specialised agencies and have been recognised

"full treaty-making capacity" but are neither member states nor non-member observer states.
- Dependencies (dependent territories, dependent areas or dependencies) and Areas of Special Sovereignty (autonomous territories).

References

Andreasen, N. C. (2022). Collected research. https://www.researchgate.net/scientific-contributions/Nancy-C-Andreasen-38685593

APA Dictionary of Psychology. (2022). American Psychological Association. www.apa.org

Baby Centre. (2022). How does my baby learn? https://www.babycentre.co.uk/a25014815/how-does-my-baby-learn

Bringuier, J C. (1980). *Conversations with Jean Piaget.* University of Chicago Press.

Carnie, F. (2017). Alternative approaches to education: A guide for teachers and parents. Routledge

Chambers, B., Cheung, A. C. K., Slavin, R. E. (2016). Literacy and language outcomes of comprehensive and developmental-constructivist approaches to early childhood education: A systematic review. *Educational Research Review*, 18, 88–111. https://doi.org.10.1016/j.edurev.2016.03.003

Duffell, N., & Basset, T. (2016). A guide to therapeutic work with boarding school survivors (p. 200). Routledge.

Fadel, C., Bialik, M., & Trilling, B. (2015). *Four-dimensional education.* Centre for Curriculum Redesign.

Gladwell, M. (2009). Outliers. Penguin.

Gopnik, A. (1999). How babies think. Weidenfeld & Nicolson.

Greenberg, J. (1985). Rites of passage. Henry Holt & Company.

Harvard. (2020). https://psychology.fas.harvard.edu/people/b-f-skinner

Hattie, J. (2012). Visible learning for teachers: Maximizing impact on learning. Routledge.

Healthy Children. (2022) The Good Childhood Report. The Children's Society. (childrenssociety.org.uk)

Holt, J. (1977). How children learn. Pelican. ISBN 0-1402-1133-0

Innerarity, D. (2012). The future and its enemies: In defense of political hope (cultural memory in the present). Stanford University Press

Jaehnig, J. (2022). Better help. https://www.betterhelp.com/advice/therapy/how-does-freudian-therapy-work/

Juskalian, R. (2018). Rebuilding Germany's centuries-old vocational program MIT Technology Review. https://www.technologyreview.com/

Kaufman, S. B. (2018). Enough with the "learning styles" already! New research adds to the skepticism surrounding the adoption of learning styles in education. Scientific America Blog Network.

Kuzujanakis, M. (2021). Anxiety in today's children and young adults. *Gifted Education International*, 37(I), 54–65.

Mair, D. (2019). The student guide to mindfulness. SAGE.

Maslow, A. H. (1970). Motivation and personality (2nd ed.). Harper & Row.

Maslow, A. H. (2022). https://en.wikipedia.org/wiki/Abraham_Maslow

Mcleod, S. (2022). Lev Vygotsky's Sociocultural Theory of Cognitive Development (simplypsychology.org)

Merikangas, K. R., He, J.-P., Burstein, M., Swanson, S. A., Avenevoli, S., Cui, L., Benjet, C., Georgiades, K., & Swendsen, J. (2010). Lifetime prevalence of mental disorders in US adolescents: Results from the National Comorbidity Survey Replication-Adolescent Supplement (NCS-A). Journal of the American Academy of Child & Adolescent Psychiatry, 49(10), 980–989.

NHS. (2022). Anxiety disorders in children – NHS. www.nhs.uk

Oxford Shorted Dictionary. (1993). Oxford University Press.

Perls Fritz. (1989). *The Gestalt approach and eye witness to therapy*. Science and Behavior Books. ISBN 083140034X

Perls, F., Hefferline, R., & Goodman, P. (1992). *Gestalt therapy: Excitement and growth in the human personality*. Gestalt Journal Press.

Piaget, J. (2022). Piaget Theory: Childhood cognitive developmental stages (cognifit. com)

Piaget, J. (1964). "Development and learning." In R. E. Ripple and V. N. Rockcastle (Eds.), *Piaget rediscovered: A report on the conference of cognitive studies and curriculum development* (pp. 7–20). Cornell University.

Piaget, J. (1998). Piaget theory: Childhood cognitive developmental stages. (www.cognifit.com)

Porter, K. A. (1987). *Conversations*. University Press of Mississippi.

Pringle, Z. I. (2022). https://www.researchgate.net/profile/Zorana-Ivcevic-Pringle

Robinson, K. (2006). Sir Ken Robinson's legacy on creativity in education, innovation. (www.learntechasia.com)

Rogers, C. (1967). Person to Person: The Problem of Being Human-A New Trend in Psychology. Real Person Press. ISBN 9780911226010

Senior, J., & Gyarmathy, É. (2022). *AI and developing human intelligence*. Routledge.

Sisk, D. (2002). Spiritual intelligence: The tenth intelligence that integrates all other intelligences. https://doi.org/10.1177/026142940201600304

Socrates. (2023). https://en.wikipedia.org/wiki/Socrates

Sternberg, R. (2022). Gifted for whom? Individualism, dyadism, and collectivism in the definition of giftedness. *Gifted Education International*, 38(3), 391–396.

Vygotsky, L. S. (1978). *Mind in society: Development of higher psychological processes*. Harvard University Press.

Wilde, O. (1890). The Picture of Dorian Gray. *Lippincott's Monthly Magazine*

Zhao, R., Tang, Z., Lu, F., Xing, Q., & Shen, W. (2022). Frontiers | An Updated Evaluation of the Dichotomous Link Between Creativity and Mental Health (frontiersin.org). Front. Psychiatry 12:781961. doi: 10.3389/fpsyt.

Further reading

Andreasen, N. J. C., & Canter, A. (1974). The creative writer: psychiatric symptoms and family history. *Comprehensive Psychiatry*, 15(2), 123–131. https://doi.org/10.1016/0010-440X(74)90028-5

Bloom's taxonomy. (2023). Bloom's taxonomy – Wikipedia

Glazzard, J. (2018). *Supporting mental health in primary and early years*. SAGE.

Hoskins, S. (2020). *Growth mindset for teachers*. Corwin.

Jones, J. (2014). A short history of mental illness in art. *The Guardian*. Manchester. https://www.theguardian.com/society/christmas-charity-appeal-2014-blog/2015/jan/13/-sp-a-short-history-of-mental-illness-in-art

Reiss, S., Gelbar, N., & Madaus, J. (2020). Pathways to academic success: Specific strength-based teaching and support strategies for twice exceptional high school students with autism spectrum disorder. *Gifted Education International*, *39*(3), 378–400.

Schein, E. (2004). *Organizational culture and leadership*. Jossey-Bass.

Schein's model of transformative change. (2023). Edgar Schein model of organization culture. https://www.managementstudyguide.com/edgar-schein-model.htm

VARK Learning Styles. (2023). VARK Learning Styles. www.vark-learn.com

Wadsworth, B. J. (2004). Piaget's theory of cognitive and affective development. Pearson/A and B.

2
MENTAL HEALTH AND SELF-EFFICACY

The activities in this chapter all aim to support the learner to maintain good wellbeing not only as a means to improve their learning but also as part of learning in itself; learning about how to maintain and improve wellbeing is a bedrock skill for every learner's present and future. For the individual learner, managing anxiety, learning emotional regulation skills and aiming to create a safe, encouraging psychological environment to learn in are all important both for good learning and for positive feelings about the self to develop. Taken together, the skills and habits that the activities in this chapter cover will support the individual learner to be confident to learn, to take the risk of trying and, through this, to build their self-efficacy which in turn will support further self-development and learning.

These skills will be beneficial to and supportive of co-learning because when a group of learners are all developing their learning and wellbeing together, the psychological environment in which co-learning happens is mutually beneficial and self-sustaining. The activities that follow do interrelate to each other, but can be tried in any order, as appropriate to the individual or group. The activities also relate to other activities in later chapters; where there is a particularly complimentary activity in another chapter, a reference is given at the end of the activity, as "works well with: Activity x/y/z." There are of course wider links and connections between many of the activities throughout the book, and some of these links will be idiosyncratic to the reader; therefore, don't limit yourself to the suggested links and make your own connections and pathways through these activities. The "Going further" sections offer ideas to broaden out the individual activity to promote and support your extended learning. Not all activities will have referenced material, where however references relating to the individual activity exist, they will be shown after the "Going further" section. Occasionally, the suggestions for "Further reading" will have additional suggestions for "Further viewing" as appropriate.

ACTIVITIES

1. MAXIMISE YOUR MEMORY

Time: flexible; from 10 to 15 minutes to read about memory to longer if trying an idea to boost memory

Who this could be for: anyone who wants to find out more about how memory works and wants to improve their ability to retain and retrieve knowledge as part of learning

Resources needed: internet access; then any additional resources will depend on the ideas you select to try

Why do this: understand how you form memories and try techniques to maximise your memory and boost your learning

This activity is a chance to find out more about what memory is and how we form memories and to try out some strategies to maximise your memory as part of improving your learning.

Memory is our ability to retain and store information from the experiences we have, combined with the ability to re-access that retained information at a future date. It is a highly important and useful skill that helps us survive, and memory often also is fundamental to our sense of identity; we might hold what we remember as a significant part of who we are. We use our memories to learn: to take in information, retain it and retrieve it later (for instance during a test) are important for learning. Even though technology advances have allowed us to externalise some of the functions of our memories, for instance social media can hold information about what we were doing, and when, in a timeline, we still have an essential need for using our memories.

We think of memory as divided up into two parts: short-term memory (STM) and long-term memory (LTM). You can think of your brain as a kind of information processing and memory-creating factory, processing the raw material of your daily experiences into long-term stored information. The parts of our brains that take in information, through our senses, need to pass this on to our LTM; a part of our brain called the hippocampus helps with this. We have one region like this in each of the two hemispheres of our brains, and the name for these hippocampi originates in the Greek name for seahorse, which the brain regions resemble in shape. It's quite pleasing to think of a small seahorse-shaped bit of your brain helping you to build memories. Our hippocampi are also quite busy during sleep; it seems likely that we are consolidating memories during sleep and especially when dreaming, and the hippocampi seem to be active during dream stages of sleep.

Maximising your memory: the basics

The most important things you can do to support your memory are ensuring you get enough rest and sleep, ensuring you eat a healthy diet and ensuring

Mental health and self-efficacy   **41**

you take regular physical exercise. These building blocks will help you to move information you are taking in during your waking experience from short-term storage to long-term storage: from STM to LTM. The information that makes it into your LTM will be available to you for far longer than information that only makes it as far as short-term storage that will decay very quickly.

Another important thing you can do to support your memory is to manage stress effectively; the parts of our brain that seem to be involved in memory creation and retrieval, especially the hippocampi, are impaired in their function by stress. Taken together, sleep, good diet and stress management are the fundamentals of supporting your memory.

Some memory-improving techniques to try

- To help retain new information, see if you can attach it to any information you already have well-retained in your LTM
- Use "chunking"; breaking up information into sub-categories and treating each sub-category as one group
- Try the "method of loci"; think of somewhere you know well, and take a mental walk around it, placing the things (information, facts, etc.) you want to remember in well-known places along your walk (when you re-walk it, you should be able to see the items you've "left" in the visualisation)
- Use your senses; we are better at remembering information that has a visual image associated with it
- Create a narrative or story about the information you want to commit to memory; this is the mnemonic link system (or chain method) of remembering; we're better at remembering a series of associations than unconnected facts

Going further

If there is anything you have tried in the main part of this activity that has been effective, see if you can go further by using it in another area of learning that you are working on at the moment. Can you boost your memory to help yourself learn more, or more effectively? Keep practicing and build the cognitive habit!

Further reading and resources

"You Would Forget Your Head …" Improve Memory With These ADHD-Friendly Tricks: additudemag.com

How memories are formed: https://qbi.uq.edu.au/brain-basics/memory/how-are-memories-formed

Look after your memory as you grow older: https://www.health.harvard.edu/topics/memory#memory5

Stress effects on the hippocampus: https://www.ncbi.nlm.nih.gov/pmc/articles/PMC4561403/

The hippocampus, memory and dreams: https://elifesciences.org/articles/58874

2. MANAGING ANXIETY TO BOOST YOUR SELF-EFFICACY

Time: flexible, from ten minutes to ongoing in relevant situations

Who this could be for: anyone who wants to understand how anxiety can impact on learning and how to cope with anxiety to benefit learning

Resources needed: no resources needed

Why do this: understand anxiety and how managing it well can help you boost your self-belief

To begin this activity here below is some background information.

Self-efficacy and learning

Self-efficacy refers to any individual's belief in their ability or capacity to achieve particular goals. Having a positive belief in our self-efficacy is clearly of importance to us as learners; if we believe we have the capacity to achieve a particular goal, we are more motivated to try and strive towards it. Alternatively, if we do not have much belief in our potential to achieve a goal (or goals), we might not even get around to trying; we don't really believe that we can do it. Anxiety can interfere with building our sense of self-efficacy, and this activity is a suggestion to work through (or with) anxiety to boost self-efficacy in order to benefit your learning.

Anxiety: overview of thoughts, feelings and physical sensations

Anxiety can be described as a feeling of unease which ranges in intensity from slight or mild to very intense and severe. It can be felt physically, for instance through tense muscles, feeling nauseous or headaches; it can be felt emotionally, through a feeling of dread or fear of something we can't quite name; it can be noticed in our thoughts, which when we are feeling anxious can have themes of catastrophe and potential problems arising, and we can have low estimations of our ability to cope with these potential problems. Overall, our thoughts linked to anxiety can be focused on the future, with a negative flavour.

What can trigger anxiety

Anxiety is an experience often set off by feeling that there is some kind of danger or threat around us; it may not be imminent or nearby because we would be likely to react by running away or fighting (the "fight or flight" response as it is often called) in order to survive. With a broader feeling of anxiety, the threat or danger we are detecting might be situated a little further away from us than right now; for instance, we can feel anxious about a situation we know is coming up for us in the near future. It's very common to feel anxious about performance situations such as interviews and assessments of any kind, medical appointments or tests and social situations with others. We can also feel anxious about situations we have found difficult in the past, as we anticipate feeling the same, or maybe worse, the next time.

How anxiety can sometimes feed on itself: thinking and avoidance cycles

It's clear to see that anxiety can sometimes feed on itself; our negative and/or catastrophic thoughts and predictions about the future can seem likely and even like facts about what will definitely happen rather than possibilities that are as yet unproved; the more the predictions seem real, the more tense and anxious we can feel both physically and emotionally in the here-and-now, which in turn feeds our sense of threat and increases anxious thoughts.

Another way that a feeling of anxiety can feed on itself is in what we do in response to it; if, for instance, we become so anxious about a future event that we become convinced is going to go badly or even catastrophically, we might decide not to go along at all. This removes the possibility of disaster that we have imagined; however, it also takes away our chance to find out what other things could happen instead of a disaster – for instance, it going well, us coping, enjoying the event, or even it just going neutrally rather than catastrophically. If we avoid the event altogether, it also takes away our chance to find out that the imagined disaster might not be so disastrous or to find out that we are able to cope with some adversity and cope well. Avoidance of anxiety-provoking situations can therefore lead to more anxiety; although it briefly removes a source of anxiety (a feeling of relief when we don't have to go along to the appointment anymore, for instance), in the longer term, avoidance serves to maintain our belief in the difficulty or even impossibility of coping in the avoided situation and over time reduces our belief in our ability to cope.

Anxiety and self-efficacy

This is where anxiety management and learning are linked together. Learning often involves putting ourselves in anxiety-provoking situations, most obviously examinations and tests, but more widely, any time we embark on learning something, we are having to move from a position of not knowing much (or maybe not anything at all!) about a subject and move towards knowing more. To do this, we have to take some risks; we have to be able to say we don't know and not to feel we have to hide our lack of knowledge; we may have to let go of some things we thought we knew because this new learning is going to potentially lead us to question some assumptions we have about things; we have to take the risk of getting it wrong, and if we feel self-conscious about looking stupid or asking a stupid question, this can be really difficult. The traps that anxiety can set us, as above, include believing our negative or catastrophic predictions about the future to be true, and seeing avoidance of anxiety as a way of reducing it, when in fact avoidance often maintains, and can even increase, anxiety.

Consider how you can create a positive cycle of coping with the anxiety that learning situations may give you, using the ideas included above (and under tips as below) to support yourself as a learner. What do you need to be able to go towards situations that you can learn from, to boost your self-belief in your ability to achieve what you want?

Use Table 2.1 to capture some relevant information about yourself relating to anxiety and self-efficacy.

TABLE 2.1 Anxiety and self-efficacy

General situations that make me feel anxious:
Learning situations that make me feel anxious:
What I believe about my own ability and capacity to achieve my goals:
What I could do to increase my belief in my own ability and capacity to achieve my goals:

Some tips for managing anxiety and boosting your self-efficacy when learning

- Approach, do not avoid
- Take the risk of asking questions, even if you feel self-conscious
- Notice your catastrophic predictions about the future; keep asking yourself, even if this feels like a fact, is it just a prediction I have made?

- Seek to create a positive, approach-based cycle to gather evidence that you can cope with difficulty and achieve your goals
- Remember to notice your successes and feel proud of yourself; do not just focus on where it went wrong if you try something and have difficulties

Going further

As you have considered in this activity, anxiety can have negative impacts on us and be a difficult experience to tolerate; however, there is benefit to experiencing some anxiety in some settings and situations. Rather than seeking to eliminate feelings of anxiety from your life, a better aim is to be able to tolerate helpful amounts of anxiety in order to access new experiences and to learn.

To go further with this activity, read about the strengths-based concept (see further reading and resources) and consider, if you were using this strengths-based thinking about yourself, what would you identify as your strengths relating to anxiety management and toleration and to your belief in your own capacity to achieve (your self-efficacy)? Does this way of thinking which focuses on your strengths make you feel differently about yourself?

Further reading

Foulkes, L. (2023). Has Mental Health Awareness Gone Awry? https://profectusmag.com/has-mental-health-gone-awry-an-interview-with-lucy-foulkes/#:~:text=Lucy%20Foulkes%3A%20I%E2%80%99m%20concerned%20that%20these%20campaigns%20have,This%20is%20unhelpful%20for%20a%20number%20of%20reasons

Strengths-based approach: https://info.nicic.gov/sites/default/files/Strength-Based%20Approach.pdf

3. PERFECTIONISM AND PROCRASTINATION

Time: ten minutes or longer

Who this could be for: anyone who would like to understand more about perfectionism and how it can slow us down in what we are trying to learn or do

Resources needed: no resources required

Why do this: understand more about perfectionism and how it affects what we do; experiment with some ideas to challenge perfectionistic thinking and doing (or not doing, i.e., procrastination!)

Perfectionism is a human characteristic comprised of thinking and behaviours with an unrelenting focus on high standards for ourselves and potentially others too. High standards, and striving to achieve high-quality work, are in themselves not necessarily bad things of course! Perfectionistic thinking and behaviour can become problematic when it pushes us (or others around us) too much and to an unrealistic degree; when it sets impossible-to-reach finishing lines for achievement, that if they are ever achieved immediately get moved out of reach again; and when it becomes so tied up with our self-worth that we find ourselves feeling despairing and defeated before we've even begun a task because we know it will never be good enough, and in fact eventually we can become defeated, hopeless perfectionists who don't even try because there's just no point – we know perfection is expected, and it can't be achieved.

Perfectionism can be quite a debilitating characteristic if unchallenged and if present in many, or even all, areas of our day-to-day activity and efforts. Here are some typical perfectionistic beliefs:

- It must be done perfectly, or not at all
- If it can't be perfect, there's no point in doing it
- High expectations at all times are the correct expectations
- If a goal is achieved, it's likely it wasn't challenging enough in the first place
- There is no such thing as "good enough"
- To have value, something must be perfect
- My worth is closely related to whether I achieve my high standards or not

These examples of perfectionistic beliefs are as you will be able to see, quite extreme, and show all-or-nothing thinking without much room for subtleties or value ranges.

Perfectionistic beliefs can fuel behaviours and responses, such as procrastination, overworking and over-checking our work, avoidance of completion (because we're dreading the negative judgement of the work), avoidance of trying at all (because we just can't tolerate the distressing feelings of it "not being good enough"), checking with others if something is good enough (and then not believing them if they say it is), comparing even our best efforts with other people's efforts and judging our efforts not good enough in comparison and holding on to all tasks because "nobody else will do it perfectly."

These perfectionistic thinking styles, beliefs and behaviours can result in negative and difficult emotions such as anxiety and worry (we know it's just never going to be good enough and we're dreading being (self-)appraised on our never-good-enough efforts), feeling low and defeated (when we know there's no point even trying because the bar is just too high), angry (when even despite a lot of effort, we're told it's just not good enough – whether it's someone else is saying this to us or we're saying it to ourselves) and exhausted (if we are trying to do too much because we feel it's down to us to do something perfectly, as nobody else will).

Considering the above, it's clear that perfectionistic characteristics can potentially cause difficulties for us if we let them run out of hand. It's also clear that to learn effectively, we need to challenge perfectionism, especially if it's getting in the way of our trying to learn and develop in a particular subject or activity. The perfectionistic beliefs as above would really hinder us in having a go at any learning activity. And the perfectionistic behaviours could clearly hinder us in getting on with, for example, an assignment. And the emotions that might also be part of perfectionism will obviously hinder our learning.

Is perfection possible, however? And more than that, is perfection even truly desirable? We might perhaps say yes! to this, but if we really think about it, life and the world around us are in a constant state of flux, change and disorder, and for anything to achieve a "perfect" state is for it to become fixed in one immovable state that is no longer subject to change of any kind. Ultimately, the idea of perfectionism contains a kind of unlifelikeness at its heart, a stillness that is really the opposite of how the world is, and in fact in many senses, the opposite of what is great about the world. That constant flux, change, possibility and happy chaotic imperfection is what makes everything tick; one thing with the potential to be another, always ready to grow and evolve and surprise us. Perfection is quite brittle; reality is much more interesting and much sturdier!

Having considered the above, take some time to identify whether you have any perfectionistic beliefs of your own. If you identify any, see if you can come up with an alternative, more flexible belief. Use Table 2.2 to capture your thoughts. Here are three questions to consider to prompt your thinking:

- What would keep the perfectionistic goalposts stiller/set the bar in one place/stop the finishing line moving all the time?
- What if you don't even need goalposts, a bar or a finishing line at all?
- What makes a good enough rather than a perfect outcome?

48 Mental health and self-efficacy

TABLE 2.2 Perfectionist beliefs

My perfectionistic beliefs	My alternative beliefs

Now take some time to identify whether you have any perfectionistic behaviours or responses of your own too. If you identify any, see if you can come up with an alternative behaviour or response to try, that is more in line with your alternative, non-perfectionistic beliefs as above. Use Table 2.3 to capture your thoughts.

TABLE 2.3 Perfectionistic behaviours

My perfectionistic behaviours	What I could try doing instead

Going further

If you have identified any perfectionistic beliefs and behaviours of your own, you could experiment with trying the alternatives you have proposed. What can you try out from your alternative behaviours list? Is it making some "good enough" work rather than trying to make it "perfect?" Rather than trying to identify the "perfect" place or point to make a start on a learning task or activity you are stuck procrastinating about, can you just start anywhere and go from there?

You could also experiment with invoking the unpleasant feelings you might try to avoid if you find yourself doing something that isn't meeting your expectations of perfection. Can you stay with and weather these feelings, like standing in an emotional storm? If you play an instrument, and hate playing it badly, can you play badly deliberately for a while? If you are perfectionistic about your artwork, can you spend some time doing your art badly on purpose? Experiment with staying with the feelings rather than escaping from them, until they settle, even if it takes a while; you might be surprised at what you find on the other side of the storm.

Looking back across this activity, are there other ways that you could apply what you have found out to your approach to learning?

Further reading and resources

Centre for Clinical Interventions. (2023). Self Help Resources for Mental Health Problems. https://www.cci.health.wa.gov.au/Resources/Looking-After-Yourself

Kintsugi as a way of embracing imperfection, see Going further, Activity 32, Grief and loss: what was and what is

4. VISUALISATION: YOUR IDEAL LEARNING SUPPORTER

A visualisation exercise to help you identify the qualities your ideal learning supporter would have.

Time: five to ten minutes

Who this could be for: current learners (pupil, student and adult learner); learning supporters wishing to reflect on their own approach to supporting the learning of others

Resources needed: five to ten minutes or more of quiet time, as free as possible of interruptions/distractions

Why do this: if you want to get ready to learn and need some motivation and encouragement, if you tend to motivate yourself in a harsh or critical way, if you do not have learning supporters around you at the moment or if you only have harsh or critical learning supporters, or if you have experiences in your past of unkindness or bullying in a learning context and you have noticed this can get in the way of new learning now

Description: it is really important to be supported and motivated to learn. Sometimes support and motivation can be really tricky to find! This exercise helps you get in touch with what your ideal learning supporter might be like.

You might have had good experiences of being encouraged to learn, or you might have had negative experiences of being pushed, criticised or even bullied as part of getting you to engage in learning. We can all take on these ways of motivating ourselves as a result, even when others aren't around. Depending on what we have experienced, we might use self-talk that is encouraging and supportive ("come on, I know you can do it!"); sometimes we might use self-talk that tries to be encouraging but somehow doesn't quite support us ("why are you struggling with this? It's easy!"), and we can even end up saying really unhelpful and unkind things ("you're too stupid to understand this, you'll never get it!").

To start this exercise, find a quiet space where you will not be interrupted and make yourself comfortable. You can sit or stand wherever is most comfortable for you. If you feel safe to, closing your eyes can help. The visualisation is in two parts.

Visualisation part one

Take a few deep breaths and concentrate on slowing down and breathing deeply before you start to visualise. Once you are ready, think for a moment of how you tend to motivate yourself to approach learning, whether it's reading, research or trying an activity. What helps you to make a start and to keep going when it's challenging?

Now think back to a time when you felt really encouraged and safe to learn or a time when you were trying something new and felt supported and trusted to have a go. It might have been learning a practical skill, trying a sport or craft activity, playing an instrument, understanding a theory or idea as part of study or a range of other possibilities. The main point is to identify a time when you felt good about learning. Once you've identified a memory, can you notice what it was about the situation that helped you to feel safe, encouraged, supported and trusted? In particular, can you think back to who supported you to learn – what was it about them that helped you? In your mind's eye, try to notice how they looked, how they sounded and what they said. If you can notice colours, shapes, sounds and any sensory details, bring them to your attention and hold them in mind. Also try to notice how you felt in that moment. What emotions and sensations were you experiencing?

If you struggle to think of a positive experience, as an alternative you can bring to mind something you've seen in a film, game or TV programme if anything fits for you. Have you ever seen a fictional character being supported to learn? Notice all the details of that situation as above, colours, shapes, sounds and any sensory details. Imagine how the character felt in that moment. What emotions and sensations might they have been experiencing?

Take a good look around what's in your mind and notice as much detail as you can.

Visualisation part two

Continue with some calm, deep breaths. Take your time to build a picture in your mind's eye of what your ideal learning supporter looks like, drawing on what you've thought of so far if it helps. Are they human, or are they another species or even a combination of different species?

How do they stand, sit or move? What tone of voice do they have (if they are saying anything)? What kinds of things do they say? Overall, how do they behave? Are they supportive and kind?

See if you can distil these ideas into a single image, and a single phrase, or even one word. If you want to, say the phrase or word out loud a few times and notice how it feels to hear it aloud.

Once you've completed the visualisation, bring yourself back to the here-and-now by noticing what's around you and stretching or moving.

Going further

The next time you are in a situation where you need to motivate yourself to learn something or to try something new, bring your ideal learning supporter to mind. See if using this ideal learning supporter helps you with your learning.

You can also use the ideal learning supporter you have created to help you with any memories of difficult learning experiences in the past if there is anything that you often think of and you find it holds you back in your current learning. Visualise the ideal learning supporter helping out past you in the difficult situation. You might find this helps to "unstick" the problematic memory a little and help you to move on from it.

Further reading

Lee, D. (2005). The perfect nurturer: A model to develop a compassionate mind within the context of cognitive therapy. In P. Gilbert (Ed.), *Compassion: Conceptualisations, research and use in psychotherapy* (pp. 326–351). Routledge.

5. DISTRESS TOLERANCE AND EMOTIONAL REGULATION SKILLS

Time: from a few minutes to longer, depending on the activity you try

Who this could be for: anyone who would like to try out some ideas for managing and regulating emotions

Resources needed: a quiet safe place to try out the activities

Why do this: understand more about how our emotions can affect our learning and try some activities to build emotional regulation skills

Being able to tolerate distress and regulate our emotions are important skills and will support learning in fundamental ways. When we're distressed and overwhelmed by emotions, our brains are not in a calm state that supports good, useful learning; we're in survival mode, feeling threatened and needing to get away from the overwhelming feelings, rather than engaged and ready to learn. We will learn only one thing when we're in this state – that this situation is dangerous and distressing, and we need to avoid it in future! If we want to take in, understand and incorporate new information into our existing learning and to make connections, challenge ideas and all the things that learning involves, we need to be in a state that supports this. Distress tolerance and emotional regulation skills are therefore really helpful for every learner of every age.

In his letter of 12 August 1904 to Franz Xaver Kappus, poet Rainer Maria Rilke offers this perspective on experiencing and tolerating emotions:

> So you must not be frightened, dear Mr. Kappus, if a sadness rises up before you larger than any you have ever seen; if a restiveness, like light and cloud shadows, passes over your hands and over all you do. You must think that something is happening with you, that life has not forgotten you, that it holds you in its hand; it will not let you fall.

It's worth remembering that the process of learning in itself can often include emotional reactions (maybe excitement at finding out a new, interesting thing or anger at finding out about something unfair), and these emotions can be useful, and part of learning – a spur to find out more, or take action in the world, or just a motivation to continue learning, in the case of the emotions around feeling excited or engaged. However, if the process of learning triggers distress and overwhelming emotions, we might be motivated to try to get away from these feelings – and if that results in us wanting to get away from the process of learning, this can really get in our way. What might be helpful is to find a way to experience the important emotional components of the learning experience, without being overwhelmed if difficult or negative emotions, or distress, arise, and then trying to escape or avoid.

The techniques included here are therefore all different ways to try to reach the same place – being able to manage distress and to regulate emotions. It is worth experimenting with these to see if any work for you. If they do, once you have learned the technique, you can keep practising it and use it any time that it might be helpful to you. The techniques don't require any resources other than, usually, a few minutes somewhere quiet and safe to just try them out.

If you read about these techniques and feel very sceptical, you are not alone! It's worth giving your sceptical self a little time off, just to try these out. If you don't find them useful, that's fine – your inner sceptic can say "I told you so!" to their heart's content. But if you do find something useful, what a great outcome! And your inner sceptic will forgive you, eventually.

Flip your feelings

This is an exercise to try for changing how you are feeling. Use it to experiment with paying attention to and altering your emotions, especially if you are feeling stuck with or in a difficult emotional state.

1. Firstly, notice any difficult, negative or upsetting emotion you are feeling. It might be linked to a situation or memory; the main thing is to notice what you are feeling in the here-and-now
2. Take a few deep breaths and pay attention to how your feelings are affecting your body; you might notice them mainly in your chest, for instance, or more in your head. Just notice where they are and breathe into them. It can help to close your eyes while you try this
3. Now take a moment to name this emotion (or emotions) to yourself. Notice what the emotion is and where and how you are feeling it in your body
4. As you notice, ask yourself, what would the opposite of this emotion (or emotions) be? And what would the opposite physical sensation to go with that opposite emotion or emotions be?
5. Now breathe into this part of your body, and imagine the flip, or opposite, of this sensation happening. You can imagine breathing it in, if you like, letting the opposite sensation also bring in the opposite emotion(s)
6. Keep breathing and just notice what happens to your physical sensations and to your emotions
7. When you're ready, open your eyes and move about to bring yourself back to the here-and-now

Butterfly hug

This technique can help with self-soothing and with managing distress and overwhelming or very difficult emotions. It was developed by Lucina Artigas to help survivors of Hurricane Pauline in Mexico in 1998. It's now often used to help people manage the impact of trauma. It works by stimulating both sides of the body. Our brains are divided into two hemispheres, left and right, and each hemisphere controls the opposite side of our body – so, broadly speaking, left brain hemisphere controls right of body and right brain hemisphere controls left of body, with some functions controlled by both hemispheres at once. The butterfly hug, by crossing the midline of the body, stimulates and gets all of your body to work together.

Give yourself a butterfly hug

Make yourself comfortable and take a few slow breaths.

Cross your arms over loosely in front of your chest, as if you are using your arms to make a multiplication sign across your body. It does not matter which arm is over which, just they need to cross over.

Rest the fingers of each hand lightly just below your collarbone, so your left hand is resting below your right-side collarbone and your right hand is resting below your left side collarbone. Interlock your thumbs (which will be pointing up to your chin). If you look down, you can see where the name for this exercise comes from; your hands have made a butterfly shape, with your thumbs like the thorax and your fingers like the butterfly's wings. It's not the most accurate representation of a butterfly but you get the idea!

Keep breathing deeply and flap each "butterfly wing" up and down in turn, so that the fingers of your right hand tap the left side of your chest and then the fingers of your left hand tap the right side of your chest. Keep going with this, each side in turn, so each side is tapped at least eight to ten times. Try to adopt a steady rhythm as you do this, you can count aloud if it helps you to set up a rhythm, as the time it takes to say "one" should be enough to tap once each side.

Keep breathing slowly and deeply while you do this and notice what happens to any difficult or distressing emotions you are dealing with as you move the butterfly's wings up and down in turn.

You can keep going with this if you are noticing good effects or if any distress is lessening or moving away from you.

Make a calming/comforting/soothing box

This activity is a chance to put together a resource that you can use to help yourself feel calmed, soothed and comforted at times when emotions are overwhelming or difficult or when you are feeling distress. When we're feeling bad, it can sometimes be difficult to remember the things that help us feel better – a calming/comforting/soothing box is a useful way of having what you need easily to hand, without having to remember what you find helpful, for any time you might need it.

You can make this a physical container, or if you prefer, you could assemble a virtual version – maybe a list of things that help that you save on your phone, so it's accessible anytime for you.

You can also come up with your own name for this resource – you might want to call it a rescue box rather than a calming/comforting/soothing box, for example, or anything else that best sums up what you've put together to help and support yourself with feeling good.

Purpose

Create an easy-to-find resource box with items that you find calming, comforting and soothing. Items should trigger good feelings for you in each of the five senses. Interacting with these items when you are feeling distressed or overwhelmed should help you feel better, and having them to hand if needed means you don't have to remember what works when you're feeling overwhelmed – you can just reach for the resource box.

Resources

- One container, big enough to hold the items you select
- Example items from each of the five senses

Selecting items for your calming/comforting/soothing box

One way of identifying items to include is to work through each of the five senses. Below are some suggestions for each of our five senses to prompt your thinking. Even if it's difficult to think of things at first, persevere, and you will start to remember or to think of things as you go.

Sight

Is there anything you like looking at? Any particular colours? Are there photographs of something beautiful or a happy time with others (or alone) that would trigger good feelings if you looked at them? Would pictures of companion animals, or the natural world, be soothing to look at? (See further reading at the end of this section for how viewing images of the natural world can improve our wellbeing.) Is there an item that you find beautiful and soothing to look at (such as a pebble or stone, a pattern on material, a painting or an image of an artwork)? Is there somewhere you've visited or an event you went to that you associate with feeling really good, and if so, can you identify a photograph or other visual cue that you associate with that experience (it could be a photograph, but it could equally be a ticket, a postcard, a menu and so on).

Sound

Is there a particular piece of music you like listening to? Or a sound that makes you feel good? You might not want to put an actual recording of it in the box, so instead you could write down the name of the music or sound and include where you can listen to it (i.e., online or saved on your phone). This is an area where assembling a virtual calming/comforting/soothing box is really good because you can include links to lots of music and sounds to make them easily reachable.

Is there an item that makes a noise you find soothing or pleasant? It might be a seed pod that rattles or something that crinkles up. There may be something that is a combination of sound and touch here of course such as a piece of material that is nice to touch and makes a pleasing sound when you brush your hand over it.

The concept of autonomous sensory meridian response (ASMR) has gained a lot of popularity in recent years, and you can read more about this and the potential soothing effects it elicits, see further reading.

It's worth considering that when you are distressed and overwhelmed, you might find a lot of noise makes you feel even worse and if so, you could include noise-cancelling headphones or earplugs (or even fluffy earmuffs) in the box to put on if you need.

Touch

Are there materials, items or objects that you find soothing and calming to touch? It might be that particular textures feel good. Sometimes very smooth surfaces feel good, such as an exceptionally smooth stone. Something squashy can also be good. Bubble wrap might work for you; the bubbles can be popped, and this also gives you something to focus on that's tactile while you seek to calm and soothe yourself. There might be an item that has particular significance for you, or an item of clothing, that has tactile qualities you want to include in this resource. Lots of people find making a fuss of a companion animal soothing; don't put your pet in the box, obviously, but you may want to include a piece of material that feels similar, if your pet isn't around when you need to use this resource! A hand cream or moisturiser might be something you could include, where the action of rubbing this into your skin can help with focusing on something and could therefore bring calm. If you select this, it may be that the cream also has a pleasing and soothing smell, so this also fits the next sense area.

Smell

Are there particular smells that you find soothing, calming or associated with good times? Many people find herbal or floral scents soothing, and essential oil dispensers with rollerballs are available. Items such as books can have a scent of their own that can be associated with good feelings. If the smell you want to include in the box is very ephemeral (a food item for instance that you can't store), then you could add a note to yourself that names the scent to remind yourself. Something you could include is mint-flavoured chewing gum or sweets, as a powerful smell such as mint can help to bring us back to the here-and-now when we're feeling distressed. This suggestion also fits with Taste, of course.

Taste

As above, a strong-flavoured sweet might be something you want to include. There may be tastes you associate with feeling calm and soothed; these might be very personal and idiosyncratic to you and depend on your experiences. For instance, if you have a really happy memory of a particular meal, the taste you might want to include could be anything associated with that experience. You might think of a beach holiday as a time when you felt soothed and relaxed; if so, a beach-related taste such as sea-salt might be your choice.

Assembling your calming/comforting/soothing box

Put the item or items you have identified from each of the senses as above in the box and store it somewhere easy to get to if and when you need it. You don't need to have something for every sense – even just one item, if it works for you, is enough.

You may have identified items that fit under more than one sensory area, in fact it's very likely that you will have done. This is fine – include them! This is your resource box, and you can make it to fit your needs.

Don't forget you can add to this box (or remove something) any time you want to.

Building your emotional awareness

Sometimes just working on becoming more aware of your emotions can be a useful part of emotional regulation. If you are someone who tends to either minimise, ignore or push through your emotions, you might not be in the habit of even being able to notice how you are feeling until the feelings are really overwhelming and can't be pushed away. Or it might be that you are someone who doesn't feel "entitled" to your emotions, especially if you are feeling distressed; you might tell yourself that you shouldn't, or do not deserve to, feel bad, when others are worse off. If you notice you do hold a hierarchy of acceptable emotional reactions in your mind, it can be that as a result you push your emotions away.

Trying out increasing your emotional self-awareness can have some interesting benefits. Spend a few days checking in with yourself and noticing how you are feeling; you can keep a brief mood diary during this time to help you. See the emotions wheel in further reading and resources to help you really put your emotions into words. You can also experiment with telling someone else how you are really feeling. During your time trying out this idea, find out what it's like to respond when someone asks "how are you?" with a word or two that does actually accurately describe your emotional state. Rather than "I'm fine!" might you be saying, "I'm feeling a bit short-tempered," or "I'm feeling quite peaceful," or "I'm feeling a bit sad but also quite optimistic." Notice what it's like, and how it feels, to share how you're feeling with someone else during this time. It would be interesting to notice how other people react to this, too.

Going further

Try out some of the ideas given above and keep practicing for a month. At the end of the month, review whether you feel different overall to how you did at the start of the month, and note whether there have been any changes in the way that you manage emotions or in the way that you react to situations. Are there any helpful changes that you would like to maintain?

Further reading and resources

ASMR (autonomous sensory meridian response). (2023): https://en.wikipedia.org/wiki/ASMR

Distress tolerance resources and ideas to try: https://www.getselfhelp.co.uk/docs/DealingwithDistress.pdf

EMDR: Origins of butterfly hug technique used in EMDR trauma therapy: https://emdrfoundation.org/toolkit/butterfly-hug.pdf

The EMDR Association: https://emdrassociation.org.uk/

The emotions wheel: https://practicalpie.com/the-emotion-wheel/

Works well with

Activity 5, Chapter 2: Distress tolerance and emotional regulation skills
Activity 10, Chapter 6: … and breathe

6. HOW TO VALUE YOU FOR YOU AND NOT JUST FOR WHAT YOU ACHIEVE: HUMAN BEINGS NOT HUMAN DOINGS

Time: 20 minutes reading; one week or longer if trying the activities

Who this could be for: anyone wishing to think more broadly about how to live and how to value themselves, beyond examination results, grades or scores; anyone who finds their To-Do lists never gets any shorter

Resources needed: a method for recording your To-Be list to refer to it when you wish to

Why do this: if you want to develop a sense of your value without linking this to examination results, grades or scores, achievement or activity; if you tend to value yourself only conditional on what you achieve or if others do

It is very easy, especially if you are engaged in learning that is measured via exam success, tests, scores and assessments, to find yourself equating your own worth as a person with your marks, grades and scores. It is especially difficult to keep a sense of your own inherent worth and value separate from marks, grades and scores when you are constantly being told that your future is going to be decided by those outcomes and when you are under pressure from all sides to achieve the most you can. This can lead to difficult emotions. Consider the following, written by an O-Level student in the 1970s:

> It Is not
> How do I feel?
>
> Is this
> important to me?
> No questions asked.
>
> It is only:
> She is
> property.
>
> It is not
> do I think?
> Have I feelings
> at all?
>
> Only there is a
> brain in there
> somewhere.
> Plain academic.
>
> It is not
> help me,

help me
to be happy.

It is only:
her exam results will
reflect well on us.

(Anonymous 15-year-old O-Level student, 1970s, Wallace, 1983)

This activity is not about deciding that those achievements you are working towards don't have meaning, nor is it suggesting that you should not strive for success in what you are studying. Instead, it is a chance to consider how you can find and then maintain a sense of your own inherent, unchallengeable worth and value as a human being, whatever directions your learning takes you in and whatever marks, grades and scores you get or don't get in the future (or did or didn't get in the past).

Two ideas relevant to how you might value yourself are introduced below, and following this are three activities to try, as ways to build your sense of self-worth just as you are, without linking it to any particular achievement.

Carl Rogers and humanistic psychology: who is worth what and when?

Psychologist Carl Rogers developed person-centred therapy, putting the individual at the heart of the therapy process. Rogers saw our essential natures as seeking to achieve "self-actualisation": a reaching of our own potential to be the human beings we are capable of becoming. Rogers considered that we need a positive regard for ourselves, feeding a sense of self-worth, to be able to achieve self-actualisation (being all that we can be). An important element of the person-centred approach was developing an understanding of what ideas of self-valuing or self-worth an individual has developed.

Rogers saw these as influenced by how important people in our early lives interacted with us and showed us "positive regard": that is, let us know that they loved, valued and regarded us well. Rogers considered our two fundamental psychological needs as children as being to gain positive regard from others, and from this to gain a sense of self-worth. So, we are highly motivated to seek positive regard. Rogers considered that there were two types of this important stuff: unconditional positive regard and conditional positive regard. Unconditional positive regard is given without conditions, it's not dependent on doing or not doing particular things; it's not stopped in the face of mistakes or doing something wrong. Conditional positive regard in contrast is given conditional on certain behaviours, responses and ways of being. If those aren't present, the positive regard is withdrawn.

Rogers saw these two types of positive regard as having different effects on our developing sense of self-worth; plenty of unconditional positive regard would be likely to lead to us building a sense of self-worth that isn't capricious or dependent on us doing the "right" thing; we know we'll be well-thought of even if we make mistakes. This is likely to feed into us having confidence to try because failure isn't going to lead to withdrawal of positive regard. Plenty of conditional positive regard, on the other hand, is likely to lead to us building a sense of self-worth that's much more linked to whether we do well or get things "right": we'll be likely to feel we will only be thought well of if we do these things. And because it's so unpleasant for us, especially when we are very young, to lose positive regard, we might seek to avoid getting it "wrong," and strive really hard to get it "right," because we don't want to be out in the emotional cold!

It's apparent that the way we organise our world is often very aligned to the idea of conditional positive regard; much of our experience can reinforce the idea that our worth is conditional on us doing certain things and/or doing well. The way we esteem and value each other, the way we conceptualise success and many other things can reinforce that we might have value in certain circumstances and with certain conditions, but the idea of us having inherent value is often lacking. Having read the above, could we benefit from a more unconditional valuing of each other?

Human beings not human doings

The statement "we're human beings, not human doings," attributed to different sources, is worth consideration in relation to how we value ourselves. In adult life, it is very typical to define ourselves by the kind of work we do when asked about ourselves, the classic question being "what do you do for a living?" When we are children and into our teenage years, a question we are typically asked by people wanting to find out more about us might be, "what do you want to be when you grow up?" The expected answer usually is related to what kind of work we might want to do.

These work-oriented mindsets are embedded in the way we think about ourselves, other people and the world. In fact, it is arguable that the social and economic developments of the last few hundred years have required this elision of work and self, being and doing. The future, however, is going to present some significant challenges to these self-concept and world-concepts; projections of how work will change in the near and further future suggest huge shifts in what kind of work will be required and the potential alteration or even disappearance of many current areas of human employment and work activity as machine and AI developments take on many of the roles previously undertaken by humans. If work changes in the future, and in fact becomes less of a relevant definition of us, and if what we do stops defining who we are (if it ever did, all that much), where does that leave us – and who does that leave us as?

Activity 1: positive regard: no conditions!

Spend a week thinking of yourself in a positive, accepting, non-judgemental manner; keep in mind that you are going to feel proud of yourself and think well towards yourself, no matter what, not because you've done certain things but just because. Especially if you tend to value yourself on the condition that you achieve certain things (for instance getting through the To-Do list), try out seeing yourself as of value to yourself and others completely independently of what you do. At the end of the week, how do you feel? Do you feel different? If so, in what way?

Activity 2: write your To-Be list

Having read about the ideas in this activity (and also in further reading and resources), take some time to create a "To-Be" list for yourself, instead of your usual To-Do list. What are you going to give some time to that's not an activity related to achievement, doing things or the completion of which is connected to your value as a person? In other words, what is your human being-centred To-Be list going to include in contrast to a more typical human doing-centred To-Do list? It might be that you will include things like spending time not doing anything, using some mindfulness of breath practice, going for a walk, swim or cycle ride or doing something you enjoy that doesn't have any sense of achievement attached to it at all.

Proposed To-Be list:

- Be realistic in my expectations of myself
- Be surprised by others
- Be at peace with what I can't get done
- Be relaxed
- Be in a quiet place

Spend a week (or longer) using your "To-Be" list as a guide for how you want to use your time. Note how you feel at the start of this and how you feel at the end of this process. Do you feel different? If so, in what way?

Activity 3: alternative questions to find out about who someone is and alternative things to learn ready for the future

If "what do you want to be when you grow up" and "what do you do" are questions you think could do with some updating, have a go at coming up with some alternative, less work-oriented ways of asking someone about themselves. "How do you want to feel when you grow up?" and "what makes you happy?" perhaps?

Given the potential shift in the nature of and need for many kinds of work in the future, what in your view is the most helpful thing to learn about in the here-and-now to be ready for a future in which work may no longer be a defining characteristic for us? Is learning about how to manage our time to ensure our wellbeing more relevant than, for example, learning how to do a particular job?

Having generated some alternative questions to ask someone about themselves, find someone to try them out on and listen to what they have to say. Considering your thoughts about what is most useful to learn as a skill ready for the future, you could also seek ways to bring learning about that into your life now.

Going further

See what happens if you spend a week offering the other people in your life, and that you interact with, unconditional positive regard. How do you (and they) feel at the end of the week? Do you notice any differences? Is there anything you would like to keep doing in the future that you've tried in this experimental week?

Reference

Wallace, B. (1983). *Teaching the very able child*. Ward Lock Educational Limited.

Further reading

Mcleod, Saul. (2023). Person-Centred Therapy And Core Conditions. Simply Psychology. https://www.simplypsychology.org/client-centred-therapy.html

How the COVID pandemic changed American attitudes to work: https://www.theguardian.com/money/2021/nov/28/goodbye-to-job-how-the-pandemic-changed-americans-attitude-to-work

You are a Human Being, not a Human Doing. (2022). https://www.psychologytoday.com/intl/blog/the-power-of-prime/202205/seven-ways-to-change-from-a-human-doing-to-a-human-being

7. ASSERTIVENESS

Time: 15–30 minutes reading time, longer for trying the assertiveness ideas

Who this could be for: anyone who would like to know more about assertiveness and to try out some ideas for increasing assertiveness

Resources needed: others to interact with for practicing assertiveness skills

Why do this: understand more about assertiveness and how it supports both wellbeing and learning; try out some ideas to boost your assertiveness

Assertiveness is a communication skill that is worth developing. In addition to being a really useful skill in life generally, being able to be assertive is also greatly beneficial for your learning journey. If you are able to identify your learning needs and then communicate them to relevant people in order to get your learning needs met, you will be able to make better progress than if you can't assertively say what you need. Asking for help and support in learning requires assertiveness and confidence, as does being able to say you don't understand something or need more information, or a different type of resource or learning method. Assertiveness skills will improve your learning and increase your confidence and sense of self-efficacy, and all of these taken together will be good for your wellbeing.

Assertiveness is about being able to state your thoughts, needs and opinions, without either dominating others or being dominated by others. If you are assertive, you can also stand up for others as well as yourself. In an ideal situation, you are able to balance asserting yourself with compromising with others while neither fading into the background nor taking over completely! This can be a tricky balancing act, and this activity is a chance to consider the idea of assertiveness and identify if there are things you can do to get the balance right.

Assertiveness can be seen as in the middle of a communication style continuum that runs from passive to assertive to aggressive:

PASSIVE	ASSERTIVE	AGGRESSIVE

FIGURE 2.1 Assertiveness communication style

Communicating with others in an assertive way is in the middle of the passive-assertive-aggressive continuum. Some ways different parts of the communication continuum might look, feel and be evident are set out below:

TABLE 2.4 Communication continuum

	PASSIVE	ASSERTIVE	AGGRESSIVE
Things you might say (or not say):	Apologise a lot Seek permission a lot from others Put yourself down often Not mention your needs or dismiss them ("don't worry about me") Not express an opinion even if it's sought by others Rambling, roundabout way of speaking, dodging the issue Seek permission from others	Make your opinions, needs and choices clear to yourself and others Speak in short clear statements; "I think," "I need," "I feel" Flexible thinking Be able to say how you feel Be able to state your feelings and emotions ("I feel" and "that makes me feel")	Tell others rather than ask Say "I" a lot Statements rather than questions Assume others agree or insist that they should Rigid/inflexible rules If asking questions, insisting on/ framing for particular answers that you want to get (leading questions)
Things you might do:	Avoid putting yourself forward or taking the lead Let others decide for you Hope others will guess what you would choose rather than actively explain it Avoid-oriented behaviour	Seek others' opinions Listen Ask questions Seek compromise Approach-oriented behaviour Able to give and accept constructive criticism without becoming defensive or taking it very personally Approach-oriented behaviour	Be dismissive of others Talk over or interrupt others Insist on your way Refuse to compromise, be uninterested in finding a compromise or common ground
Ways you might feel:	Threatened Uncertain Of low value Not listened to Not considered Frustrated Resentful Safe from being criticised or denied what you might need (because you haven't made it clear) Negative about others	Calm Confident Safe Brave Optimistic Resilient Realistic Interested Positive about others Respectful of others	Angry Fearful Inflexible Powerful/important Frustrated

Mental health and self-efficacy **67**

A few ideas for practising your assertive communication skills

Here are some ideas for practising your assertive communication skills. Depending where on the assertive communication spectrum you are, you may want to practise skills that increase your assertiveness or lessen your aggressive communication style and move it more towards assertive instead. The ideas below offer some ideas for each possibility. There are many more ways to practise assertiveness skills, and having read the above continuum, you might also have some ideas of your own.

Sorry not sorry

Spend some time (a day or a few hours) noticing how often you apologise when you speak; not when you've done something wrong that merits an apology but when you are just sharing some information, asking something or explaining what you think. Do you find yourself saying, "no I'm sorry, I don't like those biscuits" or "sorry, could you tell me what the time is" or "I'm sorry but I really think that's not a good idea" or some similar phrases?

If you notice you do this a lot, experiment with not saying this quite as often, just for a few hours at first. You could practice saying some of the above examples without the apology, so "no, I don't like those biscuits" or "can you tell me the time?" or "I don't think that's a good idea." Notice how it feels to stop pre-emptively apologising for what you are about to say and notice how others react. If you like this communication style with less apologising, you could stick with it for more than just a few hours or a day!

Assertive body language

Try some assertive body language. Sitting or standing up with your back as straight as you can make it, making eye contact (if that would be very stressful, try looking near someone's eyes or to their forehead) and putting your shoulders back can all help you feel more confident and present. If you notice you are holding your body tense, try to drop your shoulders and let go of the physical tension. Take slow steady breaths and use your diaphragm to draw air into your lungs (put one hand on the top of your stomach and feel your abdomen inflating and deflating like a balloon to practice this kind of breathing). When you speak, speak calmly and from your centre, using your breath, rather than in a rush.

Express an opinion

If you tend to leave others to decide on plans or choices, and don't express an opinion, practice expressing an opinion to others: friends, family, learning or working peer group. Notice how it feels to express your opinion and how others react. It might be that your predictions of how you will feel and how others will react are different to what actually happens.

Give others space

If you have noticed any of the aggressive communication behaviours or ways of speaking in Table 2.4 in yourself, some ideas to try to move your communication style towards assertive instead: ask open questions of others; allow others space to speak, and try not to interrupt; try to flex any immovable rules you might have about what others "should" be saying or doing; try to get comfortable with not knowing, and adopt a curious mindset; see if you can find value in the opinions of others, and consider if their perspective could teach you something or help you. It might be that your communication style is defensive because you are seeking to protect yourself from something; if so, and you can identify what it is, it might be worth considering if there are ways to test out if what you fear is really something to be frightened of or not.

Going further

To take this activity further, you could keep an assertiveness diary over a week or two; make a note of the assertive skills you used, what situations you used them in, how you felt and what the result or outcome of you being assertive was. Review the information you gather at the end of the week or two. What have you learned? How are you feeling? How are you feeling about yourself and about other people? Has anything surprising happened or changed?

Further reading and resources

Self Help Resources for Mental Health Problems. (2023). Center for Clinical Interventions. CCI - Self Help Resources for Mental Health Problems: https://www.cci.health.wa.gov.au/Resources/Looking-After-Yourself/Assertiveness

8. APPROACH/AVOID AWARENESS: GOAL ORIENTATION THEORY AND YOUR LEARNING

Time: depending on the approach-oriented experiment you choose to try; from a few minutes to as long as is relevant to your chosen experiment

Who this could be for: anyone who would like to be more active and approach-oriented in their learning behaviours

Resources needed: depending entirely on the approach-oriented experiment you choose to try

Why do this: recognise when you are avoiding something you either need to do to learn or would benefit from doing, and find ways to stop avoiding and start approaching

> You gain strength, courage, and confidence by every experience in which you really stop to look fear in the face. You are able to say to yourself, 'I have lived through this horror. I can take the next thing that comes along.' You must do the thing you think you cannot do.
>
> *(Roosevelt, 1960)*

Eleanor Roosevelt's assertion, that by looking fear in the face and doing the things we think we can't do, we can gain strength, courage, and confidence, may seem rather daunting! Avoidance, or at least doing our best to avoid, or, if complete avoidance is not possible, at least minimise, is a very normal and understandable response to difficult situations that may give rise to aversive or unpleasant feelings such as fear. It gives us a short-term benefit, too, in that we don't have to manage the unpleasant and aversive feelings the situation we are avoiding may give us; what a (short-term) relief! However, we know that avoidance can have some unhelpful outcomes; for instance, continued avoidance of a particular situation can remove our opportunity to find out that the avoided situation isn't as difficult or frightening as we predict or that it is difficult but not intolerably so and we can cope with it. Continued avoidance can also, over time, reduce our belief in our ability to cope with the situation, and in fact, this belief may start to expand to cover more, and different, situations to the one that we initially started avoiding. In fact, it can become a habit, and our default mode of responding, particularly to new or unknown situations. We can start to default to assuming that (1) we can't cope with it and (2) we should probably therefore avoid it.

This is where having an understanding of how avoidance can become a loop (itself maintaining and increasing avoidance, increasing anxiety and reducing our self-confidence), combined with an understanding of goal orientation theory and in particular the approach/avoid orientations, can be helpful to you as a learner. This activity is a chance to read more about goal orientation and about approach/avoid in relation to goal orientation, and also a chance to identify your own behaviours related to approach and avoid as you notice them in your own learning.

Goal orientation theory was developed through the work of educational psychologists and psychologists such as David McClelland, James Eison, John Nicholls and Carol Dweck. Initially, the theory identified two types of goal orientation:

- **mastery orientation** (also referred to as **learning orientation**), where an individual is motivated by wanting to acquire new knowledge or new skills
- **performance orientation**, where an individual is motivated by wanting to demonstrate their ability, knowledge or competence to others

A mastery orientation in relation to your goals is likely to mean you are motivated by self-decided measures or standards; you want to achieve the goal or goals, to develop your skills or to gain competence for yourself more than for others.

A performance orientation in relation to your goals is likely to mean that you are more motivated by gaining skills, competence and knowledge in relation to how your achievements will be judged by, and in comparison to, other people. Your motivation to reach goals is therefore more relative to how you are doing related to others, for instance you might be motivated to try to be the best in a group who are all seeking to improve in the same area. In addition to wanting to be good (or the best) in relation to others, this goal orientation can also include a motivation not to be the worst, to avoid ending up judged as less good (or even the least good!) in relation to others in a particular activity or learning area.

Further theoretical development has added the concepts of approach orientation and avoidance orientation to the initial mastery and performance orientations, resulting in four goal orientation profiles: mastery-approach, mastery-avoidance, performance-approach and performance-avoidance.

The possible combinations of goal orientation are defined by Wolters (2004) as:

Mastery-approach: those focused on learning, application of effort, gaining and increasing competence
Mastery-avoidance: those motivated to gain mastery in order to avoid doing less well than previously or in order to avoid failing to learn enough/as much as they can
Performance-approach: those motivated to evidence their ability and skill to others
Performance-avoidance: those motivated to avoid seeming unskilled/not competent/less able than others, to others.

Activity: what's my goal orientation profile?

Take some time to identify where your own goal orientation is within the matrix above. It may be that it depends on the situation; it may be that you find your style is consistent across many situations. There are goal-orientation quizzes and questionnaires available online. Here are two examples:

https://www.sfu.ca/~jcnesbit/EDUC220/StratRef/GOQ.htm
https://scales.arabpsychology.com/s/achievement-goal-questionnaire-revised-agq-r/

Alternatively, having read the above information on goal orientation theory, you may prefer to consider your behaviours and decide for yourself what seems most like you.

Activity: identify an approach-oriented experiment and try it out for yourself

This activity is in two parts and is a chance to explore the ideas around goal orientation theory further, in relation to your own experiences. Whether you have established that you are more mastery-oriented, or more performance-oriented in relation to working towards goals, you can also now consider whether you are more approach-oriented or more avoid-oriented within your mastery/performance orientation too. Keeping in mind the ideas at the start of this section on how avoidance can result in more avoidance, this activity is a consideration of how to identify a more approach-oriented mindset.

1. Nurturing an approach-oriented mindset is of help to you as a learner. To put this into practice, consider your current learning circumstances and spend some time considering how you are displaying approach-oriented behaviours in your current learning. Now also consider how you are displaying avoidance-oriented behaviours in your current learning.

TABLE 2.5 Learning and avoidance behaviours

My approach-oriented learning behaviours:
My avoidance-oriented learning behaviours:

2 Review the avoidance-oriented behaviours if you have identified any above. Consider whether there is anything there that you would like to experiment with moving into the approach-oriented zone. What would you need to do? Is it as simple as doing the opposite of avoidance, or is there a need to identify how an approach-oriented alternative behaviour would happen or what it would comprise? For example, if there is something you have avoided because you don't understand how to do it, would your approach-oriented learning plan be to find somebody to ask?

Make a plan for the avoidance-oriented learning behaviour you want to "flip" and make a prediction for how you think it will go. Then, put your plan into practice. Review what actually happened in comparison with your prediction and capture your thoughts about what you have learned (about yourself, others, the world, learning and a specific subject) through trying this activity. If you get to this stage, you've practised a bit of approach-orientation, so do not forget to be proud of yourself for being brave enough to try this!

TABLE 2.6 Learning behaviours

My avoidance-oriented learning behaviour that I am going to flip:
How I plan to flip it to an approach-oriented learning behaviour:
My prediction of what will happen when I try this:
What actually happened when I tried this and what did I learn?

Going further

Keep practising your approach-oriented learning behaviours if you have found them helpful; you may have found them helpful in unexpected ways.

You can go further with this idea by considering if there are other situations in your life that you can bring your new understanding of goal orientation theory into. As a further development of this activity, you could also keep a wellbeing or mood diary concurrently with trying these approach-oriented behaviours. What effect does this practice have on your mood day-to-day and on your wellbeing overall? Keep the diary for a week, for instance, and then review what you have found and consider what you have learned and what, if any, changes you might want to make from considering your learning. Table 2.7 is a suggested structure; you may wish to record the information in a different way.

TABLE 2.7 Diary reflection

	My approach-oriented learning behaviour	*My mood during the day*	*Self-rating of overall wellbeing*	*Notes and thoughts*
MON				
TUES				
WEDS				
THURS				
FRI				
SAT				
SUN				
After one week: Reflection on my diary: what have I learned? What changes do I want to make, considering what I have learned?				

Works well with

Activity 2, Chapter 2: Managing anxiety to boost your self-efficacy
Activity 2, Chapter 6: Going further, Self-directed learning – where (and how) do I start?

References

Roosevelt, E. (1960). *You learn by living: Eleven keys for a more fulfilling life*. Harper & Brothers.

Wolters, C. A. (2004). "Advancing achievement goal theory: Using goal structures and goal orientations to predict students' motivation, cognition, and achievement." *Journal of Educational Psychology*, 96(2), 236–250. https://doi.org/10.1037/0022-0663.96.2.236

Further reading

Elliot, A. J., & Murayama, K. (2008). On the measurement of achievement goals: Critique, illustration, and application. *Journal of Educational Psychology, 100*(3), 613–628. https://doi.org/10.1037/0022-0663.100.3.613

Growth mindset. Psychology Today (2023). https://www.psychologytoday.com/us/basics/growth-mindset

Roosevelt, E. (1960). You learn by living: Eleven keys for a more fulfilling life. Harper & Brothers.

9. THINKING STYLES

Time: ten minutes reading time, then flexible, depending on for how long and how often you would like to pay attention to your thinking styles to notice what habits of thought you might have

Who this could be for: anyone who wants to gain understanding of what thinking styles they have and how they might influence their mood and the choices they make

Resources needed: no resources required

Why do this: learn more about your habits and styles of thinking and the effect they have on your state of mind and what you do (and don't do)

We all have habits of thought and styles of thinking. Sometimes our habits of thinking can be less than helpful to us, and it is worth considering if any of the thinking habits we use are contributing to, or increasing, our difficulties. We are often not aware of these habits of thought when we slip into them, particularly when the outcome of using them results in us feeling bad in some way or more emotional – our wise, logical thinking might shut down and we can then struggle to see things from a calm perspective.

Read through the left of Table 2.8 and see if you can recognise any of these thinking styles. On the right are some ideas for more helpful or alternative thinking styles – there might be some that you already use or some you would like to use more often.

TABLE 2.8 Thinking styles

Unhelpful thinking style	*More helpful/alternative thinking style*
All or nothing thinking Thinking in extremes, black-and-white thinking, absolutist thinking. Seeing things as at one end of a long spectrum or another rather than somewhere in between. For instance, either success or failure, good or bad, win or lose, a complete disaster or an unmitigated triumph.	**All-encompassing thinking** Nuanced, flexible thinking, thinking on a continuum, seeing a spectrum of possibilities, experimenting with holding several things to be possible, replacing "but" with "and" when thinking about situations or information.
Over-generalising Taking a specific situation and over-applying it to all situations, perceiving a pattern that might not be there.	**Specific and general thinking, each when relevant** Keeping it specific to the situation, generalising only when relevant. For example, keeping in mind that failing at one thing, once, does not equal always being a failure.

(*Continued*)

TABLE 2.8 (Continued)

Unhelpful thinking style	More helpful/alternative thinking style
Mental/cognitive biases: using a selective mental filter Paying attention to one type of information and ignoring other types of information. Our mental filters can lead to us discounting clearly present information because it doesn't fit with our biases.	**Paying attention to all the available information** Being wary of discounting information that contradicts biases; allowing other possibilities; holding strong opinions lightly; asking, is there another way of looking at this? Am I missing anything because of a "filter" I may be looking at the situation through?
Discounting positive information Having an overtly negative focus when noticing information; only paying attention to information that confirms a negative interpretation and ignoring information that might challenge that interpretation.	**Accepting a range of information** Being willing to accept a range of information, being hesitant to discount or dismiss positive information too quickly.
Magical thinking Believing that just the power of thinking, wishing, envisaging or imagining can achieve a direct change in the world outside our own minds, specifically due to our thoughts rather than any other external cause.	**Realistic thinking** Recognising that influencing the world or effecting change requires thought combined with action, not just wishful thinking.
Jumping to conclusions I: mind-reading Believing we can see inside other people's heads and know exactly what they are thinking; assuming we know what they're thinking accurately, based on minimal information, and not considering that our guess might be wrong.	**Knowing it's hard to be certain what others are thinking** Accepting we might infer or guess what others are thinking, but that we're doing so on incomplete information. Considering that we might not have all the information about what's going through someone else's mind.
Jumping to conclusions II: fortune telling Confidently predicting what will happen in the future, based on what's happened in the past.	**Realistic appraisal of the future** Thinking about what the future might hold while holding onto the knowledge that we can't be certain we're right in our ideas.
Catastrophising or over-minimising Imagining that the worst possible outcome is the likeliest or jumping to the worst-case scenario when thinking what might happen. Alternatively, dismissing a situation that is significant to minimise its significance inappropriately. Either response may be an exaggerated style of thinking in the circumstances being considered.	**Realistic appraisal of situations** Remembering that a range of possible outcomes in any situation includes positive or neutral outcomes, not just highly negative or catastrophic ones. Remembering that just because a really disastrous scenario gets our attention and makes us feel alarmed, doesn't mean it's more likely to happen. Being wary of exaggerating in either direction, good or bad.

(Continued)

TABLE 2.8 (Continued)

Unhelpful thinking style	More helpful/alternative thinking style
Emotional reasoning Understanding situations through a transient emotional state; assuming that emotions are giving us accurate information about a situation.	**Wise reasoning** Acknowledging emotions while knowing that they can give us some inaccurate or skewed feedback; trying to think in a wise way that combines logical thinking with how we feel. Considering if our emotional reaction to a situation is distorting our view of it.
Using harsh, inflexible rules; should, must Either harsh rules for self, or for others; we or they must, should, ought to do something or behave in a certain way; not being flexible about these rules or considering how differing circumstances might impact on how easy or difficult these "rules" might be to stick to.	**Using flexible rules and compassion towards self and others** Being aware that we can often use "could" where we might use "should"; letting our rules for ourselves and others be flexible where this is indicated and useful.
Labelling Giving others, or ourselves, labels that define what they or we are like in a narrow, global, consistent way, not allowing the potential for either change or for a complex identity.	**Label-free thinking** Thinking of ourselves and others as not stuck with a narrow label and accepting we're complex and even contradictory.
Personalisation Identifying blame and fault inappropriately, either to self or others, placing responsibility with too narrow a range of others or just with ourself.	**Sharing the responsibility** Thinking of responsibility as very often shared between different people, and situations as complex and multi-influenced; being aware of different influences and factors on outcomes.

Going further

To go further, once you've read about thinking styles, try noticing your unhelpful thinking styles and practising new, more helpful thinking habits. Use Table 2.9 to gather some information about situations when you might notice you are using one or more of the above thinking styles. If you notice feeling emotional or upset, it might be that one of the unhelpful kinds of thinking is a factor. Table 2.9 also gives some space to consider if one of the more helpful or alternative thinking styles as above could be something to practice instead in similar situations.

TABLE 2.9 Thinking styles activity

Situation (time, place and who was there)	Thoughts	Feelings	Physical sensations	Thinking style (refer to the table in this activity)	Alternative thinking style (refer to the table in this activity)

After a week of noticing your unhelpful and helpful thinking styles, and trying to reduce the first and boost the second, what's happened? How do you feel? Are there any helpful thinking styles that you have found beneficial to your week?

Further reading

Psychology Tools. All-Or-Nothing Thinking. (2023). All-Or-Nothing Thinking (psychologytools.com) https://www.betterup.com/blog/all-or-nothing-thinking

10. SELF-ESTEEM AND SELF-EFFICACY

Time: 15 minutes or longer

Who this could be for: anyone who would like to understand how the concepts of self-esteem and self-efficacy can influence wellbeing, and to try some ideas for building good self-esteem

Resources needed: depending on what self-esteem-related activities you try

Why do this: understand what self-esteem is and try ideas for building good self-esteem

The concepts of self-esteem and of self-efficacy are both of great relevance to us as learners and as individuals seeking to support our wellbeing. Learning is supported by both good self-esteem and good self-efficacy, and struggling in either of these areas is likely to make learning difficult for us. This activity considers the meaning of these terms and offers some ideas for building good self-esteem as part of having a good sense of self-efficacy.

Self-esteem and self-efficacy meet in our progress as learners, and you could see having positive self-esteem and positive self-efficacy as basic building blocks for our learning journey at any age. If we have positive or good self-esteem, we will think well of ourselves, and if we have good self-efficacy, we have a positive belief in our ability to undertake and achieve tasks and activities and meet our goals and aspirations. It's clear that having a positive sense of both self-esteem and self-efficacy is a really helpful combination for being a successful learner. Equally, if we have poor or low self-esteem, and a poor sense of our own self-efficacy, we might struggle to initiate learning tasks or to build on learning progress; we just really don't believe in ourselves or our fundamental ability to take effective action. It's clear that if we feel that way, we are less likely to even start; we just do not believe we can do it.

Anything we can do to improve our self-esteem and our sense of self-efficacy is therefore helpful to supporting ourselves as effective learners, both right now and in the longer term; positive habits of thought about ourselves, and positive habits of learning, can make a long-term difference both to our happiness and contentment with ourselves and our efforts, and to our progress over time in any direction, or directions, we wish to go in. Good self-esteem and self-efficacy beliefs are especially important if we do not, or did not in the past, get much support or encouragement; sometimes, we might have to be our own supporter and cheerleader if others are either neutral or actively negative about us and our abilities.

Self-efficacy

Self-efficacy is our belief in our own capacity to reach our goals. It was a concept proposed by social psychologist Albert Bandura as part of his social cognitive theory. Bandura described self-efficacy as an essential part of how we learn and develop our personalities.

Self-esteem

The concept of self-esteem was originally defined by William James in The Principles of Psychology (James, 2022) as an output of the ratio of our successes when compared to our aspirations for success, and he even gave a formula for working this out:

Self-esteem = success/pretensions

So, in William James's way of understanding it, self-esteem, is all of our successes divided by what we want to be successful in but haven't been yet.

Although William James's self-esteem equation is interesting, it might be that you have a better idea of how to calculate it for yourself. What would your self-esteem equation be? What do you need to focus on or notice to feel good about yourself?

My self-esteem = _____ × _____ + _____ / _____

My self-esteem = _____ − _____ − _____ + _____

My self-esteem = ?

Some ideas for boosting your self-esteem

Positive reflection: get into the habit of noticing your good qualities, achievements, and positive feedback from others. We can be very well-practiced at noticing and dwelling on our mistakes, perceived faults and failures and on things we feel make us less good than others. Get into the habit of dwelling on the opposite; dwelling on the good stuff. The more you build this cognitive habit, the easier you will find it to notice the good things about yourself and to believe in a more positive self-concept.

Feel proud of your achievements, and forgive yourself for your slip-ups; keep in mind that you, along with everyone else, are only human. Celebrate what has gone well, and notice and learn from, but don't get completely overfocused on, what's gone wrong.

Remember that you are inherently worthy and valuable without needing to achieve anything in particular! Build a sense of your fundamental worth that doesn't require specific achievement. Then, achievements can be good, but they don't equate to you.

Practice self-compassion; if you are continually harsh on yourself, you'll learn over time that you don't deserve kindness.

If possible, withdraw from, or limit, relationships with people who lower your self-esteem; interacting with people who are unkind, thoughtless, demanding or otherwise treat you badly will lower your self-esteem.

If your self-esteem isn't currently where you would like it to be, try running your life "as if" you thought better of yourself. Be assertive in saying no, and don't let others use your time and resources so that you have none left over for yourself.

Try thinking of someone you really like and value, who you know now or knew in the past. Spend a day behaving as if you feel about yourself the way that you feel (or felt) about them. During this day, you have to treat yourself as you'd treat them.

Going further

To go further with this activity, you can read about low self-esteem, and some ideas for improving self-esteem, here: https://www.nhs.uk/mental-health/self-help/tips-and-support/raise-low-self-esteem/

Reference

James, W. (2022). *The principles of psychology (1890)*. Legare Street Press.

Further reading

Fennel, M. J. V. (2009, June 16). *Low self-esteem: A cognitive perspective* (online). Cambridge University Press.

Deepstash. (2023). Improve Your Self-Esteem With the William James Formula Self-esteem information sheets and worksheets. https://www.cci.health.wa.gov.au/Resources/Looking-After-Yourself/Self-Esteem

3
STEPS TO MENTAL WELLBEING

The NHS identifies "5 steps to mental wellbeing" as:

- Connect with other people
- Be physically active
- Learn new skills
- Give to others
- Pay attention to the present moment (mindfulness)

The evidence for the benefits to wellbeing of these five areas of activity are set out in research by the New Economics Foundation (see further reading and resources). This chapter draws on these five steps to mental wellbeing and on other cornerstones of maintaining our wellbeing. The activities below offer some ideas for how you can bring more of these important wellbeing-boosters into your own life and are also a chance to consider how these ideas can support and improve effective learning. Often wellbeing-boosting activities such as those outlined below go hand-in-hand with learning or are learning activities in themselves; some areas of wellbeing, for example getting good sleep and rest, are supportive of learning.

As you look through this chapter, keep in mind that you don't need to do everything at once, and if your wellbeing is not where you want it to be currently, don't be overwhelmed by this chapter! Pace yourself and keep in mind that maintaining your wellbeing is a journey, not a destination. You could see this chapter as a resource to dip into to build your understanding of what is fundamental to maintaining and improving your wellbeing; you can choose which activities to try in order to put the building blocks of your wellbeing in place. Good foundations are known to be vital to stable and safe buildings;

DOI: 10.4324/9781003326786-4

the same goes for our own wellbeing. Get the foundations of your wellbeing right through the following activities and ideas and you will be well-set up to feel good, and to learn effectively, into your future.

Further reading

Aked, J. (2011). FIVE WAYS TO WELLBEING: New applications, new ways of thinking. https://neweconomics.org/2011/07/five-ways-well-new-applications-new-ways-thinking/

New Economics Foundation wellbeing research: https://neweconomics.org/section/all/wellbeing

NHS 5 steps to wellbeing: https://www.nhs.uk/mental-health/self-help/guides-tools-and-activities/five-steps-to-mental-wellbeing/

ACTIVITIES

1. SLEEP

Time: suggested minimum of one week to gather information

Who this could be for: anyone interested in understanding and/or improving their rest and sleep

Resources needed: sleep diary template (given below) or sleep tracker app

Why do this: if you want to understand your current sleep patterns and identify changes to your routine or sleep set-up that may improve the quality of your rest and sleep

Getting sufficient good quality sleep is fundamental to our wellbeing. Both physically and mentally, sleep and rest help us to stay well and to thrive. Sleep and rest are also vital for successful learning; as learners, we need sleep in order to take in and incorporate the new information learning brings us and to make connections with the learning we already have. Very often our lifestyles, and the pressures on our time, serve to decrease both the quantity and the quality of our sleep and rest times. This activity is in two parts and offers ideas for improving sleep in order to support both our overall physical and mental wellbeing and to enable us to get the most from our learning. The first part is a sleep and dream diary to help you notice your current patterns and habits; the second part offers some suggestions for good "sleep hygiene" in order to maximise the benefit of your sleep and rest times.

Sleep and dream diary

Often a first step in understanding your sleep patterns is to keep a diary capturing information about your sleeping routine. Capturing what your patterns and habits are around settling down and getting ready for sleep, in addition to when you get to sleep, how long you sleep for, when you wake up (including if you wake at different times during the night) and associated information can help you see patterns, identify what may be helping (or hindering) your sleep, and to understand what might need to change to improve your sleep and rest. This sleep diary also gives you space to capture your dreams. It may be that keeping a record of your dreams, should you have any while keeping your sleep diary, will also provide some data for you to consider and you may notice connections between your daily experiences and the subject matter of your dreams.

A sleep and dream diary template is included below as a guide (Table 3.1); you may wish to design a more personalised template to capture your sleep information. There are also a range of sleep tracker apps available as an alternative method of gathering information.

TABLE 3.1 Sleep and dream diary

	Mon	Tues	Wed	Thurs	Fri	Sat	Sun
Activities in 30 mins before going to bed							
Mood during time before going to bed							
Life stressors/events today							
Positive events today							
Relevant physical health factors impacting today							
Time to bed							
Time to sleep (estimated)							
Time(s) of wakefulness during night							
- Duration							
- What I did during time(s) of wakefulness							
Time waking up							
Time getting up							
Estimated time asleep							
Dream content							
Any other comments/ observations							

Sleep hygiene: some ideas for getting the best sleep possible

There are some fundamentals that we need to attend to as part of getting the best sleep and rest we can. Some suggestions for good sleep hygiene are offered here. If appropriate or possible, you could use some or all of these ideas to make any changes you consider could be beneficial for your sleep and rest times.

- **Wind-down/relaxation routine before sleep**
  If possible, between an hour and 30 minutes before going to bed, try to relax and slow down, ready for sleep. If you tend to keep going with activities and preparations for the next day, experiment with stopping these with enough time to give yourself relaxation/wind-down time before bed. A shower or bath can help.
- **Lessen or avoid before bed: food, drink and exercise**
  Food that contains stimulants (e.g., caffeine, which can linger in our bodies for up to six hours, in tea, coffee, chocolate), alcohol and smoking may all interfere with being able to relax and sleep; avoid these in the time before going to bed. Exercising is also likely to keep us wakeful, so exercising immediately before bed is to be avoided.
- **Sleep environment: light, temperature and noise**
  Check your sleep environment. Are the light levels right – does light disturb your sleep, and if so, do you have the option of reducing light levels? Lower light levels are a cue for sleep. Is the temperature suitable for sleep? Our body temperatures begin to drop in the evening, ready to sleep, so hotter temperatures can disrupt getting to sleep; 16–18° is considered the ideal room temperature to aid sleep (although very young or older people may need a warmer environment). Do noises cause disruption to your sleep? If so, are there options for reducing or removing these or wearing earplugs if that is not possible? Attending to light levels, temperature and noise levels may help to improve your sleep.
- **Keep the bedroom for rest and relaxation only**
  To help you build an association between where you sleep and relaxation and rest, aim to only do bedroom-relevant activities in your bedroom: relaxing, sleeping, intimacy and undressing or getting dressed and not writing your To-Do list or using the bedroom as a space for any stressful or wakeful activities! If space pressures mean it's difficult or impossible to do this, consider if it would be possible to screen or cover over anything that prompts you to think about projects, stresses or daytime activities at times when you are using the bedroom for resting and sleeping.
- **Distractions and screens**
  Computer, laptop, smartphone and any other electronic screens emit light that mimics the effect of sunlight on us, waking us up and making us more alert. For this reason, it's advisable to avoid screens when getting ready

to go to bed and when in bed. If you have to or can't resist looking at a screen, try to set it to a night-time setting to reduce the impact of the light on your ability to get to sleep. In addition to the light, the content of any screens may also interfere with getting to sleep; for instance, if you are reading stressful or alarming news or looking at work-related information.

- **Watch out for clock-watching**
  We often need to set an alarm to get up at a particular time; however, if we wake in the night and hope to get back to sleep, looking at the time can sometimes induce additional stress if we start calculating how much (or little) time we have left to get some sleep. If you use an alarm clock, try turning the clock away from you so you can't see it overnight, but it will still go off when you need it to. If you set an alarm on your smartphone, try turning it face down so you don't check the time if you wake overnight.

- **Regular sleep and wake times**
  Trying to keep as regular a pattern as possible of going to bed and getting up can help to stabilise sleep patterns and ensure you get sufficient rest. It's not always possible to keep these times the same however as far as possible, sticking to similar sleep/wake times can be beneficial.

- **Worry management**
  Thinking over the day can be a part of switching off ready for sleep; however, worry (future-based thinking, often with a very negative or catastrophic flavour, accompanied by physical tension and negative emotions in the moment) can disrupt relaxing ready for sleep. If you find it difficult to switch off from worry, try refocusing on non-worrying thought content or try a physical relaxation exercise such as progressive muscle relaxation (PGMR, see Activity 14, Relax). Externalising any specific worries by writing them down or saving them on your smartphone can help to "get them out of your head" if they are not shifting prior to sleep.

- **If you can't get to sleep or if you wake and can't re-sleep**
  Staying in bed when you are wakeful and can't sleep can start a cycle of associating the bedroom and your bed with stress rather than rest and relaxation. This may make it more difficult to sleep the next time you are in the same place, as you're starting to associate it with not sleeping. If you can't get to sleep within around 20 minutes of getting into bed, or if you wake overnight and cannot return to sleep within around 20 minutes, try getting up, going to another room and doing a quiet activity like reading in low/dim light until you feel sleepy again. At that point, return to bed and try re-sleeping.

- **I have tried all of these things and I still don't get good sleep!**
  If you have tried the above ideas, and are still having difficulty with getting enough sleep, see the further resources below; there is support available for sleep difficulties and insomnia, and you may be able to access this through your general practitioner (GP) or via online self-help resources.

Going further

Insomnia help and information: https://thesleepcharity.org.uk/information-support/advice-sheets/

NHS advice and information for better sleep: https://www.nhs.uk/every-mind-matters/mental-health-issues/sleep/

The Sleep Charity: https://thesleepcharity.org.uk/

Free access to a programme for sleep improvement via NHS GP prescription is available in some areas of the United Kingdom (eligible areas can be checked on the site): https://www.sleepstation.org.uk/

Further reading

Alvarez, A. (1995). Night an exploration of night life, night language, sleep and dreams. Jonathan Cape Ltd.

How rest and sleep helps learning: https://healthysleep.med.harvard.edu/portal/

Negative impacts of blue light: https://www.health.harvard.edu/staying-healthy/blue-light-has-a-dark-side

Shakespeare on death, sleep and dreaming: https://www.poetryfoundation.org/poems/56965/speech-to-be-or-not-to-be-that-is-the-question

The Dreamachine immersive experience: https://dreamachine.world/

Walker, M. (2018). *Why we sleep*. Penguin.

2. EXERCISE

Time: from a few minutes to whatever time you wish to dedicate to exercising and getting moving

Who this could be for: anyone who wants to start exercising or moving more or to incorporate physical activity into their daily life as part of supporting both their physical and mental wellbeing and effective learning

Resources needed: depending on the exercise or activity chosen

Why do this: exercise and physical activity supports your physical health both in the short and long term and improves your wellbeing and ability to learn

We know that physical activity offers a wide range of benefits to both our physical health and our interlinked mental health and wellbeing. This activity is a chance to find out more about the benefits of physical activity and to consider how you could bring some of those benefits into your life. Physical exercise is likely to reduce your chance of major illnesses such as heart disease, stroke, diabetes and cancer and also may reduce your chances of early death. Exercise offers benefits to your health at all stages of life, and in older adults, it is associated with a reduction in the risk of falls.

Physical activity also offers many benefits to the learner: from improving concentration and cognitive function to boosting our ability to work with others. You can read more about the benefits of physical activity for learning here:

https://theeducationhub.org.nz/the-importance-of-physical-activity-for-learning-and-wellbeing/
https://www.who.int/europe/news/item/17-02-2021-who-reviews-effect-of-physical-activity-on-enhancing-academic-achievement-at-school
https://www.sportengland.org/news/physical-activity-can-help-children-catch-missed-work

Use this activity to audit your current activity levels. There are online tools you can use too, and here is one example:

https://livelighter.com.au/physicalactivity/calculator

Use this, or another tool, to work out your current activity levels.

There are also resources available online to help you find out more about the benefits of exercising. Here are some examples:

https://www.nhs.uk/live-well/exercise/
https://www.activepartnerships.org/
https://www.activenorfolk.org/activity-health/benefits-of-physical-activity/

https://www.activenorfolk.org/app/uploads/2021/04/physical-activity-guidelines-for-adults.pdf

The UK Chief Medical Officer's recommendation for levels of exercise is that adults should aim to have some activity level every day and ideally reach at least 150 minutes (2.5 hours) of physical activity across a week using different types of activity. Ensuring that your week includes physical activity goes some way to mitigate against the health damage of a sedentary lifestyle; a lot of sitting still is bad for our physical health.

The recommendations of the Chief Medical Officer for exercise, including for children and older adults, can be read in detail here:

https://assets.publishing.service.gov.uk/government/uploads/system/uploads/attachment_data/file/832868/uk-chief-medical-officers-physical-activity-guidelines.pdf

You can also find out more about ways to exercise and to introduce more activity into your life, some examples are here:

https://www.nhs.uk/better-health/get-active/how-to-be-more-active/
https://www.bhf.org.uk/informationsupport/heart-matters-magazine/activity/8-ways-to-get-active-every-day
https://www.bhf.org.uk/informationsupport/heart-matters-magazine/activity/6-ways-to-get-active-this-spring

You could even access some free exercise plans to help you structure what you might want to try:

https://www.nhs.uk/better-health/get-active/how-to-be-more-active/#exercise-plans

Apps are an option for supporting your activity; some free apps are included here:

https://www.bhf.org.uk/informationsupport/heart-matters-magazine/activity/8-free-fitness-apps

Review as much of the information above as you wish and consider if you would like to bring more physical activity into your life as a result of what you have found out, in order to benefit your physical and mental wellbeing.

Going further

Having read and found out all about the benefits of physical activity to your physical and mental wellbeing, going further with this activity is of course to identify a way to be more active, and then to bring it into your life. Try it and check in with how it's affecting how you feel physically and mentally. If you are in doubt about trying any particular activity, for instance if you have any physical health issues, check with your GP or a relevant medical professional before trying out the activity.

Further reading

Active Partnerships. (2023). Active partnerships, offering information on activity across England, including walking: https://www.activepartnerships.org/active-partnerships

Physical exercise is more effective than therapy or medication at managing mental health difficulties such as anxiety and depression: https://neurosciencenews.com/exercise-mental-health-22566/

3. EAT

Time: depending on the time available for research/reading, 30 minutes to an hour; longer can be spent on this if you find it useful

Who this could be for: anyone who wants to explore the role of diet in supporting wellbeing and learning

Resources needed: several A4 pieces of paper/card, split pin

Why do this: if you want to build an understanding of how diet can impact your physical and mental wellbeing and your learning performance and if you want to develop a personalised guide to a good diet to support yourself in your physical and mental health and your learning performance

The interaction between our brains and our bodies is fascinating and complex. This activity provides a chance to consider how our brain and our body interacts and in particular what we understand of how diet can affect not just our physical health but also our wellbeing and readiness to learn. Research has found that there are connections between our digestive systems, our emotions and our cognitive functions. Our gut microbiota (the population of microorganisms that live in our gut) can produce substances like serotonin and gamma-aminobutyric acid, which are both neurotransmitters; chemical substances that serve as messengers within our brains. In other words, our gut microbiota is capable of communicating with our brain. This communication also works the other way, too; the two-way communication between our gastrointestinal system and our central nervous system (our brain and spinal cord) is known as the "gut-brain axis," and the communication pathways are believed to start developing from the very start of our lives. Our gut has its own nervous system, the enteric nervous system, and is sometimes described as a "second brain" or "little brain;" if you've ever tried to concentrate on learning something when you're hungry, it might not in fact seem like such a little brain at all! We are starting to understand how changes to our gut microbiota can influence our wellbeing and our mental health; see further reading for more on this.

The wealth of information and research into diet and physical and mental wellbeing and the impact of our diets on the development of or lessening the chance of disease are impossible to summarise here. Instead, this activity is a chance to seek out some information that is personal and relevant to you and to incorporate this into your own wellbeing-learning dietary wheel; an eatwellbeing-learning plate. Building a dietary plan can be accomplished via apps and online resources of course; however, this activity is instead an on-paper exercise, so there is a physical and visual example of what you could incorporate into your diet to refer to at the end of it. You could if you would prefer use the idea within this exercise to develop an online or computer-based resource for yourself.

1 Firstly, for some research, see further reading and resources for some starting points on identifying foods that benefit physical and mental health and learning
2 Make three paper or card circles of concentric sizes so there is one large, one medium and one small circle
3 Secure them together through their centres using a split pin
4 Label the largest circle "physical wellbeing," the middle circle "mental wellbeing" and the smallest circle "learning"
5 Now add the foods you identify for each section either as words or images (or both)
6 Once you have enough added to each wheel for a reasonable choice, turn the wheel around to see if you can come up with some ideas for meals or recipes that incorporate foods that benefit your physical and mental health and your learning too – and hopefully taste good!

Be aware: food intolerances and allergies

When trying this activity, be mindful of any food intolerances or allergies you have and ensure you only include foods you are able to eat on your eatwellbeing-learning plate. If you are considering preparing food for others using this activity, you should also ensure that any food intolerances or allergies that others you may prepare food for are considered and excluded as necessary. If in doubt, always check with others first.

Going further

You could consider a more comprehensive and complex eatwellbeing-learning food wheel with a circle for each of the food groups on the eatwell plate and a segment of each circle divided into general wellbeing, learning, etc, as relevant for you. You could then, turning the wheel and reading from the outer edge to the middle, choose a food from every food group to assemble your beneficial meal. This would need to be a bigger wheel than the initial part of this activity unless you have very small handwriting!

Further reading for creating your own personalised wellbeing-learning food wheel

https://bmcmedicine.biomedcentral.com/articles/10.1186/s12916-023-02772-3
The Guardian. (2023). Benefits of a Mediterranean diet in reducing dementia risk: https://www.theguardian.com/society/2023/mar/14/mediterranean-diet-may-lower-dementia-risk-by-a-quarter-study-suggestsBenefits of a Mediterranean diet in reducing dementia risk: https://www.theguardian.com/society/2023/mar/14/mediterranean-diet-may-lower-dementia-risk-by-a-quarter-study-suggests
The MIND (Mediterranean diet Intervention for Neurodegenerative Delay) diet to boost cognitive function: https://www.health.harvard.edu/topics/memory#memory5

Further reading

Carabotti, M., Scirocco, A., Maselli, M. A., & Severi, C. (2015 April–June). The gut-brain axis: Interactions between enteric microbiota, central and enteric nervous systems. *Annals of Gastroenterology, 28*(2), 203–209.

Evrensel, A., & Ceylan, M. E. (2015). Gut-brain axis: The role of gut microbiota in the psychiatric disorders, *Current Approach Psychiatry, 7,* 461–472.

Evrensel, A., & Ceylan, M. E. (2015, December).The gut-brain axis: The missing link in depression. *Clinical Psychopharmacology and Neuroscience, 13*(3), 239–244.

The gut-brain axis: https://en.wikipedia.org/wiki/Gut%E2%80%93brain_axis

NHS Eatwell Guide

Eat Well Guide. (2023). https://assets.publishing.service.gov.uk/government/uploads/system/uploads/attachment_data/file/528193/Eatwell_guide_colour.pdf

Eat well Guide. (2023). https://www.nhs.uk/live-well/eat-well/food-guidelines-and-food-labels/the-eatwell-guide/

Gut health: https://www.theguardian.com/lifeandstyle/2023/mar/19/chew-slowly-keep-moving-and-eat-30-plants-a-week-12-rules-for-gut-health

Williamson G. (2017). The role of polyphenols in modern nutrition National Medical Library. (nih.gov)

4. RELAX

Time: each relaxation activity can take from 15 to 30 minutes depending on the time you have available

Who this could be for: anyone who wants to build more relaxation into their daily life; anyone who struggles to relax and unwind or would like to try specific, active techniques for relaxation

Resources needed: no resources required other than time to practice the relaxation techniques

Why do this: to gain good habits in relaxation, to find out if you can notice immediate benefits from using these relaxation techniques and to build good habits of relaxation for your longer term health, wellbeing and learning

Finding ways to relax both physically and mentally is vital for our wellbeing and for our ability to learn successfully. Relaxation helps to slow our heart rate and our breathing, and to lower our blood pressure, and by relaxing tense muscles, it can reduce muscle pain and reduce tension headaches (as we often hold a lot of tension in our upper body and especially our back, neck and jaw). Relaxation can create a positive cycle where we physically relax and in parallel with that mentally relax too.

Being stuck on one setting all the time, particularly that of striving/trying/being on-guard or focused on problems or achievements tires us out and reduces our ability to stay well and learn well. Learning to relax is a skill that will benefit us and our physical and mental health both immediately and, by building good habits, in the longer term across our lives. We also need to learn the value of relaxing, especially if we have picked up on messages about it being a waste of time, or not a valuable use of time, compared to focusing on striving or achieving or "getting on with something." Relaxation is something we could benefit from learning to value in itself as pleasant and also for the benefits it can bring to our holistic wellbeing.

This activity offers three options for relaxation: two visualisations (colour breathing, and safe, calm place) and one physical relaxation exercise (PGMR). If none of these activities work for you, see further reading and resources for other options; it's worth exploring more relaxation activities to find something that works for you.

Visualisation: colour breathing

This relaxation technique invites you to imagine breathing in a relaxing and calming colour of your choice. It is easy to try and can help you relax, feel calm and let go of stress and tension.

Getting started

Sit or lay down anywhere that's quiet and comfortable. It helps to close your eyes for this exercise to help you visualise better. If you really don't want to close your eyes, try just defocusing.

Think of a colour that you find especially pleasing, relaxing, calming and good to look at. It can be any colour you like – the most important thing is it is associated with relaxing and calming feelings for you.

Once you've made yourself comfortable and chosen your colour, start to work on your breathing.

Slowing down your breathing

Turn your attention to your breathing. As you breathe in, and out, slow your breathing down until it's at a slow, even pace. You can use a 1, 2, 3, 4 count for your in-breath, holding it briefly, and then another 1, 2, 3, 4 count for your out-breath if it helps, but do not get too hung up on counting if it makes you stressed! Just slow is fine. Use your diaphragm (the muscle below your lungs that is the main muscle involved in breathing) to draw breath in, hold it for a moment and then let it out again. If you put a hand over your stomach, you can feel it expanding and contracting like a balloon.

Continue slow breathing for a minute or two until you can feel yourself becoming calmer and more relaxed.

Breathing in your chosen colour

Continue with this calm slow breathing, and now imagine your chosen colour.

Firstly, imagine it's in the air around you as a very beautiful colour-cloud. As you breathe in, imagine the colour-cloud moving towards you and gently enveloping you. Each in-breath you take draws some of this beautiful colour into you; visualise it being drawn into your nose, then down into your lungs, and all the intricate passages and spaces within them being filled with this beautiful colour.

Notice the sensations in your chest as you breathe this relaxing colour in.

Now imagine your colour gently diffusing and spreading out from your chest into the rest of your body, into your arms and legs and upwards into your head.

Imagine the colour flowing into and all through your brain.

As you breathe slowly and calmly, notice the sensations in your body as this beautiful, relaxing colour flows through all of you.

If your mind wanders away from your colour, don't be concerned, just notice where your mind has gone, and then return it to the colour you have chosen. You could also return your attention to your breathing to help with getting your mind back to the relaxation exercise.

You can stay with these sensations and this colour for as long as you like, just noticing the good feelings it gives you.

Finishing the exercise

When you are ready, bring yourself back to the here-and-now, maybe by moving your hands and feet, stretching and, when you are ready, slowly opening your eyes.

Using colour breathing any time you need it

If you practice this relaxation technique a few times, you might find it's easy to bring the calming, relaxing sensations it gives to mind, quite quickly, any time you need it, by just visualising a colour and breathing it in.

Visualisation: safe, calm place

This is a useful visualisation to help you feel calm, safe and at peace. It involves visualising somewhere that evokes feelings of safety, calmness, tranquillity and happiness for you. Once you've developed your visualisation, you can bring it to mind as and when needed, and it's especially useful for times when you need to feel better and manage stress.

What you imagine is completely up to you, and you don't have to share the details of this place with anyone (unless you want to). It's your place for your own comfort and relaxation.

You can use a place you have a memory of for this visualisation or a combination of places where you have felt safe and calm. You can also imagine a place; it doesn't have to be somewhere real. Draw on whatever you want to in order to create the place in your imagination. If anything you bring up from your memory has difficult or upsetting associations, you might want to choose another place. The main thing is that it should feel truly safe and calm, and it should give you a feeling of happiness and contentment to imagine being there.

Getting started

Find some time when you can have five minutes or so undisturbed.

Sit comfortably, or lay down, and close your eyes.

Take a slow, deep breath; hold it for a moment; and let it out slowly. Breathe slowly and calmly for a little while and relax as you sit/lay where you are, releasing any tense or clenched muscles in your body as you breathe.

When you feel relaxed and calm, you are ready to start the visualisation part of the exercise.

Visualisation – safe, calm place

Now bring to your mind a place that makes you feel calm, safe, content, peaceful and relaxed. It may be a combination of places you know, or somewhere you've seen in something you've watched, or read about and imagined. It may be somewhere real or somewhere completely made up – it's up to you, this is your place, just for you.

Keep breathing slowly and calmly, and work on noticing what this safe calm place is like. Work through each sense in turn.

Sight – look around in your imagination – what can you see? Is it light or dark? Are you outside and can see a long way, or is it somewhere cosy and contained? Are there any colours that stand out? Look around and take in as much visual detail as you can.

Sound – listen to your safe calm place. What can you hear? Is it very quiet, or are there noises? Are they from far away or nearer? Listen and take in as much sound detail as you can.

Smell – take a deep breath in through your nose and notice how your safe calm place smells. Does it have any particular smell? If your safe calm place is outside, can you smell something of the world around? Do you want to add in any scents you find calming or associate with happy feelings? Notice as much detail of the smell of this safe calm place as you can.

Touch – keep breathing slowly and calmly and in your imagination, reach out to touch some part of this safe calm place you are imagining. What can you feel? How does it feel against your skin? Notice as much as you can about this feeling.

Taste – is there anything in the safe calm place that you can taste, that can add to all the good feelings this place is giving you? If so, imagine this too and notice how this feels.

Everything at once and noticing how being here feels – take a good look around the safe calm place you are working on and notice all the sensory details – sights, sounds, smells, touch and taste – take it all in and just be with the feelings this give you for a while. You might notice feelings of calm, warmth and relaxation in your body – if so, just notice them for a while and soak them up.

Naming the safe calm place – if you want to give this place you've created a name, or if there is a short sentence that sums up what this place is like and what it means to you, say the word or sentence over in your mind while you take in all the sensory details. If you like, you can say it aloud as well to increase the strength of the association.

Getting back to the here-and-now – in your own time, bring your attention back to the world around you. You can do this by paying attention to your breathing again, and then noticing how your body feels where you are sitting or laying. Take your time and when you are ready, open your eyes and move or stretch yourself to get back to the here-and-now.

Using your safe calm place visualisation any time you need it

Once you've worked on this visualisation, you can practice bringing it and the feelings it creates to mind as and when you need it. You can close your eyes and bring an image of the place to mind, or perhaps say the word or phrase either in your head or out loud to help. If you keep practising, you will find it easy to bring the safe calm place to your mind when you need it.

Progressive muscle relaxation

When we're feeling stressed and anxious, we can tense up physically. Physical tension can in turn make us feel there is something to be concerned about, which can set off more thoughts that make us feel more stressed and anxious – it can be a bit of a spiralling situation. As a result, we might stay physically quite tense, as if keeping ourselves ready to respond to a perceived (and often non-specific) threat or difficulty that's always just over the horizon.

Over time, if we keep holding a lot of physical tension in our bodies, it can get quite difficult to let the tension go, or even to notice how tense we are at all as we've got used to this as just the standard way we feel. What we might notice is that we're tired and headachy, holding our shoulders hunched up nearly to our ears, with sore backs, shoulders and necks, and sometimes sore jaws, too – tensing our jaws and even grinding our teeth overnight is something we might do when feeling stressed and anxious. We might not even be fully aware we're doing some of these things, and if so, we don't notice we need to let go of some of the tension we're carrying around with us.

This exercise is a way to relax so that the physical tension we are carrying reduces, which in turn can help to reduce feelings and thoughts related to tension, stress and anxiety.

As with all physical exercise, if you are concerned about undertaking it, or have any injuries or physical issues that may be impacted, seek medical advice before using this technique.

Get ready

Firstly, find some time in your day when you will be able to spend around five minutes without interruptions. Don't try this when you are already very tired or after eating a big meal.

You can sit down or lay down to do this – go with what makes you feel comfortable. You do not have to close your eyes, but if it helps you to concentrate, you can try it.

Relaxing your muscles progressively

Start by taking a few deep, slow breaths and getting comfortable where you are sitting or laying. Once your breathing is calm and slow, you can start to work through tensing up and relaxing your muscles. The order here is a suggestion, and you can work the other way around (feet to head) if it suits you better.

In this exercise, you are going to tense up each muscle area in turn. Tense the muscle area you are working on until you can feel the tension in it and hold for a few moments before releasing. Feel the tension release before moving onto the next muscle area.

Head, face and jaw

- Start with your forehead muscles (and this will also reach your scalp a little too). Tense your forehead up by raising your eyebrows as if you are extremely surprised. Hold in tension for a few moments, then let your eyebrows drop and feel the tension release.
- Close your eyes very tightly and squash your cheeks up at the same time. Hold tense, then release, blinking a few times if it helps to let go of extra tension.
- Pull your mouth into a grimace and hold tense for a few moments before releasing.
- Open your mouth wide (but don't strain your jaw) and hold tense for a moments before releasing.

Neck

Take care when tensing and relaxing your neck muscle and don't force yourself to do more than is comfortable.

- Lower your chin gently towards your chest and feel the tension in the back of your neck. Tense those muscles as far as is comfortable, hold a moments before releasing. Slowly raise your chin back upwards.
- Tip your head gently backwards as if you're looking at the stars on a clear night and hold for a few moments before returning your head to level.

Upper torso

- Pull your shoulders up towards your ears and hold tense for a moments before releasing
- Push your shoulders back (you can use your arms to help by moving them back too) and hold tense for a moments before releasing
- Hunch your shoulders forwards and hold tense for a moments before releasing
- Tense your upper chest muscles and hold tense for a moments before releasing

Arms

Work on each arm in turn; it doesn't matter if you start with your left or right arm, choose what works best for you.

- Ball one of your hands up into a fist and squeeze as tightly as you can. Hold tense for a moments before releasing.
- Hold the same arm out in front of you and tense the muscles in your forearm. Hold tense for a moments before releasing.
- Working on the same arm, tense the muscles in the upper arm. Hold tense for a moments before releasing.
- Now work through the above sequence for your other arm.

Lower torso

- Take a very deep breath in, by expanding your lungs fully using your diaphragm. You can do this by imagining your stomach is an inflating balloon and keep expanding it out to fill your lungs. Hold for a few moments, then release.
- Tighten your stomach muscles and hold tense for a moments before releasing.
- Tighten your buttock muscle on one side and hold tense for a moments before releasing. As with your arms, choose which side of yourself to start on and do the same with the other buttock muscle in turn.

Legs and feet

Choose one leg to start on.

- Tighten the muscle in your thigh and hold tense for a moments before releasing
- Tighten the muscle in your calf on the same leg (gently) and hold tense for a moments before releasing
- Point your foot and toe on the same leg and hold tense for a moments before releasing
- Raise your foot towards the front of your leg and hold tense for a moments before releasing
- Rotate your foot gently
- Now repeat this sequence for your other leg and foot

Keeping going with muscle relaxation

If you notice this exercise is helpful, you might want to try it again. With some regular practice, you will probably notice it gets easier to do and also easier to drop the tension out of your body as and when you need to.

Another thing you might notice if you practice this regularly is that it becomes easier to deliberately tense up specific muscles in your body. At first, it can feel very difficult to tense up different leg muscles deliberately, for instance. Over time, this gets surprisingly easier.

As mentioned at the outset of this activity, if in any doubt about using this technique, or if it makes any injury or physical difficulty worse, or you are concerned it might, seek medical advice and don't push yourself or your body. Slowly and gently is always better.

Going further

In addition to the above ideas for relaxation practices, there are many online resources available such as guided meditations, guided mindful practices and guided relaxation exercises. See further reading for more relaxation resources, and you can also find much more for free online. Keep experimenting with different relaxation activities and exercises; something will work for you, even if not all of them do. The overall benefit of relaxation to your physical and mental wellbeing in the short term and over time is worth it.

Further reading

Breathing exercise for stress, NHS (2023). https://www.nhs.uk/mental-health/self-help/guides-tools-and-activities/breathing-exercises-for-stress/

Relaxation interventions can reduce anxiety and depression in older adults: https://pubmed.ncbi.nlm.nih.gov/25574576/

Relaxation techniques from MIND: https://www.mind.org.uk/information-support/tips-for-everyday-living/relaxation/relaxation-exercises/

Relaxation techniques from Harvard Health Publishing: https://www.health.harvard.edu/mind-and-mood/six-relaxation-techniques-to-reduce-stress

Relaxation techniques reduce anxiety in younger adults: https://pubmed.ncbi.nlm.nih.gov/35765083/

5. MANAGING ANXIETY

Time: from a few minutes to longer, depending on which anxiety management strategy or strategies are selected

Who this could be for: anyone who would like to understand anxiety better and find ways to manage it

Resources needed: depending on strategies selected, no resources beyond time required for trying the strategies

Why do this: understand anxiety and experiment with ways of managing and lessening anxiety, to benefit both your immediate learning and wellbeing and your long-term health

To start, here are some descriptions of anxiety:

> Anxiety is the dizziness of freedom.
>
> *(Kierkegaard, 2015)*

> Anxiety is the reaction to the threat to any pattern which the individual has developed upon which he feels his safety to depend.
>
> *(May, 2015)*

> The self is made up, on its growing edge, of the models, forms, metaphors, myths, and all other kinds of psychic content which gives it direction in its self-creation. This is a process that goes on continuously. As Kierkegaard well said, the self is only that which it is in the process of becoming.
>
> *(May, 1994)*

> I have only now realized how anxiety has devoured my life, thinned my blood, destroyed my pleasures. Everything was contaminated. The rarity was the moments of peace, of enjoyment.
>
> *(Nin, 2015)*

These are all different and perhaps surprising perspectives on the idea of anxiety and what it might be or mean. Do any of these descriptions change the way you might think of anxiety; as problem, opportunity, limiting factor or in some other way?

Understanding and managing anxiety are core skills that will be of ongoing benefit to anyone at all stages of life. Anxiety can be thought of as a feeling of unease and can be further defined via identifying its physical, cognitive and emotional effects. Aspects of anxiety can include feelings of unease, dread, tension both physical and emotional and worry. Worry is often a fundamental part of feeling anxious. Worry is typically a style of thinking about potential or hypothetical events in the future and often involves scenario-building via a series of "what if…?" questions that result in hypothetical scenarios with a negative or even catastrophic quality.

This kind of thinking about potential future situations is usually accompanied in the present by physical tension and fear-based emotions. We might, for instance, start by thinking, "what if something goes wrong tomorrow?" and then find this leads to a series of further what-ifs, such as "what if the something that goes wrong is really bad," "what if I can't cope with it," "what if it triggers a whole load of other bad things" and before too long we've reached "what if my life and everything that's good in it is lost because of this rolling series of catastrophes?!" At that stage, we're likely to be feeling really stressed and possibly even distressed. But it's all hypothetical; none of these things we've what-iffed have happened.

It's perhaps rarer for us, if we tend to this kind of thinking pattern, to build a hypothetical scenario around "what if things go OK tomorrow?" or even "what if things go brilliantly tomorrow?" See cognitive anxiety management strategies below for some ideas to try around changing anxious thinking patterns into less anxious ones (Table 3.2).

Anxiety: cognitive, emotional and physical factors, typical responses, and potential impacts on learning

TABLE 3.2 Impacts of anxiety on learning and wellbeing

Thoughts	Worry; what-if thinking, scenario-building with negative/catastrophic themes; seeing threats in the environment we are in and over-estimating those threats; over-focusing on problems and difficulties; underestimation of our own coping abilities
Feelings/emotions	Unease, fear, dread, alertness and feeling threatened/in danger/unsafe (often in an undefinable way where the threat or danger isn't clear)
Physical sensations	Physical tension, especially upper body tension; neck, shoulder and back tense muscles; tension across head and headache
	Nausea and loss of appetite
	Churning stomach
Responses, coping	Being tense/on edge and unwilling to relax, staying vigilant for potential problems
	Spending time trying to problem-solve catastrophic future scenarios once imagined despite not actually needing to deal with the hypothetical situation
	Seeking reassurance from others, such as reassurance that things won't go wrong
	Avoiding situations and scenarios that are associated with increased anxiety

(*Continued*)

TABLE 3.2 (Continued)

Impacts	Difficulty relaxing
	Being restless, unable to settle and agitated
	Sleep disruption
	Appetite loss and digestive disruption
	Concentration difficulties
	Difficulty focusing on the here-and-now
	Struggling to take in new information (see cognitive load theory regarding this)
	Being on a short fuse/impatient
	Losing time to worry
	Avoiding situations that increase anxiety may result in missing out on enjoyable activities
	Anxiety sustained over time can potentially contribute to physical health problems

Impacts of anxiety on learning

As learners we can be particularly impacted by anxiety and its negative effects. If we consider how Rollo May (2015) defines anxiety, "Anxiety is the reaction to the threat to any pattern which the individual has developed upon which he feels his safety to depend," it is clear that learning may well create the conditions for anxiety to be experienced by its essential nature; when we learn, we are experiencing a change to what we know; we may be adding to what we know, and often that also involves questioning what we thought we knew or discarding previously held understandings. Learning can disrupt our patterns of knowledge and understanding; this is what makes it worthwhile and also what means it brings potential for anxiety with it. Often as learners, we are challenged to choose; do we hold onto our existing understanding, or do we take the risk of challenging that and incorporating new information? Can we change our minds? Anxiety management is a skill that is supportive of our experience as learners and finding ways to cope with anxiety can help us to become better learners.

Managing Anxiety

There are many strategies that can help with anxiety management. Some options are included here for you to select those relevant to you and give them a try. Many of the other activities in this book are also methods of anxiety management, so you can also refer to other sections and activities as part of building your understanding of anxiety and anxiety management, depending on what aspect of anxiety is most relevant to you and your experience. The most important thing is to keep experimenting until you find something that works for you. The ideas below are divided into cognitive, behavioural, physical and emotional themes; of course, these themes do cross over and influence each other (see going further activity). The thematic section each strategy is under reflects the main component of each strategy. Each idea is described briefly.

Cognitive anxiety management strategies: thinking differently

Noticing and challenging catastrophic thinking styles (what if something good, or neutral happens, rather than a catastrophe?).

Reducing "what-if" thinking spirals that build anxiety; refocusing attention onto the here-and-now and being more focused on the present.

Reappraising your perception of your own resilience and ability to cope with potential future difficulties; visualising and thinking of yourself as strong and capable, for instance, rather than weak and incapable; and bringing to mind times in the past when you have coped well with difficulties rather than focusing on times when you have coped less well.

Mindfulness practice in order to notice your anxious thoughts and let them go to be replaced with others rather than becoming caught up in them.

Meanings of anxiety, part one: become aware of the meanings you are making of different anxiety-provoking situations; are you reading a particular situation as full of threat and doom when this is a subjective view and not based in what's actually going on? Keeping in mind that the more anxious we feel, the more physical sensations can create a feedback loop and add to our anxious thinking. Keep your head up and notice what's actually going on.

If what others might think of you really fires up your anxiety, keep in mind that we can actually be really bad at mind-reading and at working out what other people are "really" thinking. Trying not to make assumptions about what is going through the minds of other people, especially about us if we fear being disliked or rejected, is a really valuable anxiety-management technique using thoughts.

Asking yourself, "is there another way of looking at this?" or "what would a friend say to me about this?" can be powerful cognitive techniques; taking a step back or another perspective, can untangle us from anxious spirals of thinking.

Meanings of anxiety, part two: try keeping Søren Kierkegaard's description in mind; "Anxiety is the dizziness of freedom." We can often frame these feelings as negative; what happens if you change the meaning you are making of the anxious sensations you are experiencing from negative to neutral or even positive? For example, does changing from "I am feeling anxious and apprehensive and I don't know what is going to happen this is bad" to "I am feeling excited about this because it's unknown and there may be a pleasant surprise" change anything? Is it helpful?

Behavioural anxiety management strategies: doing differently

The central behavioural strategy to keep in mind with anxiety management is "approach, don't avoid." Avoiding anxiety-provoking situations we know is a fundamental contributor to the maintenance of anxiety about those situations; the short-term relief avoidance gives us can in fact increase anxiety about those situations the more avoidance is used as a coping strategy. Exposing yourself to the difficult feelings and experiences of anxiety-provoking situations is a key strategy for managing anxiety.

Experiment with doing differently in relation to anxiety; identify something you feel anxious about and make a plan to change your behaviour in relation to it. Is there something you are putting off going to, someone you need to speak with, a task you are avoiding? Try a different behaviour to avoidance and notice what happens.

Notice anxiety but don't let it put you off. Our internal alarm system can be set off by the idea of changing. Stay with the feelings, don't push them away, and stick to your behaviour change plan anyway.

Be aware of the impact on anxiety levels of overloading yourself. Especially if you have a lot of responsibilities, and/or tend to "take everything on," or like to please people and to be thought well of, so say "yes, of course I can help you with that/do that/sort that out for you," when you might really need or want to say "no, sorry!," a behaviour of overloading yourself can lead to feeling constantly anxious about not being able to do the impossible, and fatigue (which in itself can make anxiety heightened), and eventually burn-out. Behavioural change here might mean establishing different boundaries, or being assertive, or valuing your time and energy differently.

Physical anxiety management strategies

There are also some building blocks of anxiety management on a physical level that could be your first considerations. Getting enough sleep and rest, having a nutritious diet, taking regular exercise and lessening or avoiding the use of artificial stimulants such as caffeine can have a big influence on our anxiety levels.

There are many other strategies for managing anxiety in its physical manifestations; some are found elsewhere in this book or are in further reading and references below, so refer to the relevant sections if any of these strategies sound useful and worth trying:

- Relaxation
- Mindful breathing
- Square breathing/box breathing
- Exercise

- Meditation
- Walking or being outdoors
- Muscle relaxation
- Listening to music
- Identifying sensory triggers that reduce anxiety for you: smells, sounds, sights, textures and tastes

Emotional anxiety management strategies

Self-compassion: having compassion for your anxious self, rather than telling yourself off for your anxious feelings, or being harsh with yourself or self-critical. Instead of taking a "stop it!" or a "pull yourself together!" or a "you shouldn't feel like that!" approach, because this stokes anxiety and distress further, try being kind as you would to someone you love dearly. Tell yourself that it's understandable this is difficult and anxiety-provoking and that you are doing really well. Try asking yourself, what do I need right now? Bearing in mind that if you are trying an "approach, don't avoid" technique, and the response is "I need to get out of here immediately!" then the compassionate response might be "I know this is really difficult, but try to stay" rather than "OK, let's go!".

Don't avoid emotions, especially positive emotions. Holding ourselves in an anxious state is sometimes linked to a dislike of the experience of shifting emotional gears from a calm or happy or relaxed state to an upset or distressed state. Building up the habit of allowing ourselves to experience more intense emotions can be helpful in managing anxiety. You could try this via listening to music that brings up emotions for you (you might need to experiment a bit to find what music does this) or watching an emotion-packed programme or film for instance.

Becoming more aware of your emotions: paying attention to your emotions can be helpful in managing anxiety; if you tend to not notice how you are feeling, you might miss the clues that anxiety is building up. Practice noticing how you are feeling day-to-day and build your overall emotional self-awareness.

Going further

Select one anxiety management strategy from one of the thematic sections given above and give it a try. You might want to try the ideas across a week, and note how you find them; helpful/unhelpful, easy/difficult? If there is anything you find useful, keep using it to build a good anxiety management habit and notice if this makes a difference to your overall wellbeing across some time.

You could also try a combination of techniques: select a combination of strategies that sound most useful to you, considering your own experience of anxiety. Are you going to sample a more physical-emotional type of technique or would the thought-focused ideas be most helpful to you? Keep experimenting; something will work for you!

References

Kierkegaard, S. (2015). *The concept of anxiety: A simple psychologically orienting deliberation on the dogmatic issue of hereditary sin.* Liveright.

May, R. (1994). *The courage to create.* W. W. Norton & Company.

May, R. (2015). *The meaning of anxiety.* W. W. Norton & Company.

Nin, A. (2015). *Mirages: The unexpurgated diary of Anais Nin, 1939-1947.* Swallow Press.

Further reading

Cognitive load. (2023). https://en.wikipedia.org/wiki/Cognitive_load

Hawthorne, B. S., Vella-Brodrick, D. A., & Hattie, J. (2019). *Well-being as a cognitive load reducing agent: A review of the literature. Frontiers in Education, 4.* https://www.frontiersin.org/articles/10.3389/feduc.2019.00121/full

Square breathing/box breathing: https://www.nhs.uk/mental-health/self-help/guides-tools-and-activities/breathing-exercises-for-stress/

6. KEEPING PERSPECTIVE

Time: 15–20 minutes

Who this could be for: anyone who would like to try a perspective-taking technique on a challenge they are dealing with

Resources needed: some quiet interrupted time to try the activity

Why do this: get a fresh or different perspective on a situation you are in or a difficulty you are faced with in order to either make changes or to move on

Helicopter view: getting some perspective

As learners, we are often working closely on a subject or area of learning and it can sometimes be difficult to keep perspective, especially when the learning pressure is on and what we're working on is right in front of our faces (and brains). Perspective is important however, and a broader view is beneficial; for instance, if we're engaged in one element of a course of study, it's helpful to keep in mind what else we are going to be covering, in future weeks and months; we can hold an awareness of the learning direction we are travelling in, in other words. Being aware of wider patterns and connections can also be useful to us, and making links between different areas of one subject, or even between different learning subjects, can benefit our learning overall. Perspective is also important for our wellbeing while we are learning; getting too caught up in the close details and missing the bigger picture can make us feel overwhelmed and a bit lost.

The helicopter view technique is a good way to get some perspective on a learning situation or challenge. You can also use the helicopter view to get some perspective on any situation you are involved in or that you are thinking about. Looking at things from a different angle and at a distance can sometimes help us to unstick our thinking if we're getting caught up or tangled in what we're working on; this technique may help you move on with your learning.

When to take the helicopter view

You can try the helicopter view to find a different perspective on any situation or learning activity that you are involved in. This technique is particularly useful if you notice that you are getting too over-focused on details and missing the bigger picture; it's also useful if you are getting too tangled up in emotions and reactions and want to get some distance between the situation and yourself so that you can think a bit more clearly. In a learning setting, the helicopter view might help you literally step back and see the bigger picture; this can help you get past something you might be stuck with or perhaps realise that there is a different piece of the picture you can work on to help get un-stuck.

How to take the helicopter view

Firstly, identify the learning situation or problem that you are encountering. Imagine it's directly in front of you, maybe on a desk or on the floor. Try to imagine the distinct aspects of the issue you are working as physical items laid out as component parts, like an engine, or maybe a piece of flatpack furniture that needs assembling. The parts might include things like:

- the hand-in deadline for a piece of work
- the reading you need to do to prepare for writing what you need to submit
- the aspect of it you really don't understand and are a bit worried about
- any important emotions that you are dealing with connected to the situation, such as excitement or anxiety
- barriers or things that are getting in the way of resolving the situation, such as the other calls on your time between now and the deadline
- … and anything else that's part of the situation

Really notice how you are feeling about everything you are noticing; notice the intensity of the emotions and any thoughts running through your mind.

You are starting off up close to the situation. Have a good look at it closely, then take a deep breath. Now imagine zooming back like a camera changing focus; the elements of what you are considering are going to get a bit smaller. As you do this, see if there are any patterns or connections between the elements of the situation as you have laid them out before you that you hadn't noticed when you were looking very closely. As you take a wider focus, you can also notice any intense emotions you are experiencing changing to feel a little further away.

Now imagine you're in a helicopter, with the ability to go even higher about the situation you are considering. Imagine flying up higher, and as you move higher, you can see more of the situation and all its aspects. At this height, you might be able to see other parts of the situation that are now apparent with a broader view. It might be that if you look beyond the edges of this situation, you can see links to other, similar situations you have experienced before or anticipate experiencing again; can you see some similar worries about things you did not understand from similar situations in the past? Can you see possible future scenarios that will have similar components, such as a deadline? At this height, you might be able to observe the emotions you have noticed so far from a cooler distance. It can help to keep imagining, for example, the worry and anxiety that's part of the situation you are looking at as one component of it, that's currently quite a long way away.

While you're up in your helicopter, you can ask yourself some questions to help with gathering as much information as you can from your new perspective. For instance, how does it feel to be able to see all aspects of the situation at once? Is there anything you would change now that you can see the bigger picture? What might somebody who was a passenger in this helicopter with you have to say about what they are looking down at? What connections might they make, or what details might they notice? How would they describe what they are seeing to you?

You can zoom in on any aspect of this scene and fly upwards again if you want. When you're ready, imagine landing your helicopter back gently on the ground. See what your new perspective has brought you. If the exercise has suggested any action that you need to take, such as seeking more or different support, or making changes to how you are approaching the situation, go ahead. You might also take a moment to notice if your emotions have changed since the start of this exercise and, if so, to notice in what way.

Helicopter view summary

- Observe the situation
- Notice its component parts, including your emotions, and imagine them laid out in front of you
- Take a deep breath
- "Pull focus" to see the wider view
- Imagine your own personal helicopter to lift you high above the situation, and look down at it, taking the widest possible view
- Notice how you're feeling, make connections, gather information and zoom in where you want
- Land safely back on the ground ready to hold your new perspective in mind as you move forward with your situation

Going further

You could try using the helicopter view in a learning setting, to get a perspective from another subject – that is, what does this learning situation or dilemma in maths look like from the perspective of biology? This might result in connections between areas of study that you hadn't made before. It might also give different perspectives on what's difficult within one area of study, as what's important in another area of study might be quite different!

Further reading

Grand unified theory (the ultimate helicopter view?). (2023). https://en.wikipedia.org/wiki/Grand_Unified_Theory

Hall, K. (2021). Psychological Flexibility and Mental Wellness. The importance of psychological flexibility: https://www.psychologytoday.com/gb/blog/constructive-controversy/201906/the-importance-taking-the-perspective-others

https://www.sciencedirect.com/topics/psychology/psychological-flexibility

7. REST

Time: open-ended

Who this could be for: anyone who needs to build more rest time into their daily lives

Resources needed: no resources required

Why do this: benefit from understanding the value of good quality rest for your general wellbeing, physical health and ability to progress as a learner

Getting good quality rest is an important part of maintaining both our physical and mental wellbeing. Rest is not just sleep; it can incorporate a state of relaxation and feeling safe and soothed. We need to feel it's safe to rest – not under threat of any kind. Rest can help us learn better, too; see further reading and resources for more on how getting some rest can help with acquisition of, consolidation of and recall of new learning. Not having good quality rest can have some quite significant impacts on our physical and emotional states, too; if we are not well-rested, it can become increasingly difficult to regulate our body temperature, our appetite and our emotions. Our bodies seek to maintain homeostasis, and being fatigued can make this difficult. Rest therefore is vital to us.

Despite this, we may undervalue the concept and practice of rest in our lives, especially if we are focused on achievement and driven to make what we perceive as progress in our day-to-day activities. This activity introduces the concept of rest being as valuable a use of our time as achieving and striving. This is because resting supports our being able to achieve by helping us to recover and recuperate from our efforts and to feel safe and able to "stand down" from a setting of try/strive/achieve, or a defensive, threatened state of stay-alert-to-danger-and-threat/survive/defend. If we are continually stuck in the mode of trying/striving/achieving, or of surviving/defending, we can become fatigued over time, and eventually the harder we try to progress, the slower our progress and the more our minds and bodies are shouting at us to take a breather. Sometimes we work hard to distract ourselves from this warning and push through it because we are very invested in continuing to achieve or to survive; sooner or later though, the message gets through and we find we have to stop, whether due to complete exhaustion or a physical illness that leaves us simply no choice but to rest.

Although a short-term stress response (such as a "fight or flight" adrenaline burst to help us survive a threat by getting away from it or fighting it off) can be beneficial for us, there is evidence that chronic stress has a deleterious effect on our immune system and may contribute to the development of illness and disease in the long term. There are a lot of good reasons, therefore, to find ways to rest and to value the idea of rest as an important part of our daily lives. In an ideal world, we don't run ourselves completely into the ground, and instead run a more balanced schedule of resting along with working hard and achieving.

Take some time to read about the Gilbert "three systems" model of emotional regulation. See further reading and resources, or view the model here: https://www.nicabm.com/3circles/. The model argues that we have three emotional regulation systems: "drive," "threat" and "soothing" and that we move between them. The different responses associated with each system are fitting in different situations; being in "drive" means you are task-, goal- or activity-focused; you are expending energy to reach something you want or need. In "threat," you are responding to dangers and threats to you; you are expending energy here too, and your responses are intended to ensure your survival (fight, flee, defend, find safety). In "soothe," you are out of danger and also not striving to achieve anything; you are resting and recuperating and generally feeling safe. This is where you might be recouping all that energy used up on the other two systems. And here is where the Gilbert model suggests we might have a challenge; many of us have an unbalanced relationship between these three systems and spend too much of our time in either "drive" or "threat" mode. As a result, we might not manage to recover from our energy depleting experiences and can end up feeling low, run down and exhausted. We might also find it difficult to actually get into a "soothe" system response, as we're so unused to it, we can find it almost alarming! Our lives can encourage us to de-prioritise the "soothe" part of these emotional regulation systems, and in fact, we can be rewarded for doing so (an achievement such as a promotion at work might follow "putting in the hours," for example).

Having read about the Gilbert three systems idea, take some time to survey your own life, over the past month (or less if you prefer). Try to estimate how much time you have spent in each of the systems and make some notes of what you were doing that put you into each of them, for instance, having a deadline for an assignment; getting into an argument with a friend or family member and having a week off and going to the beach every day and just doing nothing. Use Table 3.3 to capture what you have noticed. Once you have done this, you can have a go at drawing the three circles as in the Gilbert model, with their sizes reflecting the amount of time you have spent in each mode. It might be that your diagram looks very equally balanced or it might not!

TABLE 3.3 Three threat model

DRIVE:
when I have been in drive mode this month (or week) and what I was doing
THREAT:
when I have been in threat mode this month (or week) and what I was doing
SOOTHE:
when I have been in soothe mode this month (or week) and what I was doing

Going further

Having reflected on what you have noticed about your own three systems experience in the first part of this activity, you might feel that it would be good to try to rebalance things. Do you need to spend more time in "soothe" mode? If so, how are you going to do this? Make a plan (and make the changes you need to make) and then try it. Don't forget to review how it works out and notice if you feel any different as a result of what you have changed.

Further reading

AGE UK. (2023). MIND. How rest and sleep helps learning. (2023). https://healthysleep.med.harvard.edu/healthy/matters/benefits-of-sleep/learning-memory

Dhabhar, F. S. (2014, May). Effects of stress on immune function: The good, the bad, and the beautiful. *Immunologic Research*, 58(2–3), 193–210. https://doi.org/10.1007/s12026-014-8517-0; https://pubmed.ncbi.nlm.nih.gov/24798553/#:~:text=In%20contrast%2C%20long%2Dterm%20stress,and%20function%20of%20immunoprotective%20cells

Dhabhar, F. S. (2018, April). The short-term stress response – Mother nature's mechanism for enhancing protection and performance under conditions of threat, challenge, and opportunity. *Frontiers in Neuroendocrinology*, 49, 175–192. https://doi.org/10.1016/j.yfrne.2018.03.004; https://pubmed.ncbi.nlm.nih.gov/29596867/

Gilbert, P. (2019). *The compassionate mind: A new approach to life challenges.* Constable and Robinson Ltd.

Psychological Therapy. (2023). Emotion regulation systems: The three circles model of Paul Gilbert (psychologytherapy.co.uk)

Three-systems model of emotional regulation: https://ppss-static.cumbria.nhs.uk/files/patient-resources/Worksheet-5.3-Threat-drive-soothe-system.pdf

8. CONNECT WITH OTHERS AND GIVE TO OTHERS

Time: flexible, depending on the amount of time you have available and on what if any of the activities to decide to get involved with

Who this could be for: anyone who would like to explore connecting with other people as a way to support and improve wellbeing and to boost learning

Resources needed: internet access if taking part in any virtual activities; any other resources will depend on what activities you wish to try

Why do this: benefit from the ways in which connecting with other people and giving your time and company to others can improve your own wellbeing too, and give you opportunities to learn

Connecting with others and giving to others are two of the cornerstones of good wellbeing as identified in the NHS's five steps to mental wellbeing. This activity outlines why these are beneficial activities for your wellbeing and offers some ideas for you to consider on how you could bring more connection and giving to others into your own life.

The NHS's five ways to wellbeing states that connecting with other people can:

- help you to build a sense of belonging and self-worth
- give you an opportunity to share positive experiences
- provide emotional support and allow you to support others

It also states that giving to others can improve wellbeing by:

- creating positive feelings and a sense of reward
- giving you a feeling of purpose and self-worth
- helping you connect with other people

This activity takes these two ideas together; as is shown above, one supports the other. It can be challenging to find ways of bringing this way to wellbeing into your life, especially if you have a lot of pressure on your time from commitments and responsibilities. Even if this way to wellbeing isn't something you feel you have time for now, it's worth understanding the positive impact it can have on your wellbeing for consideration in the future. If this is something you would like to move towards in your life, see "values based living" in further reading and resources or see Activity 49: Values based living – and values based learning.

Step 1: Firstly, consider your own current life and identify what you might already be doing to connect with and give to others. Use Table 3.4 to summarise what you notice. In the first column, capture information on how you currently connect with and give to others. Give details of who, where and how often (is it a one-off or a regular event or activity?). In the second column, consider how you might like this to develop in the future. If you notice a lot of "oh but that couldn't happen because of x/y/z"-type thoughts, just notice them but try not to be too put off; sometimes we can push away even good ideas before we've given ourselves a chance to think about how they could work (or how we could get to some aspect of them, if not all).

TABLE 3.4 Current life

My current life: how I connect with other people now (who, where and when)	In future: how I would like to connect with other people more/differently
My current life: how I give to others now (who, where and when)	In future: how I would like to give to others more/differently

Step 2: Secondly, identify any obvious options or opportunities you already have easily accessible to you, to connect with others and/or give to others. Is there a friend or relative you've been meaning to get in touch with, but life is just too busy and you keep putting it off? Do you know someone who has an interesting hobby, skill or pastime and you'd like to know more about it but haven't got around to asking? Is somewhere in your local area asking for volunteers to help with a one-off project? Is there a charitable fundraising event near you that you could get involved with? Do you have anything you think might make a good donation to a charity shop, a clothes bank or another donation-receiving organisation? If there are any "easy wins," you could just try them right away.

Some ideas you have come up with might need a bit more consideration and research, however. See further reading and resources for a start in finding possible directions with, for example, skills-based volunteering, or volunteering internationally. The Charities Aid Foundation offers some suggestions for charitable giving here, not just donating money but a range of activities: https://www.cafonline.org/my-personal-giving/long-term-giving/resource-centre/ways-to-give-to-charity

To bring a learning focus to the wellbeing benefits of connecting with others and giving to others, as an alternative second step in this activity, firstly consider if you have a skill, pastime or hobby that you know improves your own wellbeing, and if so, volunteer to show someone else how to do it. Alternatively, you could ask your friends, family, fellow learners, colleagues or neighbours, whether they have a skill, pastime or hobby that they know benefits their wellbeing. If any of them do, ask them if they would consider teaching you how to do it. Do you know anyone who knits or crochets to relax and manage anxiety, for instance? Do you know something about gardening and could share it with others?

Going further

If you have found trying any of the ideas for connecting with others and giving to others beneficial to you, to take this activity further, you could consider inviting others to join you. Can you encourage anyone else to find ways of connecting with others in their own life? Can you invite someone else along to volunteer? Alternatively, you could identify a way to let others know what you have found beneficial or enjoyable and pass on your experiences through, for example, a local newsletter or magazine or a noticeboard (real or virtual!). This would add a further layer of connecting of course and increase the benefit to others and to your own wellbeing.

It is fascinating to consider the findings of the Charities Aid Foundation's World Giving Index, their 2022 report into giving around the world (see further reading and resources to read the full report). It notes that the COVID pandemic coincided with an alteration of global giving behaviour; it states that

> in 2018, seven out of the 10 most generous countries were classed by the United Nations as high-income countries. However, in 2020, during the height of the pandemic, seven out of the top 10 were low- and middle-income economies. This trend continued in 2021. Only four of this year's top 10 most generous countries are classed as high-income countries, and six are low- and middle-income countries.

An additional going further activity is to consider why this change has come about, and what, if anything, might change it again?

Works well with

Activity 2, Chapter 7: Modelling and passing it on

Further reading

AGE UK. (2023) Friendship services. https://www.ageuk.org.uk/get-involved/volunteer/telephone-friend/

RVS Virtual village hall, virtual sessions to take part in from arts and crafts to singing and technology: https://virtualvillagehall.royalvoluntaryservice.org.uk/?gclid=CjwKCAjw0ZiiBhBKEiwA4PT9z5yXFJDjpUdXQCPFSG-n7VKth_hNloKxeGHqRY_39tlSu_eftdtLGRoCwpIQAvD_BwE&gclsrc=aw.ds

RVS: why volunteer? (2023). https://www.royalvoluntaryservice.org.uk/volunteering/why-volunteer

Skills-based volunteering. (2023). https://reachvolunteering.org.uk/

The Charities Aid Foundation World Giving Index 2022: https://www.cafonline.org/about-us/publications/2022-publications/caf-world-giving-index-2022/

Values-based living. (2023). https://psychotherapyacademy.org/acceptance-and-commitment-therapy-the-essentials/the-journey-of-life-a-metaphor-for-values-in-act/

Voluntary Service Overseas. (2023). https://www.vsointernational.org/

9. BUILDING A POSITIVE SELF-IMAGE

Time: five to ten minutes to gather positive data; ten minutes to reflect on the positive data gathered

Who this could be for: anyone who would like to build a more positive way of thinking about themselves; anyone who finds it easy to notice flaws in themselves or to focus on mistakes but might find it more difficult to identify good qualities, achievements and positive aspects of the self generally

Resources needed: writing materials/other method of recording information

Why do this: build a habit of noticing positive aspects of yourself in order to feel a better sense of self-esteem and self-belief and to lessen the stress and distress that can be caused by being unrelentingly self-critical over time

Building a positive self-image

The way we think about ourselves and the habits of thought we get into can make a significant difference to our wellbeing over time. If we tend to think of ourselves in a positive manner and to notice and reflect on our good aspects, our achievements, things we are proud of and times when we have been appreciated by others or been helpful and made a contribution to the world around us, the impact on our wellbeing will be significant. Alternatively, we might get into a different kind of mental habit, where we tend to think about ourselves in a negative manner and to notice and reflect on our mistakes, on times when we fell short or let others or ourselves down, on things we regret and times when others have expressed disappointment in us or said negative things about us. This will also have a significant impact on our wellbeing.

Our habits of noticing, remembering and reflecting can make a difference to the mental picture we build of ourselves, and over time, even if that picture is skewed and misses out important information (due, e.g., to us not noticing positive aspects of ourselves), it can start to feel like a fixed and factual representation of us – in short, we start to believe the kind of story we tell ourselves about who we are. We will all have a range of different experiences as we go through life, we will all behave in a variety of ways in different situations and we will all have a range of great and perhaps not so great characteristics. How we reflect on this range of experiences, behaviours and characteristics is worth attending to as part of looking after our wellbeing. Building positive habits of thought when we think of ourselves will benefit us as learners and as we go through our lives.

This activity will help you notice and reflect on information about yourself in order to build a positive self-image. The data log is for use in helping to build a general positive self-image and invites you to capture evidence of your good qualities and to actively reflect on them.

Positive data log: gather the evidence and information

The first step is to gather evidence and information from your daily life of your good qualities, your achievements and successes, your coping skills and the positive comments and feedback from others around you that you get. Don't wait for something big to add to this log; even a small thing is relevant. And don't forget that on a really tough day, just turning up can count as an achievement! There will be something to capture in this exercise every day, even if at first you find it really difficult to notice anything. It's all part of building a habit of noticing positive things about yourself.

TABLE 3.5 Positive data log: reflect on the evidence and information

My good qualities	*My achievements and successes*	*When I have coped well*	*Positive comments and feedback from others*

Identify a time when you can read through what you have captured in Table 3.5 and set aside (for example) ten minutes to reflect on and remember each situation the evidence you have gathered relates to. It can help to visualise the scene as you remember it, as visual images are more powerful in affecting our thinking and our emotions than just words. Try to hold the good feelings in your awareness that you felt at the time and also notice the good feelings that arise while you are reflecting on the evidence.

Going further

Set some time aside every day to practice this for a week and see how you feel at the end of this process. Is there a change in how easy you find it to reflect on yourself in a positive manner or to identify positive evidence and information about yourself?

Further reading

Padesky, C. A. (1994). Schema change processes in cognitive therapy. *Clinical Psychology and Psychotherapy*, 1(5), 267–278. https://padesky.com/newpad/wp-content/uploads/2012/11/schema_change_article_permissions.pdf

10. MEDITATION AND MINDFULNESS

Time: from 5 to 30 minutes or longer, depending on time available

Who this could be for: anyone who would like to know more about and try meditation, to develop mindfulness as a way of relaxing, getting into a present-focused state of mind and increasing their ability to notice the sensory world around them

Resources needed: uninterrupted time to try the activities; access to a quiet (or less busy) space for the duration of the activities

Why do this: find out how meditation and mindfulness can benefit your wellbeing and help you refresh and clear your mind and relax your body to support you in day-to-day activities and enable you to learn more effectively

Meditation, and mindfulness, have their roots in religious traditions including Buddhism, Jainism, Hinduism and Taoism. Other major religions including Judaism, Islam and Christianity also incorporate contemplative techniques as essential parts of their practice. As concepts, both meditation and mindfulness have, over the last century or so, spread into secular society, and in recent years, mindfulness as a practice has become increasingly popular as a way of benefiting general wellbeing and to relax and connect more with the world around us and find a sense of peace.

Mindfulness is described as "paying attention in a particular way; on purpose, in the present moment, and nonjudgmentally" (Kabat-Zinn, 1994). To be mindful is to be fully present, moment to moment, with what we are experiencing; being aware of our thoughts, emotions, sensory experiences as they come and go; noticing what's going on around and within us; and without being closely caught up with it either via judgement or trying to over-control anything. If we are mindful, we are not completely lost in thoughts about the past, nor focused on thoughts about the future, but instead we are more conscious of being in the moment as it is happening around and to us, right now.

In reading this description, it might be that your mind leapt about all over the place: to something that happened yesterday, to what you need to do later on today, to that other thing that's really bothering you, to other things you've read about mindfulness or what someone you know told you about it; in other words, your mind may have wandered away from the moment-to-moment experience of reading and attending to the description. If it did, you can, if you like, try re-reading it mindfully, being fully present with each word as you read through. If you try it, see if you find any differences in how the first and second reading felt to you.

Meditation is the practice by which mindfulness is developed and honed. Meditation is therefore the process by which you can gain, develop and improve your ability to be mindful or able to pay attention to and be in the present moment without judgement. You don't need a lot of resources to try meditation; just some time, and even a few minutes will be enough to get started.

This activity is an invitation to find some time in your day to try a meditation exercise. It can be just for a few minutes, so it should hopefully be possible to find a little time even on a busy day.

- Make yourself comfortable
- notice, and then try to let go of, any body tension, especially in your arms, shoulders and upper body generally
- if it helps, close your eyes, or if that's not comfortable for you, defocus a little
- pay attention to your in-breath and out-breath; just notice your breathing, and take slow, calm breaths
- just notice your thoughts and feelings as they come and go, without getting too tied up in them and without trying to change or block them (imagining the thoughts and feelings as leaves fluttering past on a breeze or drifting along on a river is a useful way of noticing them without holding on to them).
- When you're ready, re-focus your eyes, or open them if you've had them closed, and bring your attention back to the world around you

That's it! You might have noticed this short meditation exercise has changed your mood or made you feel different. Taking just a few minutes a day to meditate can be beneficial and supportive of your general wellbeing and your readiness to learn effectively too.

There are many online resources (see further reading and resources for more) which you can use to explore meditation and mindfulness further if you found this initial exercise beneficial.

For consideration

While many people who use meditation to develop mindfulness find it beneficial, there is some evidence that it can have negative effects particularly when used very intensively. If you are concerned about meditation raising distress for you, or emotions and/or memories that are very painful or too difficult to tolerate, it may be more beneficial for you to give consideration to other forms of relaxation and being in the present moment. Discuss it with someone you trust if in doubt.

Going further

Using the mindful skills you have gained in the first part of this activity, try this listening and visualisation exercise to de-centre yourself, if you are feeling under pressure from the expectations of others or from the expectations you have of yourself. This exercise brings your awareness to the experience of being alive that others around you – human, animal, bird and insect – are living through, moment to moment.

1. Find a place to either stand, sit or recline, ideally outside (inside will work if there is some evidence of other people, animals or insects around).
2. Close your eyes or defocus your eyes if that's more comfortable for you.
3. Take a few moments to slow your breathing: taking slow, calm breaths in, holding the breath and then breathing out, until you feel your body calm and relax.
4. Let go of any physical tension you notice across your body: relax or release tensed muscles.
5. Now turn your attention from your breathing to the sensory world around you. Notice the sounds around you and pay attention to them, without judging.
6. If your mind wanders away from the sounds you can hear and you notice thoughts arise, or worries, that's fine; just notice the thought or worry that has arisen and then gently return your attention to the sounds you can hear around you.
7. It might be that, if you are outside, you can hear birds, insects and animals either nearby or further away from you. Pay attention to each sound of another being living its life, as it moves through the world. Each being with its own experience, intentions and directions to go in. Just notice these sounds of other lives about you as you breathe.
8. Now imagine looking down from above yourself. Visualise the sounds of these other beings as points on a diagram, with you as a point on the diagram too, at the centre. As you listen, it may be that the animals, birds and/or insects you can hear are moving along; visualise their point on the diagram moving along too. If you visualise joining the dots on this diagram, try to see the kind of shape that it makes.
9. Now imagine what those other points on the diagram might be able to hear if they were trying the same exercise as you; their sound map or visualisation would include you as one of the outer points on the diagram rather than in the centre. If you can, try to visualise what one of these other maps of other lives would look like. Is it a different shape?
10. You can jump to another point if you wish and try the same thing.
11. When you are ready, return to your own sound map or visualisation, looking and listening to who and what you can hear moving around you.
12. Return your attention to your breathing, and when you are ready, open or refocus your eyes.
13. Take some time to notice if this new awareness of the lives of other creatures around you and their perspectives makes you feel or think any differently to how you were feeling and thinking at the start of this exercise.

Don't forget, you cannot get this exercise "right" or "wrong"; just notice what happens, without judgement, just with compassion for yourself and your reactions, and compassion for others.

Further reading

Brown, K. W. & Ryan, R. M. (2003). The benefits of being present: Mindfulness and its role in psychological well-being. *Journal of Personality and Social Psychology*, 84, 822–848.

Germer, C. K., Siegel, R. D., & Fulton, P. R. (Eds.). (2005). *Mindfulness and psychotherapy*. The Guilford Press.

Hanh, T. N. (1987). *The miracle of mindfulness: A manual on meditation*. Beacon Press.

https://www.mind.org.uk/information-support/drugs-and-treatments/mindfulness/about-mindfulness/

https://www.nhs.uk/mental-health/self-help/tips-and-support/mindfulness/

Kabat-Zinn, J. (1994). *Wherever you go, there you are: Mindfulness meditation in everyday life*. Hyperion Books.

Keng, S.-L., Smoski, M. J., & Robinsa, C. J. (2011). Effects of mindfulness on psychological health: A review of empirical studies. https://www.ncbi.nlm.nih.gov/pmc/articles/PMC3679190/

Mair, D. (2019). *The student guide to mindfulness*. SAGE.

MIND. (2023). Deciding if mindfulness is right you for. https://www.mind.org.uk/information-support/drugs-and-treatments/mindfulness/is-mindfulness-right-for-me/

Mindfulness. https://plumvillage.org/mindfulness/mindfulness-practice/

Paid-for mindfulness resource, Headspace: https://www.headspace.com/

The Mindfulness Attention Awareness Scale: https://ppc.sas.upenn.edu/resources/questionnaires-researchers/mindful-attention-awareness-scale

4
WELLBEING IN THE CONNECTED LEARNING COMMUNITY

The settings in which we learn are already incredibly varied. It seems likely that our near future learning will take place in an ever-widening range of settings and situations. Informal and spontaneous learning networks have already formed using social media around themes and issues, and these exist and develop outside of what we might see as more formal and "traditional" learning setting such as the institutions of schools, colleges and universities. It seems likely that these networks will continue to form and develop in the near future. This chapter considers one particular aspect of the connected learning communities that are developing and are likely to continue to develop in the near future: namely the place of wellbeing within such communities. Traditional learning institutions aspire (albeit not always with success) to support the wellbeing of their members: how are more informal networks to do the same and should they aspire to do so? Can, and should, informal learning communities consider wellbeing (both the wellbeing of those who participate in the community and the impact of the activities of the community on those connected to it and outside it)? And if they are both capable of doing so, and should do so, how can they consider wellbeing?

There are potential benefits to consider for learning that happens outside formal structures as well as potential risks and pitfalls. One significant benefit may be that an informal, outside-institution learning network becomes accessible to those who might find, or have found, it difficult to access the same or similar learning via formal institutional routes, for instance due to reasons of difference (gender, ethnicity, age, sexuality, disability and neurodiversity) that may have intentionally or institutionally resulted in exclusion.

There may also be benefits to this type of learning in that it may be philosophically profoundly different in its underlying beliefs and approaches; the

DOI: 10.4324/9781003326786-5

concept of open source coding is a good illustration of the potential for a collaborative, interactive approach to learning and developing ideas together rather than an information-retaining approach with the "inner workings" either not shared or only shared with select groups. Co-creation, the concept of collaboratively developing something (object, process, product, etc.) together with those who are to interact with what is being developed, is also aligned to the idea of more informal learning and may be another aspect of what is beneficial to such learning.

The risks and pitfalls of such learning networks should be considering too, as there may be questions of oversight, consistency, ethical practice and authenticity of information to consider. There is also the question of the wellbeing of those involved in a connected learning community. In recent years, social media use has become ubiquitous; platforms such as Facebook, Twitter, Instagram and TikTok are often the means by which informal learning networks arise, for instance via a Twitter hashtag (see further reading) or a content creator with a particular theme or subject who gains followers who then interact with each other within the follower network. Twitter is estimated to have over 350 million active monthly users, Instagram around 2.35 billion active monthly users, TikTok over a billion and Facebook over 2 billion. The potential members of any connected learning community that forms and assembles on a social media platform (or across more than one) is vast.

The use and over-use of social media have been associated with a range of negative impacts on the mental health of users and have also been implicated in a range of social harms such as the development of extremist views, the sharing of false or misleading information, practices such as bullying or hounding either individuals or groups with shared characteristics and doxing. The potential negative sides of social media are impacting young people; NHS (National Health Service) Digital's report, Mental Health of Children and Young People 2022, found that one in eight (12.6%) of 11- to 16-year-old users of social media reported having been bullied online. Set against this is a majority view found via survey in 2021 (see further resource and reading) that social media platforms have a duty to take care of the mental health of their users.

This view may however be at odds with the nature of social media platforms as they currently function; often gaining and holding the attention of users as a priority and if that has a result of an increase in an emotion or state for a user that is negative for their wellbeing, such as anxiety for example, it may be that the platform benefits from the feeling the user experiences because they may, as a result of feeling anxious, spend longer attending to the information on the platform than they otherwise would. If in a state of heightened anxiety, for instance, the user may be driven to try to reassure themselves or to gain additional information about the source of their anxiety.

Platforms are also likely to benefit from the extended attention of users who are attempting to avoid more anxiety-provoking focuses for their attention; scrolling instead of getting on with an aversive task or dealing with something emotionally difficult for instance. Given this, an expectation that the types of platforms and online spaces that connected learning networks are likely to form in will be able to attend to the wellbeing of the potential members of those learning networks might be an expectation that is unrealistic. It may therefore be left to such learning communities to develop their own wellbeing-protective behaviours and safeguards. This may in fact be one of the aspects of what such connected learning communities learn together.

Further reading

2021 survey finds two-thirds of adults with social media accounts consider social media platforms have a duty to protect the mental health of users: https://press-releases.responsesource.com/news/101063/two-thirds-of-social-media-users-want-better-mental-health/

Co-creation: https://www.interaction-design.org/literature/topics/co-creation

Doxing. https://en.wikipedia.org/wiki/Doxing

How twitter fuels anxiety: https://www.theatlantic.com/technology/archive/2017/07/how-twitter-fuels-anxiety/534021/

Instagram user statistics: https://www.demandsage.com/instagram-statistics

Kumar, P. 2019. Social media for informal Learning: a case of #Twitterstorians. Proceedings of the 52nd Hawaii International Conference on System Science. https://scholarspace.manoa.hawaii.edu/server/api/core/bitstreams/229e3040-93ce-4519-889d-8ad07c2f09cb/content

Mental health of 17–19 year olds, 2022: https://digital.nhs.uk/news/2022/rate-of-mental-disorders-among-17-to-19-year-olds-increased-in-2022-new-report-shows

NHS Digital, Mental Health of Children and Young People 2022: https://digital.nhs.uk/data-and-information/publications/statistical/mental-health-of-children-and-young-people-in-england/2022-follow-up-to-the-2017-survey

Open source coding: https://en.wikipedia.org/wiki/Open_source

Social media platforms and their actions to support mental health of users: https://www.socialday.live/features/social-media-platforms-supporting-users-mental-health

Twitter users statistics 2019–24: https://www.statista.com/statistics/303681/twitter-users-worldwide/

ACTIVITIES

1. EMERGENT PROPERTIES OF CONNECTED LEARNING COMMUNITIES: WHAT WILL WE CREATE BY LEARNING TOGETHER?

Time: 15 minutes or longer for consideration time

Who this could be for: anyone who wants to think about what new phenomena connected learning communities may result it

Resources needed: internet access (optional; if wishing to research/read more relating to the activity)

Why do this: develop your understanding of the possibilities that connected learning communities may offer and consider (via going further activity) how alternative emergent properties can be generated by changing how we go about organising our world

Emergence is something that happens when something (e.g. a system, entity or object) comprised of separate parts or elements develops qualities, properties or behaviours that the separate parts didn't have on their own. Emergence is a phenomenon that can occur in different settings; life, for example, can be seen as an emergent property of chemistry. Perhaps we could see a loaf of bread as an emergent property of flour, salt, sugar, water and yeast!

Connected learning communities are complex and dynamic networks that are highly likely to give rise to emergent properties as they form and interact and learn. The separate elements of the learning community won't necessarily give rise to these properties alone; it's the coming together of the different elements to form the community that gives rise to them. There is a sense of unpredictability in what emergent properties may arise from a dynamic connected learning community; this is perhaps part of what makes such communities interesting and potentially beneficial; it is also what may make them difficult to manage and challenging to integrate into more structured or formal learning settings.

This activity is an invitation to consider what emergent properties a connected learning community of your choice may give rise to. You could choose to consider this exercise in relation to a connected learning community that you are currently involved in or have been involved in, or you could instead choose to think about a connected learning community that you are aware of, or alternatively you could think of a speculative, hypothetical learning community that you predict may arise in the near future. Some ideas to prompt your thinking are included here: don't feel limited to these if your thinking goes in other directions, they are simply prompts to use if needed.

1 Consider these examples of connected learning communities:
- A group of allotment-holders who are in contact via an online forum with other allotment-holders who are geographically distant to each other

- A group of people who share an interest in cosplay and post pictures of their costumes on Instagram
- A special interest group set up by psychotherapists who want to understand more about how climate change is impacting on the wellbeing of their clients
- Another example of a connected learning community that you have heard of, are or have been involved with, or that you predict might arise in the near future

2 What emergent properties might arise from any of the above connected learning communities; what might they create via their interactions? (Resources, plans, conflicts, ideas and awareness beyond their community?) What impact might the potential emergent properties of any of these connected learning communities have?
3 What do you think would need to be adjusted in the elements that comprise the connected learning community (the constituent parts that make it up, for instance the learners, their individual environments and the platform(s) via which they might interact) to result in an emergent property of improved wellbeing for everyone involved in the connected learning community?

Going further

Using the concept of emergence, consider the phenomenon of poor wellbeing or difficulties such as stress, anxiety and depression. Can we consider mental ill health as an emergent property of our collective way of living as it is organised now? If so, how does our way of living and organising our societies need to alter, for the emergent property to change from mental ill health or poor wellbeing to good mental health or good wellbeing? Choose five key changes to our social organisation and systems that, if made, would result in the emergent property of good wellbeing.

Further reading

Surviving or thriving: the state of the UK's mental health: https://www.mentalhealth.org.uk/explore-mental-health/publications/surviving-or-thriving-state-uks-mental-health

The concept of emergence: https://en.wikipedia.org/wiki/Emergence

2. DISTRESS TOLERANCE AND EMOTIONAL REGULATION SKILLS IN GROUPS

Time: flexible to fit time available

Who this could be for: anyone who would like to understand more about how our emotions can be triggered by others and how to keep balance and keep learning

Resources needed: no resources needed

Why do this: build your understanding of how interpersonal factors influence our emotions and how we can manage this

There are many positive and beneficial elements to co-learning, and learning in groups and learning with others are often productive of the most beneficial and richest kinds of learning. There are also potential challenges to learning in settings with others, and this activity considers some of the interpersonal factors that can potentially interfere with the learning, and reduce the wellbeing, of participants.

Whenever we experience positive interactions with others, we can benefit from a range of good things such as feelings of connection, confidence and improved self-efficacy and self-esteem. If we experience more negative interactions with others, the effect can be distressing, and if we experience negative interactions with others in learning settings, it can hold us back as learners and might even make us want to avoid similar learning situations in future, further impacting our potential learning experiences and limiting our development as learners. Potential negative interpersonal experiences in learning settings include conflict, power imbalances, bullying, exclusion or rejection, inconsistent support, unfairness, unfair or excessive criticism and disproportionately punitive responses to minor mistakes.

We can't control the behaviour of others; the best response to being treated poorly or unfairly might well be to withdraw and end our exposure to the poor treatment. However, there are times when we can experience distress and emotional responses in groups settings that are not due wholly to the behaviour of others but are contributed to by our own internal factors; previous experiences and memories, for example. Knowing what can trigger us off to react emotionally can help us to manage our responses and regulate our emotions in order to keep participating in a learning situation with others.

Take some time to identify the things that others can do in learning settings that cause a strong negative reaction in you. Use Table 4.1 to capture your thoughts.

TABLE 4.1 Learning setting

Things others do that can cause me to react strongly (negatively) in a learning setting	Why I think this causes a strong reaction in me (e.g., previous experiences, current beliefs and other factors?)	How I tend to respond to this situation	How I would prefer to respond to this situation instead

When you have identified some examples, note how you tend to respond to these button-pressing behaviours in others. You might find you tend to respond with a range of defensive or attacking strategies; once we're in a heightened emotional state, we're likely to stop thinking in a calm and wise manner and instead respond by either defending ourselves or getting out of the situation; our "fight or flight" survival response is in charge. Consider finally for each item you've identified, how you might like, if possible, to respond instead.

If your preferred responses are less emotional, then review the following emotion regulation ideas and also see links in further reading and resources. Practice some emotional regulation techniques and see if you can put these alternative responses into use in a future learning setting where you find interpersonal factors are giving rise to heightened negative emotions for you.

A few emotional regulation ideas

- Doing the opposite: try going in the opposite direction to your first instinct when you're reacting (being curious and continuing to engage rather than shutting down and withdrawing; speaking quietly and calmly when you feel like shouting; being empathetic when you feel like being sarcastic?)
- Remind yourself that thoughts are not facts; consider other perspectives and points of view; keep in mind that several things can seem true from different subjective perspectives

- Try some defusion techniques (see further reading for more) such as pausing, noticing your reactions or being mindful of the passing thoughts and feelings you are experiencing
- Notice who you are really reacting to; who's really speaking? It might be that what someone does has reminded you of a past experience with someone else that was upsetting or distressing; are you reacting to the person in front of you or to a memory you have of a situation now long past? If it's from the past, ground yourself back in the here-and-now.

Try as many of the ideas above and in further reading as you wish to. If you find something that works, keep practising; you might find after a while that you have a new habit of responding that helps you manage difficult feelings.

Going further

Consider the ideas about the impacts on our wellbeing of the high connectivity and instant sharing of information including via social media that we now live with, as discussed at the beginning of Chapter 7, the future of wellbeing and learning – your impact on the world. Is there anything you consider would be helpful in tolerating distress and regulating emotions while interacting with this global connected learning community?

Further reading

DBT: https://dbt.tools/index.php
DBT emotion regulation skills: https://dbt.tools/emotional_regulation/index.php
Defusion techniques: https://www.getselfhelp.co.uk/defusion-techniques/#:~:text=Defusion%20Techniques-,Defusion%20Techniques,%2Ffor%20the%20other%20person)
Developing emotion regulation skills in children: https://camhs.rdash.nhs.uk/wp-content/uploads/2021/04/NL-Emotion-regulation-e-leaflet-02.21.pdf
Dialectical Behaviour Therapy (DBT) emotion regulation skills: https://www.therapistaid.com/worksheets/dbt-emotion-regulation-skills
Emotion regulation skills for adults: https://positivepsychology.com/emotion-regulation/
Interpersonal learning in groups: http://psychology.iresearchnet.com/counseling-psychology/counseling-therapy/interpersonal-learning/
Interpersonal relationships in education: https://scholar.harvard.edu/files/marietta/files/king_and_marietta_-_interpersonal_relationships.pdf

Works well with

Activity 5, Chapter 2: Distress tolerance and emotional regulation skills.

3. MAKING A SAFE PLACE TO LEARN

Time: 15–30 minutes discussion time or longer if preferred

Who this could be for: any learning community that would like to consider the idea of what's needed to feel psychologically safe to learn and whether their community is good at creating that environment

Resources needed: no resources needed

Why do this: consider what is needed to make a safe place to learn and identify if your learning community has what's needed – and if not, what you can do to change

One of the most fundamental things that needs to be present for successful learning to take place is psychological safety. We need to feel that it's safe to try, make mistakes, get it wrong and try again; safe to ask, not fearing humiliation, criticism, personal attack, rejection or any of the many other ways that we can be psychologically hurt. Psychological safety encourages us to take the risk of trying and to venture out into the new; in short, we are confident that we learn without being hurt to an intolerable amount. It's not about preventing us from feeling any discomfort; in fact, it is the opposite, it will help us build our ability to find out that the discomforts of being a learner are survivable and don't result in catastrophe.

For this activity, take some time to consider with other members of your learning community whether it is currently able to offer this safe place to learn. It may be a partial yes, and you might identify ways it could improve. You could consider what's working well in making a safe place to learn and identify areas for improvement. You can use these prompt questions to capture your thoughts:

- What is our learning community currently doing well in making itself a safe place to learn?
- What could our learning community could do better to make itself a safe place to learn?

Bear in mind that if your group is lacking in psychological safety currently, it might be helpful to gather feedback on these questions anonymously in order to get a truer reflection of how things really are.

Going further

If you have identified changes that would increase psychological safety in your learning community, agree and implement a plan for making the changes and review if they have worked.

You could also consider collecting feedback from members of your group anonymously; this is particularly relevant if your group is currently further off from psychological safety than you would like it to be.

You could also read in more detail about the four stages of psychological safety – see further reading.

Further reading

Psychological safety. Wikipedia. 2023. https://en.wikipedia.org/wiki/Psychological_safety

The four stages of psychological safety: https://wind4change.com/4-stages-psychological-safety-timothy-clark-inclusion-learner-contributor-challenger

The psychologically safe learning environment: https://www.advance-he.ac.uk/teaching-and-learning/curricula-development/education-mental-health-toolkit/social-belonging/psychologically-safe-learning-environment

4. ACTIVE LISTENING

Time: from a few minutes to as long as you wish to practice active listening

Who this could be for: anyone who wants to work on the skill of listening to others in a considered way that helps to facilitate change

Resources needed: someone to listen to

Why do this: find out about the concept of active listening and what benefit it could be to both the active listener and to the person being listened to

There is definitely a lot of talking going on in the world; how much listening is done? And not just the type of listening that's about waiting for a gap so you can say what you're waiting to say (which usually means you're not attending much to what's being said as you're focused on waiting for your chance to get in!). Active listening is an idea for listening in a more intense and purposeful manner. It sounds deceptively simple; try it out, and get someone to actively listen to you, and you might be surprised by how effective it can be. How often have you had the experience of trying to say how you feel about something, but you're met with a response that shows they haven't heard what you are saying about your experience at all? How does it make you feel? The chances are, if you've had this kind of experience, you can feel ignored, dismissed and even lonely/alone. In contrast, if you have ever truly been listened to, it can have a very different effect. If it's clear, from how someone responds to you, that they have listened to what you have been trying to say, you might feel noticed, valued, heard and perhaps even less alone with whatever experience you are describing.

Active listening was first described by Carl Rogers and Richard Farson in 1957. They proposed that listening well to someone is a process that can bring about change for the person being listened to. Rogers and Farson state that active listening can have some significant benefits for both individuals and groups:

> Active listening is an important way to bring about changes in people. Despite the popular notion that listening is a passive approach, clinical and research evidence clearly shows that sensitive listening is a most effective agent for individual personality change and group development. Listening brings about changes in people's attitudes toward themselves and others; it also brings about changes in their basic values and personal philosophy. People who have been listened to in this new and special way become more emotionally mature, more open to their experiences, less defensive, more democratic, and less authoritarian.
>
> When people are listened to sensitively, they tend to listen to themselves with more care and to make clear exactly what they are feeling and

thinking. Group members tend to listen more to each other, to become less argumentative, more ready to incorporate other points of view. Because listening reduces the threat of having one's ideas criticized, the person is better able to see them for what they are and is more likely to feel that his contributions are worthwhile.

(Rogers, 1957)

It's clear from reading the above that active listening could be extremely beneficial to the potential for effective learning within, as well as the wellbeing of, groups of many kinds. Here is a summary of the elements needed for active listening. To read in more detail about the idea of active listening, see further reading and resources.

Active listening: the elements needed and key atmosphere to foster

- Aim to be non-threatening: allowing the individual to feel safe to explore their own understandings rather than being made defensive by being threatened
- Key atmosphere: equal and free, permissive/allowing and understanding, and accepting and warm
- Be reticent in offering any judgements, opinions or answers, even if the speaker is asking for this; answering "surface" questions is to be avoided as it shuts down the expression of the wants and needs that are "beneath the surface" of the questions. For example, beneath "do you think I'll be OK?" may lie the deeper thought, "I don't think I'll be OK," and deeper still may be "I'm afraid." Actively listening for what's really being communicated can uncover this, whereas responding to the surface question with "yes of course you will!" dismisses all the other layers that the speaker is trying to communicate (while also trying to hide from even themselves).
- Listen for the "total meaning" of what's being communicated; notice the inferences within and around what's being said, and the way it's being said
- Respond to feelings; the factual content of what's said is accompanied by emotions. What are they? What else is being said around this?
- Note all cues: including the non-verbal cues that are just as much part of communication, if not more so, than the spoken words. Active listening (2021) is therefore also active looking!

By actively listening, as described briefly above (and fully in Rogers' and Farson's paper in further reading and resources), we also communicate some important messages ourselves to the person we're listening to; that they are worth listening to; that you are interested in them and what they have to say; that you won't dismiss them, or their own understandings and capabilities; that their thoughts and feelings are valid and valued. Take a moment to think of a time when you have felt all of those, or some of those, things. Was it a good experience? Is it an unusual experience for you? It might be that you have very rarely, or perhaps even never, had that experience of feeling truly listened to and heard. In contrast, you may be able to bring to mind far too easily the time, or times, when you have felt the opposite of all of these things; not worth someone's time; not of interest; dismissed; belittled; with thoughts and feelings that are lacking in validity, and not valued or valued very poorly. How did it make you feel? It's likely that it didn't make you feel very good at all, and in fact, the heightened emotions of these experiences can linger with us long after the event. What a difference it could make to everyone's wellbeing if being truly listened to via active listening could be the norm rather than the exception.

Going further

Having read about active listening, have a go at trying it out. You could try it in a learning group you are involved with; you could invite friends, other students or colleagues, depending on your life circumstances, to try the idea of active listening together. Give it a go and notice the effects of active listening on the group who tries it out. If you find it helpful, keep using the idea; over time, it could become quite contagious and spread out from your group, to others linked to the participants in your group.

References

Active listening (2021) https://en.wikipedia.org/wiki/Active_listening

Rogers, C., & Farson, R. (1957). *Active listening, further reading and resources*. Mockingbird Press.

5. TAKE A WELLBEING WALK TOGETHER

Time: from 10 to 15 minutes or as long as you and your walking companions wish to walk for

Who this could be for: anyone who would like to boost their wellbeing through taking a walk in the company of others

Resources needed: appropriate walking clothing and footwear; depending on the location chosen, and the time of year, walking shoes or supportive footwear, warm/weatherproof jacket

Why do this: gain from the many benefits to physical and mental wellbeing of walking in company with others

> Solvitur ambulando
> *(Latin, trans: "it is solved by walking," Saint Augustine, attrib.)*

We know that spending time in the natural world, and especially in green spaces, such as woodland, parkland or anywhere with the natural living-growing world around and near at hand, is beneficial for wellbeing – and in fact research is showing that being around nature has beneficial effects on our physical selves such as lowering blood pressure and improving mood. We also know that connecting with others in a meaningful way is an important part of maintaining wellbeing and that taking even light physical exercise is good for our physical health too. Going for a walk together with others in a green space therefore delivers lots of benefits.

Whether your learning community is big or small, temporary or long-standing, spending time together while walking is something that will have a positive impact on everyone's wellbeing. Setting up a wellbeing walk as either a one-off or a regular event is something to consider within your learning community. Your learning community might be a group of friends who share an interest or a pastime, a class or tutorial group, a group of colleagues in your working life who are a working community, your neighbours where you live, allotment-holders or many other types of community.

Setting up a wellbeing walk or joining in with an existing walk

There are two ways of going about taking a wellbeing walk as part of a community. You can either join in with one of the wellbeing walks that are already organised (see below for sources of information on wellbeing walks and walking), or you could set up your own wellbeing walk with members of your learning community.

If you set up a wellbeing walk for your own learning community, consider who will participate in your walk and choose a walking location that everyone will be able to access. Bear in mind differing fitness levels, any access needs, public transport links to the start of the walk and any COVID mitigations your participants might want to have in place. Depending on how many are going to be involved in your walk, you may be able to decide together where to go or vote on the most popular choice if there are several options.

When you are on your wellbeing walk

You could either simply walk together with no additional activities other than enjoying each other's company and being out and about, or you could add in some additional activities during the walk that focus on wellbeing. What activities could be appropriate would vary depending on the location you have chosen for your walk. For instance, can you intersperse the walk with a breathing exercise, a mindful practice, a reading appropriate to the group or anything else? Some of the other activities in this book might be relevant to try on the walk such as anxiety management strategies, distress tolerance and emotion regulation strategies or meditation and mindfulness (Chapter 1, Activity 2, Activity 5; Chapter 2, Activity 20).

More information on wellbeing walks and walking opportunities

Active partnerships, offering information on activity across England, including walking: https://www.activepartnerships.org/active-partnerships. Each region has an organisation that provides more information on local opportunities for a more active lifestyle, Active Norfolk is one example: https://www.activenorfolk.org/

IAPT services offer Wellbeing Walks, two examples are:

https://www.wellbeingnands.co.uk/norfolk/community-development-team/social-events/
https://bmywellbeingiapt.nhs.uk/our-courses/courses/walking-groups/
National Trust for Scotland on walks: https://www.nts.org.uk/visit/things-to-do/walking-in-scotland
The National Trust on walks: https://www.nationaltrust.org.uk/visit/walking
National Trust for Ireland: https://www.antaisce.org/
Ramblers Association on wellbeing walks and finding one near you: https://www.ramblers.org.uk/go-walking/ramblers-wellbeing-walks.aspx
Walks in Ireland: https://www.theirelandwalkingguide.com/

Walking and spending time in green spaces benefit health and wellbeing

Beneficial effects of shinrin-yoku (forest bathing) and nature therapy on mental health: A systematic review and meta-analysis: https://repository.derby.ac.uk/item/93x3y/effects-of-shinrin-yoku-forest-bathing-and-nature-therapy-on-mental-health-a-systematic-review-and-meta-analysis

BMJ. (2023). Visiting green spaces is related to lower use of medication for some mental and physical health difficulties: https://oem.bmj.com/content/80/2/111

Mental health benefits of regular woodland walks: report from Forest Research (the research agency of the Forestry Commission)

https://www.forestresearch.gov.uk/publications/valuing-the-mental-health-benefits-of-woodlands/

https://cdn.forestresearch.gov.uk/2021/12/frrp034.pdf

Four poems for a wellbeing walk (of many possibilities)

Dog Days, Derek Mahon:

https://www.pnreview.co.uk/cgi-bin/scribe?item_id=7065

The Present, Michael Donaghy:

https://www.poemhunter.com/poem/the-present-26/

God Says Yes To Me, Kaylin Haught:

https://www.loc.gov/programs/poetry-and-literature/poet-laureate/poet-laureate-projects/poetry-180/all-poems/item/poetry-180-126/god-says-yes-to-me/

Wild Geese, Mary Oliver:

https://www.poetry-chaikhana.com/Poets/O/OliverMary/WildGeese/index.html

Going further

If your wellbeing walk has been a success, you might want to make it a regular event. How about a seasonal wellbeing walk to take in the changing seasons? You could read more about micro-seasons too and take some wellbeing walks to notice them.

Japan's 72 Microseasons. (2015). https://www.nippon.com/en/features/h00124/

Reference

Solvitur ambulando. (2022). It is solved by walking: https://en.wikipedia.org/wiki/Solvitur_ambulando

Further reading

Barton, J, Hine, R, & Pretty, J. (2009). The health benefits of walking in greenspaces of high natural and heritage value. *Journal of Integrative. Environmental Sciences*, 6, 261–278.

How to go outside in the cold and stay warm: https://twitter.com/BlairBraverman/status/1334163443415441409?lang=en

How viewing images of the natural world can improve wellbeing and lower stress:

Jo, H, Song, C, & Miyazaki, Y. (2019, November 27). Physiological benefits of viewing nature: A systematic review of indoor experiments. *International Journal of Environmental Research and Public Health*, 16(23), 4739. https://doi.org/10.3390/ijerph16234739

https://www.ncbi.nlm.nih.gov/pmc/articles/PMC4025002/#B11-ijerph-11-03678

NBC News. (2018). 5 good reasons to go outside even when it's freezingr: https://www.nbcnews.com/better/health/5-good-reasons-go-outside-even-when-it-s-freezing-ncna843331

Parikian, L. (2021). *Light rain sometimes falls: a British year through Japan's 72 seasons*. Elliot & Thompson.

Pretty, J, Peacock, J, Hine, R, Sellens, M, South, N, & Griffin, M. (2007). Green exercise in the UK countryside: Effects on health and psychological well-being. *Journal of Environmental Planning and Management*, 50, 211–231. https://doi.org/10.1080/09640560601156466

Thompson-Coon, J, Boddy, K, Stein, K, Whear, R, Barton, J, & Depledge, M. H. (2011). Does participating in physical activity in outdoor natural environments have a greater effect on physical and mental wellbeing than physical activity indoors? A systematic review. *Environmental Science and Technology*, 45, 1761–1772. https://doi.org/10.1021/es102947t;

6. THINKING TOGETHER: TASC

Time: 30 minutes or longer depending on time available

Who this could be for: anyone who would like to try a problem-solving and critical thinking skills technique in a small group with others

Resources needed: internet access and others to work with

Why do this: try out a problem-solving and critical thinking technique as part of a learning community; develop your learning and support your wellbeing at the same time by working with and connecting with others

TASC, Thinking Actively in a Social Context, is a creative problem-solving framework developed by Belle Wallace, designed to support learners to develop their problem-solving and critical thinking skills in a creative and interactive manner, communicating with others and developing ideas together, drawing on the essential characteristics of us all as human learners, in particular that we learn effectively together in social groups. Rather than "telling," TASC as a framework invites learners to identify and then consider the questions that need to be answered and then to work on these together. For this activity, use the TASC wheel to work on something of your and your co-learners' choice. The subject you decide to consider is entirely up to you.

Going further

You could consider working on a wellbeing-related question, situation or problem using the TASC structure. If you have a group of co-learners you would like to try out the TASC framework with, there are free resources available online (see further reading and resources) as well as training in its use for a fee.

You could also read more about Albert Bandura's Social Learning Theory to take this activity further and understand more about how social interaction and learning interlace. See further reading and resources for more on this.

Further reading and resources

Albert Bandura's Social Cognitive Theory: https://sphweb.bumc.bu.edu/otlt/mph-modules/sb/behavioralchangetheories/behavioralchangetheories5.html
Bandura, A. (1986). *Social foundations of thought and action: A social cognitive theory*. Prentice-Hall, Inc.
Social Learning Theory: https://www.simplypsychology.org/bandura.html

TASC Wheel (Thinking in A Social Context). (2018). https://www.tes.com/teaching-resource/tasc-wheel-thinking-in-a-social-context-11844428

Wallace, B. (1983). *Teaching the very able child*. Ward Lock Educational Co Ltd.

Works well with

Prochaska and DiClemente's stages of change model in Activity 9, Chapter 5, Coping with and managing change

Critical thinking skills in Activity 9, Chapter 4, Combatting dark learning

7. GETTING THROUGH, TOGETHER: DEPERSONALISING RESILIENCE

Time: flexible

Who this could be for: any learning group or community who would like to consider developing their collective resilience

Resources needed: will vary depending on any plans made

Why do this: consider how resilience can be thought of as a collective, not just a personal, quality and find ways to build resilient learning communities

The concept of resilience has gained much attention in recent years, and a common critique of how it can be considered is that too much stress can be put on us as individuals to build our personal resilience in the face of challenge and adversity. This over-personalisation of who is responsible for resilience is often a way of passing on the negative impacts of societal structures that fail to support us, or actively harm us, and making dealing with the fallout a personal rather than a collective and shared responsibility.

This activity invites your learning community or group to instead consider resilience from a shared perspective; how do we develop this quality together rather than in isolation from each other?

Resilience: meaning

Psychological resilience is the capacity or ability to cope with a crisis and to return to a "pre-crisis" status quickly: the ability to be able to adapt in the face of difficulty and challenge.

Resilience: factors that build and maintain it in individuals

- The ability to make realistic plans and being capable of taking the steps necessary to follow through with them
- Confidence in one's strengths and abilities
- Communication and problem-solving skills
- The ability to manage strong impulses and feelings
- Having good self-esteem

Fletcher (2013)

Resilience: what defines a resilient community

The charity MIND (see further reading) suggests that individual resilience is supported by a community that has the right services and support, sufficient capacity and infrastructure and that makes the things people need to build their resilience accessible and available. Other aspects of a resilient community are being able to collectively grow and adapt around change and to anticipate and respond to disruptions and emergencies without losing its core values and identity.

What does resilience mean for your learning community?

As part of this activity, consider what resilience means for your own learning community. How does your learning community support its own resilience and support its individual members to build their own resilience? Could your learning community do more? If so, what could you do?

Going further

If you have identified anything your learning community thinks it could change, or do more of, to support the resilience of itself and its members, go further with this activity by agreeing a plan together and then making the changes.

Reference

Fletcher, D, & Sarkar, M. (2013, January 1). Psychological resilience. *European Psychologist*, 18(1), 12–23. https://doi.org/10.1027/1016-9040/a000124

Further reading

A collection of essays on what we need to do to build resilience collectively: https://www.redcross.org.uk/-/media/documents/about-us/what-we-do/communities-of-humanitarian-thought.pdf

British Red Cross. Resilience building activities to improve wellbeing. (2023). Resilience understanding and building activities (redcross.org.uk)

Ideas on what community resilience might be: https://www.resilience.org/stories/2018-11-28/six-foundations-for-community-resilience/

Kumar, U. (Ed.). (2020). *The Routledge international handbook of psychosocial resilience*. Routledge.

Padesky, C, & Mooney, K. (2012). Strengths-based cognitive-behavioural therapy: A four-step model to build resilience. *Clinical Psychology & Psychotherapy*, 19(4), 283–290.

The Red Cross's 6 R's of personal resilience: https://www.redcross.org.uk/-/media/documents/get-help/fam-update-loneliness-and-resilience-toolkit.pdf?la=en&hash=47E42800AE221E08F19CADC8C003ED70D18DBEDC

8. EMPATHY AND COMPASSION

Time: flexible

Who this could be for: anyone who would like to find out more about the concept of empathy and its role in supporting collective wellbeing within learning communities

Resources needed: no initial resources needed; any resources needed might be identified as part of going further activity ideas

Why do this: understand the impact of empathy in learning communities and identify ways of increasing empathy within your own learning communities

Empathy is the ability to place oneself in the experience of another to imagine what they are experiencing. It is a profound capacity and one that is vitally important for us. It can arise between humans and between humans and non-humans, and in its broader definitions, it is potentially present in some other animals too. Being able to imagine the experience of another is a key part of interacting with others, and of course a key part of learning; to teach, learn or co-learn, is to a great extent a process of placing oneself in the position of the other to understand what their understanding is and what is required to be shared.

Empathy can help us to feel good, too; you only need to recall how you felt when you were struggling with something, and someone was empathetic to you, to know how comforting and valuable it can be to feel that someone else understands what you are experiencing. We don't need to have exactly the same experience as someone else to be empathetic to them; we all have shared experiences that give us understanding overlaps with the experience of others. Expressing empathy is more about asking than telling and more about being with and alongside someone in their difficulties than looking on from a separate vantage point. Telling someone, even if it's well-intended, that "I know how you feel!" is less helpful than asking them to say more about their experience and feelings and then listening. Meet someone where they are to be truly empathetic; even if you've been on a similar journey, they're at a different point on it to you now.

It is fascinating to read about mirror neurons (see further reading and resources) in light of the experience of empathy; when we, and some other animals such as monkeys and rodents, witness another performing certain actions, our own neurons fire as if we were ourselves performing the action we are observing. It is possible our human experience of empathy has deep evolutionary roots.

Social systems are under strain and will potentially increasingly be so in future years with the combined effects of the intersecting challenges of climate breakdown, economic pressure and a potential struggle for resources.

Adding to this, there are factors actively driving a reduction in our collective empathy for political reasons, in multiple societies. What do we need to do now to future-proof ourselves against the reduction of empathy and compassion for each other?

Read about the work of the Empathy Museum (see further reading and resources) for some ideas on what can be done to build empathy and increase our understanding of each other's experiences, for instance literally walking in someone's shoes while listening to a recording of them describing their lives. Or read about the Human Library project, a worldwide learning project created in 2000 and running since then, inviting people to "borrow" each other like books in order to find out more about their lives and challenge their assumptions about what others might be like.

Going further

Having read about the impact of empathy, consider what options you have within a learning community you are part of to bring empathy and increase empathy within the group. Is shadowing or role-swapping for a brief period of time possible? Can you find ways to share what each other's experiences are? How about an activity where one of the members of your learning community learns about and then presents a view they disagree with to the group? Is there a one-off event you can arrange or a regular drop-in with an informal structure (either physical or virtual space)? Do you want to start a Human Library within your learning community?

Do you have any ideas for building empathy not just between humans but with the wider world? Here are two ideas to consider:

Empathy tree: http://wp.lancs.ac.uk/everydayfutures/files/2017/10/Kullman-and-Stasiulyte-2017-Empathy-Tree.pdf

Forest empathy: https://designmuseum.org/your-membership/your-membership-exhibitions/designers-in-residence-2020-care-members-and-patrons/forest-empathy-understanding-the-perspectives-of-trees-members-and-patrons

Further reading

Mirror neurons: https://en.wikipedia.org/wiki/Mirror_neuron
The Empathy Museum. (2023). https://www.empathymuseum.com/
The Human Library: https://humanlibrary.org/

9. COMBATTING DARK LEARNING

Time: 15 minutes or longer depending on the time you would like to spend finding out more about the ideas explored in this activity

Who this could be for: anyone who would like to know more about how to navigate the information available in the connected learning community

Resources needed: internet access

Why do this: find ways to benefit from the availability of information in the connected information-rich online world, while avoiding the hazards of learning from unreliable online sources. Understand the role of critical thinking in combatting susceptibility to conspiracy theories

"Don't believe everything you read online."

Abraham Lincoln

Although we live in an information-rich and news-rich world, there are significant problems with the ways in which our engagement with all of this information and news is making us feel (often stressed and unable to switch off), but there is also an emergent problem relating to what kinds of learning is resulting from the interaction of information, disinformation and social media-enabled networks of interest. This activity outlines what some of the issues may be and suggests some ways to use critical thinking skills to navigate the potential for dark learning in the connected information world.

As human beings, we are sense-making and pattern-making creatures; we operate by taking in information about the world via our senses and seeking to interpret it into meaningful experience. This is, in many ways, a useful approach that helps us to survive, develop and find our way about in the world, but it does result in us tending to seek out patterns and make connections where there might not be any. One example of the tendency to perceive a meaningful pattern or meaningful connections between unrelated things is pareidolia, which is the tendency to perceive a meaningful pattern in either images or sounds that are actually random. It's likely you will have experienced a very common manifestation of this if you've ever seen a face in an inanimate object. Using "pareidolia" as an image search term is highly recommended to get a sense of this phenomenon.

This sense-making and pattern-finding approach seems to be a driver for one of the emergent problems of the quantity of information available online which has increased exponentially with the development of the internet: the growth and permeation into mainstream culture and political discourse of conspiracy theories. Conspiracy theories are defined as alternative explanations of events either in history, or in the present, with a central claim that either people or particular groups are involved in secret, or conspiratorial, plotting. Social media development has enabled a much faster and more diverse dissemination of information in recent decades but hand in hand with this has gone a much faster and more diverse dissemination of misinformation, and the increased visibility of conspiracy theories is one effect of this. The range of people exposed to such ideas has increased, and a phenomenon of people becoming drawn into quite extreme and polarised views has become more widespread and has also led to people being fully drawn into conspiracy-accepting worldviews to the extent they become very different characters from who they formerly were (see further reading and resources, "how my mum became a conspiracy theory influencer").

Here are some proposed key elements and functions of conspiracy theories:

- Belief in a secret/conspiratorial plot existing between powerful individuals, groups or organisations
- Provide alternative explanations of events and situations that challenge and run counter to "official" or "accepted" versions
- Serve to reduce the complexity of reality (thus making it easier to grasp)
- Assist conspiracy theory-believing individuals to make sense of the world
- May arise out of a desire on an individual's part to understand important or critical events taking place in the society in which they live

Considering the elements and functions of conspiracy theories as above it's clear that there is some crossover with what we might seek from learning generally; we could consider these elements of conspiracy theory thinking as dark learning or a reflection of more helpful learning. How to combat this dark learning? There are potentially social ways to work on this, for instance reducing inequality between groups in a society, increasing participation and reducing exclusion and addressing power imbalances, improving overall wellbeing and boosting living standards so that there is less need to feel that there are indefinable threats from other groups or that others have power and one is powerless and without the ability to influence one's own immediate life or the world around. Another social factor in addressing this dark learning is potentially an attitude of openness, as far as possible, within institutions and organisations and states, sharing how and why decisions are taken to reduce the space for conspiracy thinking to work within. There are also individual steps to take that could be helpful; some ideas for this are included below.

Identifying conspiracy theories

Here are some ideas and things to look for to help you spot a conspiracy theory when you are looking at information (see further reading and resources for link to EU information page on this):

Author: who is the author of the information – verifiable identity, attached to a real institution, organisation, etc.? Or anonymous (see especially social media accounts), claiming expertise without credentials?

Source: being featured by reputable, legitimate news sources? Information is supported by legitimate individuals or organisations? Or unclear/anonymous/anecdotal "friend of a friend" source?

Tone: factual, balanced, complex, critical of own limits? Or emotive, sensational, extreme, denies other explanations?

Critical thinking: build your critical skills to combat dark learning

Having and maintaining good critical thinking skills is an important way that you can combat the kind of dark learning that helps conspiracy theories take root and grow. Critical thinking is the ability to think in a rational, considered, balanced manner, noticing and weighing up evidence, being aware of your own biases and subjectiveness. Critical thinking is clearly very different to that which might indicate conspiracy theory thinking as above.

Here are some ideas for building your critical thinking skills:

- Practice weighing up information and seeking different views and opinions; not rushing to take a position, reflecting on different viewpoints
- Notice your emotive and emotion-heavy reactions, be wary of deciding your view based on heightened emotions, especially if these are negative heightened emotions (e.g., anger or fear)
- Take a curious, inquisitive approach rather than jumping to conclusions
- Read about what "critical evaluation" is and try it out on a subject of your choice
- Be aware of your own assumptions and beliefs and how these might lead you to discount some information and potentially over-value other information; how can you balance this?
- Try to identify different perspectives; take an objective not subjective approach; is there another way of seeing it? Are there multiple ways of seeing it? Can you evaluate them rationally?

See the following for some more ideas on practicing your critical thinking skills:

https://www.skillsyouneed.com/learn/critical-thinking.html
https://www.forbes.com/sites/bernardmarr/2022/08/05/13-easy-steps-to-improve-your-critical-thinking-skills/

You could also see United Nations Educational, Scientific and Cultural Organization's (UNESCO's) page for some more information on conspiracy theories and how to stop them spreading: https://en.unesco.org/themes/gced/thinkbeforesharing

Going further

If conspiracy theories are socially contagious via dark learning networks present within social media, and if their spread mirrors the spread of infectious diseases, what treatments would you propose? Using the metaphor of illness, would you prescribe a preventative medicine, and if so, what would it be? Keeping healthy – for instance via critical thinking skills-boosting, increasing trust levels in collective and authentic sources of information and reducing social isolation? What treatment would you suggest if and when an individual or a group "catches" a conspiracy? To read about research into one idea that might be relevant, see Further reading and resources, Saleh et al.'s research into playing a game as an inoculation against being drawn into extremism. Or see Uscinski's point that the conspiracy theory is a form of political dissent; is your treatment recommendation going to require a better way of giving space for dissent?

Works well with

Activity 6, Chapter 4: Thinking together: TASC

Further reading

Todd, C. (2022). Stressful news cycle tips: 13 ways to protect your mental health. SELF

How my mum became a conspiracy theory influencer: https://www.bbc.co.uk/news/av/uk-54669239

How to identify conspiracy theories: https://commission.europa.eu/strategy-and-policy/coronavirus-response/fighting-disinformation/identifying-conspiracy-theories_en

Ideas for coping with stressful news cycles and social/political turmoil: https://psychiatry.ucsf.edu/copingresources/politics

Institute for Strategic Dialogue's report into social media impact of climate denialist websites: https://www.isdglobal.org/digital_dispatches/mainstreaming-climate-scepticism-analysing-the-reach-of-fringe-websites-on-twitter/

Mahl, D., Schäfer, M. S., & Zeng, J. (2022). Conspiracy theories in online environments: An interdisciplinary literature review and agenda for future research. *New Media & Society*, 25(7). https://doi.org/10.1177/14614448221075759

McLaughlin, A. C. & McGill, A. E. (2017). Humanities education benefits critical thinking skills: Explicitly teaching critical thinking skills in a history course. *Science & Education*, 26, 93–105. https://doi.org/10.1007/s11191-017-9878-2

McLaughlin, A.C., & McGill, A. E. https://en.wikipedia.org/wiki/Source_criticism#:~:text=Source%20criticism%20(or%20information%20evaluation,in%20order%20to%20obtain%20knowledge.

NGO EU DisinfoLab Report into climate disinformation online: https://www.disinfo.eu/publications/dont-stop-me-now-the-growing-disinformation-threat-against-climate-change/

Saleh, N., Roozenbeek, J., Makki, F., Mcclanahan, W., & Van Der Linden, S. (2021). Active inoculation boosts attitudinal resistance against extremist persuasion techniques: A novel approach towards the prevention of violent extremism. *Behavioural Public Policy*, 1–24. https://doi.org/10.1017/Bpp.2020.60

Smartphones and your attention: https://www.britishcouncil.org/anyone-anywhere/explore/dark-side-web/smartphone-war

The history of online conspiracy theories: https://www.wired.com/story/wired-guide-to-conspiracy-theories/

Tim Wu, T. (2017). *The attention merchants: The epic struggle to get inside our heads*. Atlantic Books).

Umberto Eco on the elements of fascism: https://theanarchistlibrary.org/library/umberto-eco-ur-fascism

Understanding fake news: https://www.britishcouncil.org/anyone-anywhere/explore/dark-side-web/fake-news

Uscinski, J. E. (2018). The study of conspiracy theories. *Argumenta*, 3(2), 233–245.

10. VALUES BASED LIVING AND LEARNING IN THE CONNECTED LEARNING COMMUNITY

Time: 30 minutes or as long as your learning group wishes to spend exploring the ideas in this activity

Who this could be for: flexible, depending on the time you and your co-learners want to spend considering shared values and how to be in line with them

Resources needed: no resources needed

Why do this: consider what your shared values are as a learning community, and consider how you can develop to be in line with them

As part of supporting your learning community's wellbeing and identifying learning directions you may wish to go in, either now, or in future, the concept of values based living can be a helpful tool. Values based living, contained within Acceptance and Commitment Therapy (ACT), offers a structure for your learning community to reflect on what values you hold as a community. This activity follows the same structure as that of Activity 49 but here using the concept of values based living for a group rather than for an individual.

To try this idea out, firstly identify your community's values. What's important to you all? There are some prompt questions to help your thinking here: https://www.therapistaid.com/worksheets/values-discussion-questions

You can break your consideration of values down into different areas of life. Use the suggested areas available on this worksheet with adaptations of key areas to fit what's relevant to your group:

https://www.therapistaid.com/worksheets/values-self-exploration

An alternative structure is included in this worksheet, where a bullseye diagram can be used to indicate how near (or far!) your group is from living in line with its values:

https://drexel.edu/~/media/files/studentlife/counseling/bulls%20eye%20values%20exercise.ashx?la=en

(See also Activity 45, Your health and wellbeing wheel, for a similar visual tool).

Next, identify what needs to change to bring your group more towards living in line with the values you have identified. Consider what needs to change and make a plan. You could make an all-encompassing plan for values based living or take smaller steps and do some things now, with more in mind for later.

Going further

Having considered what values your learning community wants to develop in line with, have you identified any changes that you all wish to make that will move the community more in line with those values? Go further with this activity by agreeing together and then making the changes.

It might be that trying this idea has identified some conflicts of values within your group. Some values might not be universally shared, or some values might conflict with each other. Working out how to deal with this, compromise, adjustment, considering new information or seeking different perspectives, is another possible development of this activity.

Further reading

Psychology Today. (2023). Acceptance and Commitment Therapy: https://www.psychologytoday.com/gb/therapy-types/acceptance-and-commitment-therapy

5
WELLBEING AND LEARNING IN A COVID-IMPACTED WORLD

The wide-ranging and significant impacts of the COVID pandemic on learning and opportunities are beginning to be understood. Research is revealing significant negative impacts on the wellbeing and learning of young people. These impacts are likely to persist into future years and continue to affect many people in their future lives. The COVID Social Mobility and Opportunities study carried out by the Sutton Trust and UCL has found nearly 50% of young people had not caught up with learning missed out on during the height of the COVID pandemic, rising to nearly 60% of young people who had experienced Long COVID. The impact on the wellbeing of young people is also significant, with research by the Prince's Trust finding nearly 50% of the young people surveyed lacked hope in the future. The combination of missed learning, not being able as yet to catch up, and reduced or absent hope for a better future is of obvious significance to both young people themselves and to wider society.

Research is also beginning to reveal the significant negative impacts on cognition and mental functioning that COVID can cause, particularly the impacts on cognition and mental functioning that people suffering with Long COVID are experiencing. It is essential to address this in any consideration of how wellbeing and learning can best be supported in a COVID-impacted world; large numbers of learners are now, and will continue to be, impacted by the effects of having contracted the virus. Finding ways to work with and learn with the often-debilitating cognitive effects of Long COVID (such as brain fog, fatigue, and memory difficulties) will be ongoingly important to providers of learning and to learners.

Along with the significant negative impacts of the pandemic on learning and wellbeing, there are potential opportunities for development and improvement of how we as societies organise ourselves and our educational, social and governance structures. UNESCO released a report in 2020 entitled "Education in a post-COVID world: nine ideas for public action," looking ahead to a future post-pandemic and to the potential to reshape education, access to knowledge, valuing educators, children's participation and rights, accessibility of technology, scientific literacy, education funding and inequality. The UNESCO reports assert that navigating the pandemic and post-pandemic world requires us to challenge and change the inequalities that have become so significant across our world. The links between the impacts of the pandemic and global inequalities are significant; the Wellcome Global Monitor: Covid-19 (a report published by Wellcome in November 2021) found that the pandemic had "a disproportionate impact on low-income countries and people with low incomes across all countries" (Wellcome Global Monitor, 2021). Recovery and societal development in a COVID-impacted world therefore may need to prioritise lessening inequality and widening access to education; the positive impacts on collective wellbeing if we do so are significant as are the potential negative impacts on collective wellbeing if we don't.

The following activities offer a range of ways to consider how we learn, what will support wellbeing and how we might want to develop our collective learning-wellbeing futures in a COVID-impacted world. Considering these activities from the perspective of living in a COVID-impacted world hopefully puts to one side the differing conceptualisations of where we now are. Viewing our collective situation as in a "post-pandemic" phase belies the ongoing presence of disease and the long-term negative health impacts that many people are suffering with Long COVID. Public health responses and management have changed, but the impacts of recent years are with us now and seem likely to cast a long shadow into future years.

Further reading

Betthäuser, B. A., Bach-Mortensen, A. M., & Engzell, P. (2023). A systematic review and meta-analysis of the evidence on learning during the COVID-19 pandemic. *Nature Human Behaviour*, 7: 375–385. https://doi.org/10.1038/s41562-022-01506-4: https://www.nature.com/articles/s41562-022-01506-4

New Economics Foundation Five Ways to Wellbeing during COVID, 2020: https://neweconomics.org/2020/03/five-ways-to-wellbeing-at-a-time-of-social-distancing

Project on the impact of COVID on younger generation: https://www.theguardian.com/world/2021/jun/02/a-sacrificed-generation-psychological-scars-of-covid-on-young-may-have-lasting-impact

Psychological and physical effects of Long COVID: https://psychiatry.ucsf.edu/copingresources/longcovid#:~:text=Psychological%20aspects%20of%20post%2DCOVID%20conditions&text=Anxiety,Sleep%20disturbance

The increase in teenagers experiencing mental health difficulties since 2010: https://www.ft.com/content/0e2f6f8e-bb03-4fa7-8864-f48f576167d2

UNESCO, Education in a Post-COVID World: nine ideas for public action: https://www.unesco.org/en/articles/education-post-covid-world-nine-ideas-public-action

Full report: https://unesdoc.unesco.org/ark:/48223/pf0000373717

Wellcome Global Monitor: Covid-19: https://wellcome.org/reports/wellcome-global-monitor-covid-19/2020

ACTIVITIES

1. WHAT HAVE WE LEARNED FROM REMOTE LEARNING?

Time: 15–20 minutes or longer if you wish

Who this could be for: anyone who would like to consider what we've learned from the experience of mass remote learning during the COVID pandemic

Resources needed: possible Internet access if wishing to read more/research

Why do this: consider what we've learned about remote learning, and what benefits and new ways of interacting we might want to keep

Remote learning during the first lockdown of 2020 developed very quickly. Consider the following report findings:

> It is worth noting, that while the time students spent on learning did not change over the period of the initial lockdown … the quality of remote learning resources improved. As the school closures were extended into the summer term, schools and colleges reduced their reliance on offline resources and started to incorporate more pre-recorded and live online lessons into their teaching (Cattan et al., 2020; Edurio, 2020). This is shown in the increase of the proportion of parents reporting that their students were provided with online learning between April and June 2020, which rose from 44% to 51% for primary students, and 59% to 65% for secondary students.
> *(Ofqual, 2021)*

In the space of weeks and months, the necessity to develop online learning resources was met by an increase in the amount of online learning delivered to students.

Consider also the following, from the same report:

> For most students, their learning has suffered to at least some degree. Teacher estimations indicate that while a small proportion of students made learning gains, most students have learning losses, and sometimes this was severe. The literature indicates that the extended periods of remote learning are likely to account for most of the learning loss.
> *(Ofqual, 2021)*

For this activity, consider what we've learned from the experience of mass online and remote learning at very short notice for large numbers of learners. If you learned remotely during 2020 (and/or after 2020), consider your own experience in relation to this question. If you learned remotely with others during that time, you could discuss this together if you wish. You can read more in the above report about learning during the pandemic. Questions to discuss and reflect on are included here as prompts:

- What did we learn from learning remotely?
- Who benefited more from remote learning and who less?
- Given the learning losses as identified above, what could be done to limit or mitigate against learning losses in future similar situations?
- How could remote learning benefit or disbenefit: geographically remote or dispersed communities; excluded groups or individuals; anyone with a neurodiversity or anyone with anxiety?
- Does remote learning offer any ecological benefits or disbenefits?
- What positive impacts on the wellbeing of learners, teachers, others did remote learning have?
- What negative impacts on the wellbeing of learners, teachers, others did remote learning have?
- What could be done to maintain or increase the positive impacts of remote learning, and lessen or remove the negative impacts, in a similar future situation?

Going further

To go further with this activity, consider the following: what have we learned from learning remotely that will inform our potential deep space travel future? Medical advances, notably burns care and caring for multiple wounds, are often propelled by conflicts (see further reading). We have been through a mass experiment in remote learning, at very short notice. Has it catalysed the development of different learning and teaching techniques, and new ways of interacting in remote learning spaces, which otherwise might either not have happened, or only developed much more slowly?

Consider what five key things (or more if you wish) that you would like to pass on to future designers of remote learning environments for supporting learners in deep space travel situations. What should they know about what works, what is useful, what difficulties there are, what opportunities remote learning presents, and any other ideas or advice you think they would benefit from being given?

Further reading

A resource page offering many ideas for distance learning best practices: https://sendbird.com/blog/distance-learning-best-practices-how-to-build-connection-in-a-remote-classroom

Learning during the pandemic: review of research from England (Ofqual, 2021): https://www.gov.uk/government/publications/learning-during-the-pandemic/learning-during-the-pandemic-review-of-research-from-england

Medical advances during conflict: https://www.fpri.org/article/2018/02/advances-in-medicine-during-wars/

2. GRIEF AND LOSS: WHAT WAS AND WHAT IS

Time: flexible to fit the time you wish to assign for reflection and consideration

Who this could be for: anyone who has experienced bereavement, and/or a wider sense of loss

Resources needed: Internet access, means of writing notes/recording reflections if you wish

Why do this: reflect on a way of understanding grief and of considering a more general sense of loss. Develop a broad perspective on both losses and gains or other changes you may have experienced during recent years.

In 2017, Lauren Herschel posted a thread on Twitter sharing an analogy for the experience of grief and grieving and how the emotions relating to bereavement change over time. The analogy, described as "the ball and the box" conceptualised someone's experience as a box with a press button that causes emotional pain on one side and grief as a ball that bounces around within the box. The analogy suggested that in the early or acute stages of grief, the ball takes up almost all the space within the box (or within one's experience); as a consequence, it is almost constantly hitting against the pain button. Over time, this changes; the ball shrinks, and there is more space within the box that's not taken up by the grief-ball. However, it can still move around and hit the pain button; it might just do so less often or more randomly. See further resources and reading, below, to view the original thread.

Lauren Herschel's Twitter thread outlining the ball and box conceptualisation of grief has been widely shared; it clearly resonates with many people. It may be that reading the description of the ball and box grief analogy and/or looking at the accompanying illustrations in the original thread resonate with you and that you recognise this idea from your own experiences of grief and/or loss. In addition to the losses of bereavement during the first years of the COVID pandemic, many people have experienced a wider sense of loss. Particularly if your recent years have been spent in full-time study, you may be experiencing a sense of loss of matters related to your learning experience; you may feel you have missed out on key learning and life experiences and may be experiencing this loss as irrecoverable, or have a sense of not being able to catch up or regain lost ground. The loss of possibility and the loss of potential opportunities are likely to give us emotional pain, particularly if we don't feel these are recoverable.

Does the ball and box metaphor work for you in describing your experience of grief and/or loss? If not, what would your alternative expression of this be in either words, pictures, or both?

The sense of loss and/or grief you may have explored in this activity may also be accompanied by some other changes in your life and your experience in recent years. To take this activity further, you could consider if there are any gains to balance against the griefs and/or losses you may have experienced. These, of course, do not make the losses less or more tolerable, but are worth also bringing your attention to as part of developing a full and rich picture of your experiences during the COVID pandemic. It may be that you have been able to identify new insights into what is valuable to you in your life; or what we value collectively; you may have new or different insights into what you want from your current and future life, or a new perspective on how we should organise our world; you may have made new connections with others and now have new people (or animals) in your life. If you wish, use the prompts below to consider and capture any of these potential gains or changes that you notice.

TABLE 5.1 Changes

Gains/positive changes: myself	
Gains/positive changes: my future	
Gains/positive changes: others	
Gains/positive changes: the wider world	

Going further: post-traumatic growth

To go further with this activity, consider the concept of post-traumatic growth. Post-traumatic growth is positive psychological change in anyone following going through a very difficult or traumatic experience or experiences (Tedeschi, Shakespeare-Finch, Taku, & Calhoun, 2018). Such circumstances do not in themselves necessarily result in post-traumatic growth; our emotional response to the traumatic experience makes a difference to the effect the experience has on us in the long term (Tedeschi & Calhoun, 2004). Our ability to cope with and respond with resilience to even incredibly difficult life experiences is not just down to us, of course; we need support around us to be able to move towards post-traumatic growth, as well as our own inner resources. See Activity 27: Depersonalising resilience for more on how recovery from trauma can and could be a collective rather than just an individual effort.

Features that are experienced as part of post-traumatic growth include appreciation of life, relating to others, personal strength, new possibilities and spiritual, existential or philosophical change (Tedeschi et al., 2018). Try the post-traumatic growth inventory (see further reading and resources) for yourself as a tool to reflect on your own experiences. When you have done this, consider what would a post-traumatic growth inventory for a community or a society include as statements, rather than just for an individual? Post-traumatic growth is considered to be modestly related to personality factors such as extraversion. If some personality factors mean an individual is more likely to experience post-traumatic growth, what qualities would a community need to have to maximise the potential for post-traumatic growth for members of the community?

A way of thinking about the self after trauma: Kintsugi

As an additional going further, you could consider the repair concept of Kintsugi. This is a Japanese technique for repairing broken or damaged ceramics using gold lines to draw attention to, rather than seek to make invisible, the breakage lines. The results are beautiful and can perhaps challenge our ideas of damage, value and what we are really doing when we "fix" or "repair" something. Watch the video in further reading and resources to find out more about the idea of using this as a metaphor for thinking about ourselves and our traumatic experiences. Where are your own Kintsugi lines? Brain, heart or elsewhere?

Works well with

Activity 8, Chapter 5: Where do you want to go? Where do we want to go?

References

Tedeschi, R. G., & Calhoun, L. G. (2004). Target Article: "Posttraumatic growth: conceptual foundations and empirical evidence", *Psychological Inquiry*, 15(1), 1–18. https://doi.org/10.1207/s15327965pli1501_01

Tedeschi, R., Shakespeare-Finch, J., Taku, K., & Calhoun, L. (2018). *Posttraumatic growth: Theory, research and applications*. Taylor & Francis. https://doi.org/10.4324/9781315527451

Further reading and resources

Ball and box grief analogy: https://www.hopefulwarrior.com/blog/2020/2/26/unpacking-grief-the-ball-amp-box-analogy

Debilitating effects of pandemic linger on for Britain's young: https://www.theguardian.com/uk-news/2023/jan/29/debilitating-effects-pandemic-young-people-uk-health-education-careers

How we might heal from the trauma of the pandemic: https://www.bbc.com/future/article/20210203-after-the-covid-19-pandemic-how-will-we-heal

Impact of pandemic on memory formation and ideas for mitigation of negative impacts: https://edition.cnn.com/2022/02/03/health/memory-covid-19-pandemic-wellness/index.html

Kintsugi as a metaphor for our own traumatic experiences: https://www.youtube.com/watch?v=lT55_u8URU0

Kintsugi: https://traditionalkyoto.com/culture/kintsugi/

Post-traumatic growth: https://positivepsychology.com/post-traumatic-growth/

Post-traumatic growth inventory: https://results.wa.gov/sites/default/files/WendyFraser_Oct28_HANDOUT.pdf

Post-traumatic growth inventory: Tedeschi & Calhoun. (1996 Jul). *Journal of Traumatic Stress*, 9(3): 455–471.

https://pubmed.ncbi.nlm.nih.gov/8827649/

https://results.wa.gov/sites/default/files/WendyFraser_Oct28_HANDOUT.pdf

Stott, R., et al. (2010). *Oxford guide to metaphors in CBT: building cognitive bridges*. Oxford University Press.

We're on permanent catch-up: how COVID has changed young Britons' lives: https://www.theguardian.com/society/2023/jan/29/were-on-permanent-catch-up-how-covid-has-changed-young-britons-lives

3. ANXIETY MANAGEMENT IN A COVID-AWARE WORLD

Time: 15 minutes or longer

Who this could be for: anyone who would like to understand more about the different forms of anxiety in a COVID-aware world and to consider the anxiety equation

Resources needed: no resources required

Why do this: consider what kinds of anxiety experience the COVID pandemic has caused and is causing; and consider the anxiety equation as a way of understanding and managing anxiety

Someone is asleep and having a terrible dream. They see an appallingly frightening monster looming towards them, and scream "please, what do you want?!" The monster pauses for a moment in its looming and replies "well there's no use asking me, it's YOUR nightmare." Living through the experience of the COVID pandemic has given rise to many different kinds of nightmares. What each person might have found most frightening is likely to have depended on their life circumstances and how the impacts of the pandemic affected their lives. For one person, the most distressing thing might have been a fear of contracting COVID and being seriously ill or dying from it; for another person, the most distressing thing might have been a fear of losing the opportunity to be with loved ones and becoming isolated due to restrictions on travel or lockdowns. This activity considers the different kinds of anxiety that the COVID pandemic has caused and is still causing, and includes an idea for making sense of anxiety and potentially altering our anxious feelings.

Some possible types of anxiety that may be experienced and exacerbated through living in a COVID-aware and COVID-experienced world include:

- Agoraphobia
  https://www.nhs.uk/mental-health/conditions/agoraphobia/overview/
- Panic attacks
  https://www.nhs.uk/mental-health/conditions/panic-disorder/
- Health anxiety
  https://www.nhs.uk/mental-health/conditions/health-anxiety/
- OCD
  https://www.nhs.uk/mental-health/conditions/obsessive-compulsive-disorder-ocd/overview/
- General anxiety (or worry)
  https://www.nhs.uk/mental-health/conditions/generalised-anxiety-disorder/overview/

These are all difficulties that were experienced before COVID; however, the pandemic has had particular relevance to these anxiety experiences due to many factors in its nature and adds a complicating aspect to managing these specific types of anxiety. This is where the anxiety equation is a useful tool for understanding more about how anxiety can be perceived and fuelled by our experience and our thinking.

A way of making sense of anxiety: the anxiety equation

When we are anxious, we tend to overestimate danger and underestimate our coping and available resources.

Watch CBT therapist, Christine Padesky, explains how the anxiety equation (created by Dr Kathleen Mooney) can be used to understand our anxiety:

https://www.youtube.com/watch?v=jw0ivpUQ43U

The anxiety equation is as follows:

$$\text{ANXIETY} = \frac{\text{Overestimation of danger}}{\text{Underestimation of coping and resources}}$$

Using this equation, either reducing our estimation of danger or increasing our perception of our coping and resources, or both, will alter our danger perception and anxiety levels. Consider how changing the factors within the anxiety equation could be helpful for someone, for example, who is highly anxious about going out of their home due to fears of contracting COVID; someone who is highly anxious that a vaccination will cause them severe harm; someone who has become fearful of being around other people when previously they did not feel like this; someone who fears that things will never "get back to normal" and that society will be damaged as a result.

Bear in mind that the aim of using the anxiety equation is not to remove legitimate perceptions of threat; for example, if someone is immuno-compromised, or has had a previous severe infection, their perception of the dangerousness to them of COVID infection is understandably higher than the dangerousness perception of someone without their experiences might be. Rather than globally reducing the perceived danger of COVID infection, a realistic appraisal of threat might be, for instance, appraising the likelihood of contracting COVID infection from touching surfaces (such as picking up a food item to purchase) as opposed to the likelihood of contracting it via airborne particles and droplets. The aim of the equation is to seek a more realistic, balanced, accurate perception of threat, and to help yourself (or someone else) to live life with an awareness of danger but not to be so overwhelmed with it that it completely interferes with living the life you (or they) want to live. That requires in addition to getting a realistic estimation of danger, also building up our estimation of our own ability to cope, and what resources we can draw on.

Take some time to consider your own anxiety equation. What do you want to explore using this equation? When you've selected a perceived danger, see what you can do to change either side of the equation.

Further anxiety management ideas and techniques are found throughout this book, so also refer to other activities that you find helpful with anxiety management.

What might influence perception of threat: COVID experienced patients

Research (Krok et al., 2003) has identified that threat perception in recovered COVID patients is influenced by an individual's coping characteristics; resilience and problem-focused coping, for instance, and engaging in active solutions influences threat appraisal to be lowered. Part of managing COVID-related anxiety may therefore be related to building psychological resilience. See Activity 27, for more on this.

Going further

A significant complicating factor for anxiety management, for our collective wellbeing and for social cohesion related to the COVID pandemic is the politicisation of differing public health management responses and infection prevention and control public health measures.

To go further with this activity, consider whether ideas within the following activities could help us to reduce the polarisation of opinions and hostility between people with differing viewpoints around COVID impacts:

Activity 28: Empathy and compassion
Activity 29: Combatting dark learning

Further reading

Adrenaline: https://get.gg/docs/Adrenaline.pdf

Britton, J. C., Lissek, S., Grillon, C., Norcross, M. A., & Pine, D. S. (2011 Jan). Development of anxiety: the role of threat appraisal and fear learning. *Depress Anxiety*, 28(1): 5–17. https://doi.org/10.1002/da.20733. Epub 2010 Aug 23. PMID: 20734364; PMCID: PMC2995000.

Fight or flight response: https://www.simplypsychology.org/fight-flight-freeze-fawn.html

Threat appraisal in recovered COVID patients: Krok, D., Telka, E., Szcześniak, M., Falewicz, A. (2023 Feb 18). Threat appraisal, resilience, and health behaviors in recovered COVID-19 patients: the serial mediation of coping and meaning-making. *Int J Environ Res Public Health*, 20(4): 3649. https://doi.org/10.3390/ijerph20043649. PMID: 36834343; PMCID: PMC9963736.

Understanding and coping with agoraphobia: https://www.nhs.uk/mental-health/conditions/agoraphobia/overview/

Understanding and coping with panic attacks: https://www.nhsinform.scot/healthy-living/mental-wellbeing/anxiety-and-panic/how-to-deal-with-panic-attacks

Understanding our anxiety "alarm system": https://www.psychologytoday.com/gb/blog/harnessing-principles-change/202104/anxiety-gets-bad-rap-understand-your-healthy-alarm-system

Understanding the fight-or-flight response and how its chronic activation can make us ill: https://www.health.harvard.edu/staying-healthy/understanding-the-stress-response

4. BRAIN FOG AND LONG COVID: STRATEGIES FOR LEARNING

Time: flexible, from a few minutes to longer, depending on energy levels and concentration levels

Who this could be for: anyone who is experiencing cognitive impacts from Long COVID such as difficulty concentrating, brain fog, memory issues

Resources needed: no resources needed

Why do this: find out more about how Long COVID can affect your mind, and try out some ideas to help with any symptoms that are impacting your day-to-day life and your learning

Long COVID is when anyone who has had COVID finds that their COVID symptoms are persisting for three months or longer after they first became unwell. There are multiple physical symptoms that may be experienced with Long COVID, including (but not limited to) fatigue, breath shortness, changes to sense of smell, muscle and joint pain, persistent cough, gastrointestinal difficulties, Postural tachycardia syndrome (PoTS) and sleep disruption. There are also impacts on wellbeing and mental health, including low mood and anxiety, and difficulties with memory, concentration, ability to focus, and ability to retain information, collectively often referred to as "brain fog." It's worth also considering that, particularly if someone was severely unwell and needed intensive care in hospital due to COVID, it's possible to also experience Post-Traumatic Stress Disorder (PTSD), not as a symptom of Long COVID, but as a result of frightening and distressing experiences in ICU, and PTSD can negatively impact wellbeing alongside the physical and psychological impacts of Long COVID.

This activity offers some ideas to try for helping with the cognitive effects of Long COVID particularly if you are finding it's making learning difficult for you. Keep in mind that our understanding of Long COVID is still developing, and research and treatments are likely to bring new ideas in future months and years for helping with this experience. See further reading and resources for links to more guidance and ideas.

Basics of self-care for Long COVID brain fog

Getting the right amount of rest, eating a balanced diet, taking exercise and engaging with others are the building blocks of managing symptoms. Of course, the physical and cognitive symptoms of Long COVID can in themselves interfere with putting these building blocks together and this can be frustrating. Doing what you can with these in mind, and trying to minimise frustration at, for instance, slow progress in your recovery might be the way to approach these basics.

Memory

- Use external memory repositories to help you – diaries, phone reminders, alarms etc. – but do keep using your memory too. Keeping in mind that an external support can be a backup plan and you will use your own memory as and when you can. A mixture of the two is likely to be most helpful.
- Get rest when you can; sleep helps us consolidate our learning and knowledge into long-term memory. It's harder to remember with poor sleep.
- Get a support team; ask others around you (family members, friends, colleagues) to help you out with remembering relevant things.

Concentration

- Take breaks; don't push on if you're losing concentration.
- Plan study or learning at the times of the day you find it easier to concentrate; you might find it useful to keep a concentration diary over a week or so to find out if there are better concentration times for you.
- If you find external activities and noises reduce your ability to concentrate even further, try to reduce external stimulation such as noise and visual busyness around you when you're trying to concentrate. Can you find somewhere quieter, with less distractions, to help?
- Some people find that in a busy social situation when a lot of people are talking or interacting this makes concentrating more difficult. If you want to stay in the situation, see if you can find a way to enjoy it without pressuring yourself to follow everything that's going on.
- Give yourself extra time to take in information if you need to make a decision about something.
- See if you can portion what you're trying to take in, into smaller chunks of information; take breaks and come back later.

Self-compassion: valued self, whatever

- Try not to attack yourself if you are struggling cognitively, especially if you've previously found it very easy to do the cognitive things that you might find more difficult at present. Being criticised can make us feel threatened and defensive, and if we're engaged in self-attack, the defensive response is just the same; we will shut down and retreat and not feel safe. This will in turn knock our complex thinking offline; adding to our difficulty in thinking clearly.
- Keep in mind that you're of profound value to others and to yourself, whether or not you can currently perform as you could prior to Long COVID cognitive symptoms. We don't love and value other people just

because they can remember ten different facts about something! Offer yourself compassion as you would a loved friend or family member.
- Part of being compassionate to yourself as you manage the cognitive impacts of Long COVID is being proud of yourself for managing and coping. Can you reward yourself for being strong and keeping moving forwards?

Meanings of symptoms about you and your brain

Beware of catastrophic thinking; if you notice being forgetful, for instance, or notice concentration difficulties, be aware of your brain running at a hundred miles an hour towards the most catastrophic meaning of the symptom. Jumping to a catastrophic conclusion can make us feel very anxious or distressed, which can mean we find it even harder to concentrate as we're in such a heightened emotional state. Notice any meanings you make of symptoms that are 1) extremely catastrophic and/or 2) permanent rather than temporary, and ask yourself, is there another way of making sense of this? Could it be, for instance, not catastrophic, and not permanent?

In relation to this, also beware of hypervigilance: if you've concluded that a particular cognitive symptom is catastrophic, you might find that you become hypervigilant for it and that in itself adds to stress and distress. Being vigilant for symptoms or checking your cognitive function is probably going to make it more likely that you'll notice things that are problematic.

Neuroplasticity: finding ways around/finding a new neuro-pathway

Consider the idea of neuroplasticity. Our brains are very good at finding new routes to keep functioning. Read about neuroplasticity (see further reading and resources) and keep in mind that your brain is able to find workarounds and different paths, even after a damaging event such as a stroke or a traumatic brain injury, via, for instance, axonal sprouting, which sounds like a way to grow salad but is actually how your brain's neurons can grow new connecting elements, if they have been damaged, to communicate with other neurons again. Your brain will be working on workarounds; you could hold the idea of being supportive of your brain as it gets on with this.

... what have you found useful so far?

It is also worth noticing what strategies you are already using and have already identified as helpful and useful to you. Note any tricks, strategies and helpful things that you already know help you with the cognitive impacts of Long COVID:

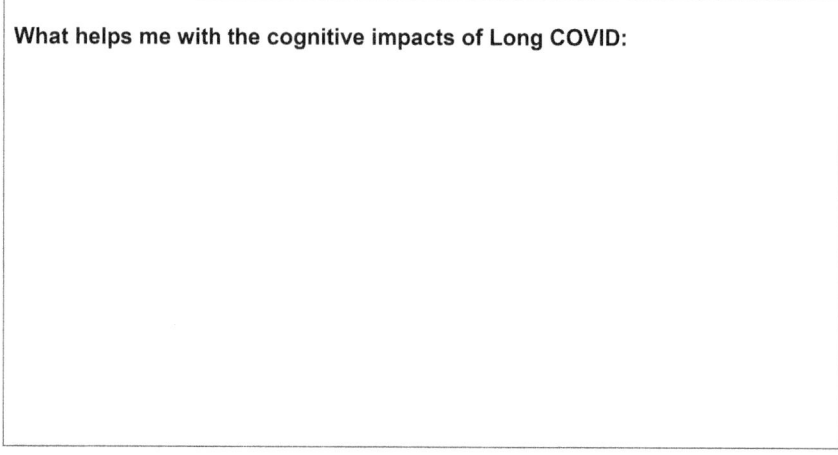

FIGURE 5.1 Long COVID

Going further

Take some time to review the video given in further reading and resources. It includes some ideas from Acceptance and Commitment Therapy (ACT) for managing the psychological impacts of changes to your cognitive abilities due to Long COVID. Is there anything here that you find helpful?

Further reading and resources

ACT-based strategies for managing the psychological and physical impacts of Long COVID: https://www.youtube.com/watch?v=0sGaq_-k9zQ

Coping with Long COVID brain fog: https://www.nhsinform.scot/long-term-effects-of-covid-19-long-covid/signs-and-symptoms/long-covid-brain-fog

Long COVID: https://www.nhs.uk/conditions/covid-19/long-term-effects-of-covid-19-long-covid/

Managing effects of Long COVID on your memory and concentration, NHS Your COVID Recovery site: https://www.yourcovidrecovery.nhs.uk/i-think-i-have-long-covid/effects-on-your-mind/memory-and-focus/

Neuroplasticity: https://www.ncbi.nlm.nih.gov/books/NBK557811/#:~:text=It%20is%20defined%20as%20the,traumatic%20brain%20injury%20(TBI)

5. MOTIVATION: FINDING IT, REVIVING IT

Time: flexible, depending on time available

Who this could be for: anyone who would like to boost their learning motivation

Resources needed: a box for the items selected as part of the activity; any items selected (what the items are will depend on your own choice)

Why do this: boost your learning motivation and create a learning motivation box for your use now and in future learning situations

What's in your learning motivation box?

Sometimes it can be difficult to find the motivation to learn. Many things can get in the way of us feeling motivated and reduce our enthusiasm and optimism for getting started with a learning activity, or for keeping going with something we are underway with already and need to continue working on. Motivation is something we need to take action towards achieving goals; the word itself contains the idea of movement, so this exercise is something to try if you want to keep a supply of motivational fuel nearby to help you get moving-learning.

Particularly in the context of this chapter, it is worth considering the impact of the COVID pandemic on motivation and learning. For many, the learning experience within the first two months of the COVID pandemic involved the opposite of getting moving – lockdowns, staying in and remote learning literally reduced moving about and going places. Staying still can be seen as a response to a threat; particularly if we can't run away from the threat and it made sense in the context of the early stages of the pandemic. It is very understandable if motivation has been impacted in line with this experience. This exercise is a chance to consider how you might engage feelings of motivation to learn now in an ongoingly COVID-impacted learning environment and world.

Resources

- A box, big enough to contain the items you select as part of this exercise
- Specific items as you select, or symbols of those items if they are too big to contain in a reasonably sized box (you might have to make do with a picture of the natural history museum, for instance!)

Putting your learning motivation box together

This activity invites you to consider what you would include in a resource box to encourage and motivate yourself to learn. This is likely to be very personal to you, and it can include anything that you find helpful. Below are some prompts, questions to ask yourself and suggestions to help. You can do this your way; it's a resource for you, so it can be what you need it to be rather than something to fit in with others' expectations. The prompts, questions and suggestions are divided into three time periods to help you think this activity through.

Past

Think back to times in the past when you have felt really enthused and motivated to learn something. Was there something that helped with those feelings and responses? See if you can find either an item or an image that represents that past experience. It could be an item related to the activity you were doing (a brush, or a pen, for instance) or something you made at the time as a result of feeling enthused and motivated.

Think back to times in the past when you were motivated to try something, and the results weren't what you hoped – is there an item or image that represents that experience? This item can represent the tenacity to keep trying and to return to something difficult in order to either improve or to reach a goal you have for yourself.

Other items you might want to include:

- Certificates (original or copy), marks, feedback on your past learning work
- Praise for your past efforts (for instance a report or other feedback that you value)

Present

Think of your present experience with learning. Is there a time of day when you feel most energy-filled and motivated? You could add in something that represents a quality that this time of day has, for instance, an image of a sunrise, if early morning is your best time.

Again, thinking of your present experience with learning, is there a place that you find gives you encouraging and motivating feelings? It might be somewhere you can actually visit and spend time in, in which case, you could include an image of the place in the box, or an item that is from there or represents it. If it's not somewhere you can visit, either because it's too far away, or because it is a fictional location, you could still find a way to represent it in order to include it in your learning motivation box.

Treats: what do you look forward to as a treat when you've accomplished a learning task or part of a task that you are working on? You could include the treat itself in the box (if it's not too tempting to treat yourself to it straight away) or a reminder of what treat or reward you would like if you can get started or make progress with the learning you are trying to motivate yourself for.

Support network: who is on your motivational team? You could include a list of others who you turn to for help, support and encouragement in your learning motivation box, to remind yourself who is on your side and rooting for you. Is it family members, friends, tutors or teachers? You can include yourself in this list (hopefully!), and even any fictional characters or people you don't know, but know of, on this team.

Future

Think of yourself in the future. What do you hope to have learned in a few months' time? How about in a year's time, or a few years into your future? You might have something you want to find out more about, or a skill you would like to discover or practice more. You may even have a career (or a career change if you are further along your learning journey) in mind. Select an item (or items) that symbolises your hopes for your future learning. It might be a pair of knitting needles, some secateurs, a musical instrument, a mode of transport, a medical device. Depending on the item(s) you may have to use a photograph or image rather than the real thing!

You could write a letter from your future learning self; imagine yourself in the future, having progressed towards your learning goals, and having enjoyed the learning journey along the way (and still being open to new directions and learning possibilities). Write a letter from your future learning self, to you, now; telling yourself what you'd most like to hear. It might be some words of encouragement, and expressing belief in you now, and that you can get where you want to get, wherever that turns out to be. It may be some news of how it's good to be where your future learning self has reached.

You could also write a letter to your future learning self. Write a letter to yourself, imagining you have progressed along your learning journey. You might want to send yourself some words of thanks for making the efforts in learning, to get where you wanted to get. You might want to remind your future self that it was really difficult at times! You might want to let your future self know what is working for you now, and where you hope to get. It's up to you.

Keeping the theme of motivation being about making a move, you could include a learning map to help guide you in future weeks, months and years. You can add details into your learning map as you go along.

```
┌─────────────────────────────────────────────────┐
│ My Learning Map                                 │
│                                                 │
│                                                 │
│                                                 │
│                                                 │
│                                                 │
│                                                 │
│ Timescale: today > 20___                        │
└─────────────────────────────────────────────────┘
```

FIGURE 5.2 My learning map

How and when to use your learning motivation box

Here are some occasions when you might consider using your learning motivation box. You are likely to have some other thoughts, so don't limit yourself to these suggestions.

- When you need to encourage yourself to get started with a learning task
- When you notice you are flagging with a learning task and need an emotional-motivational energy boost
- When you notice you are doubting yourself or your abilities
- If you need a reminder of who is on your motivational team
- If the learning task you are engaged with seems to be endless
- If you don't feel you are making any progress, despite effort
- If other(s) have expressed doubt in you or said anything discouraging
- To help you remember your goals and your hopes for your future as a learner – where you want to get to, including if you're not sure of where you want to get to and just know that you want to keep travelling in a general learning direction and work it out on the way!

Works well with

Activity 5, Chapter 2: Distress tolerance and emotional regulation skills
Activity 2, Chapter 6: Self-directed learning: where (and how) do I start?
Activity 6, Chapter 6: Who is on your learning and wellbeing support team?

Going further

See further reading for a link to read more about motivational interviewing. Does the motivational interviewing approach offer you anything helpful in building your learning motivation box?

Further reading

Motivational interviewing: https://www.homelesshub.ca/resource/motivational-interviewing-open-questions-affirmation-reflective-listening-and-summary

6. SPOONS THEORY: A WAY OF UNDERSTANDING THE IMPACT OF LOW ENERGY LEVELS WITH LONG COVID

Time: flexible; depending on time available and energy levels

Who this could be for: anyone who is currently impacted by fatigue and low energy levels connected with Long COVID

Resources needed: no resources required

Why do this: consider a way to describe the experience of managing low energy levels due to Long COVID

Long COVID is a condition where symptoms linger beyond three months (12 weeks) after having first contracted COVID. In 2022, the ONS estimated that around two million people in the United Kingdom were suffering from Long COVID symptoms. Global prevalence is uncertain; in the United States, the Centre for Disease Control and Prevention estimated that 7.5% of adults were suffering from persistent symptoms for more than three months after initially contracting COVID. In short, there are a lot of people struggling with ongoing symptoms of this disease. This activity considers an analogy for describing the experience of managing energy levels which many people coping with Long COVID are finding to be low and variable.

Spoons theory is an analogy created in 2003 by Christine Miserandino, a writer and blogger who has lupus, in order to explain to others what the experience of having to manage limited and fluctuating energy levels is like for anyone who manages a long-term physical health condition. In addition to being an effective metaphor for explaining to others what the experience of this is like, spoons theory also offers a way of thinking about your available energy levels and how to use your energy when you suffer from a physical health condition that reduces your energy levels, by causing pain and fatigue for instance. In summary, the analogy suggests your available energy on any day can be seen as a series of spoons; there are fewer available than to somebody who doesn't have to manage a health condition that drains their energy levels; and so the choice of how to use the spoons across the day is a series of decisions with an awareness that the spoons can be used up, potentially without getting through all the things that were necessary in the day. The theory suggests that borrowing a spoon from tomorrow's supply, although possible, will end up leaving you even shorter of spoons tomorrow. To read about spoons theory in full, see further reading and resources.

Going further

If you have found reading about spoons theory useful as a way of describing the experience of managing your energy levels with Long COVID, you could share it with someone (friend, family member, colleague, manager?)

whom you would like to give a better understanding of your experience to. Particularly with any "invisible" difficulty such as Long COVID, people who haven't experienced it themselves can struggle to realise quite how significant the impact is. You might have experienced someone saying to you that you look well – although kindly meant, unfortunately when you might feel anything but well, it can really underline the invisibility of what you are experiencing, and might also make you feel that other people are expecting you to be "better" just because you look it. Sometimes giving someone a clearer insight into your experience can help others be more empathetic and supportive of you and your experience. Time to explain with spoons!

You could also use the spoons theory idea to help yourself consider how you would like to spend your own set of "spoons"; especially if before Long COVID you had a tendency to push yourself on even when drained or exhausted, your habit might not be to pause and do less or differently and this can be very frustrating. The spoons theory ends with the idea of keeping back a spoon; is thinking this way something you find helpful for your own experience? Does seeing the energy available as a precious resource mean that you might think differently about how to expend it; on something worthwhile to you and important, for instance, rather than something that doesn't matter so much?

Further reading

Full description of the initiation of spoons theory by Christine Miserandino: https://butyoudontlooksick.com/articles/written-by-christine/the-spoon-theory/
NHS Your COVID Recovery: https://www.yourcovidrecovery.nhs.uk/
NHS Your COVID Recover, Long COVID support: https://www.yourcovidrecovery.nhs.uk/i-think-i-have-long-covid/
Spoons theory for energy management: https://www.thebraincharity.org.uk/whats-spoon-theory/
Long COVID effects: https://www.nhs.uk/conditions/covid-19/long-term-effects-of-covid-19-long-covid/
Long COVID experience: https://www.theguardian.com/commentisfree/2023/feb/20/long-covid-treatment-symptoms-research-uk
Long COVID prevalence globally: https://www.thelancet.com/journals/eclinm/article/PIIS2589-5370(22)00491-6/fulltext
Long COVID prevalence, UK. (2022): https://www.bmj.com/content/377/bmj.o1391
Long COVID prevalence, US. (2022): https://www.cdc.gov/nchs/pressroom/nchs_press_releases/2022/20220622.htm

Works well with

Activity 9, Chapter 7: Values based living

7. BUILDING NEW WAYS OF LEARNING

Time: 15–30 minutes or more if desired

Who this could be for: any learner or group of learners who would like to consider what new ways of learning we are going to need in the future

Resources needed: no initial resources; resources to go further will depend on any plans made

Why do this: Consider what new ways of learning we need to support our collective future

This activity is about exploring new ways of learning. It is a chance to consider the question, what new ways of learning do we need now, and in the near future?

What new ways of learning do we need?

UNESCO's 2021 report, *Education in a Post-COVID World: nine ideas for public action* gave the following nine ideas for educational change following the pandemic:

Nine ideas for public action

1. Commit to strengthen education as a common good. Education is a bulwark against inequalities. In education as in health, we are safe when everybody is safe; we flourish when everybody flourishes.
2. Expand the definition of the right to education so that it addresses the importance of connectivity and access to knowledge and information. The Commission calls for a global public discussion – that includes, among others, learners of all ages – on ways the right to education needs to be expanded.
3. Value the teaching profession and teacher collaboration. There has been remarkable innovation in the responses of educators to the COVID-19 crisis, with those systems most engaged with families and communities showing the most resilience. We must encourage conditions that give frontline educators autonomy and flexibility to act collaboratively.
4. Promote student, youth and children's participation and rights. Intergenerational justice and democratic principles should compel us to prioritise the participation of students and young people broadly in the co-construction of desirable change.
5. Protect the social spaces provided by schools as we transform education. The school as a physical space is indispensable. Traditional classroom organisation must give way to a variety of ways of 'doing school' but the school as a separate space-time of collective living, specific and different from other spaces of learning must be preserved.

6 Make free and open-source technologies available to teachers and students. Open educational resources and open-access digital tools must be supported. Education cannot thrive with ready-made content built outside of the pedagogical space and outside of human relationships between teachers and students. Nor can education be dependent on digital platforms controlled by private companies.
7 Ensure scientific literacy within the curriculum. This is the right time for deep reflection on curriculum, particularly as we struggle against the denial of scientific knowledge and actively fight misinformation.
8 Protect domestic and international financing of public education. The pandemic has the power to undermine several decades of advances. National governments, international organisations and all education and development partners must recognise the need to strengthen public health and social services but simultaneously mobilise around the protection of public education and its financing.
9 Advance global solidarity to end current levels of inequality. COVID-19 has shown us the extent to which our societies exploit power imbalances, and our global system exploits inequalities. The Commission calls for renewed commitments to international cooperation and multilateralism, together with a revitalised global solidarity that has empathy and an appreciation of our common humanity at its core.

COVID-19 presents a real challenge and a real responsibility. These ideas invite debate, engagement and action by governments, international organisations, civil society, educational professionals, as well as learners and stakeholders at all levels.

UNESCO (2021)

Having read these nine ideas through, take some time to consider them. Are they the right ideas? What would you add or change? Would these ideas help us to identify, create and nurture the new ways of learning we need in a COVID-affected world? What kinds of new ways of learning do you think we need now and may need in the future? What in particular might we need to consider and change in relation to the effects of Long COVID on cognition for learners now and in the future?

To prompt your thinking, see further reading and resources below.

Going further

To take this activity further, you and your co-learners could consider coming up with a future learning needs manifesto. Share what you have come up with and see what others think. Can you gain support for and agreement with your ideas? Is there anything you can do to put some of your ideas for new ways of learning into action in your own learning community?

References

UNESCO. (2021). Report, *Education in a Post-COVID World: nine ideas for public action*. Education in a post-COVID world: Nine ideas for public action | UNESCO

Further reading

Izzy Garbutt, MYP for Wigan and Leigh 2022–24, speaks in the Youth Parliament about the inadequacy of the current curriculum to meet the learning needs of young people: https://twitter.com/IzzyGarbuttMYP/status/1589017875750080512

Mild COVID infection is found to result in persistent cognitive impairment: https://www.brainfacts.org/diseases-and-disorders/covid-19/2023/the-risks-of-even-mild-covid19-1-in-4-showing-cognitive-deficits-011723

https://pubmed.ncbi.nlm.nih.gov/35701598/#article-details

UNESCO. (2021). Report, *Education in a Post-COVID World: nine ideas for public action*. Education in a post-COVID world: Nine ideas for public action | UNESCO

Works well with

Activity 4, Chapter 7: Going beyond problem solving

8. WHERE DO YOU WANT TO GO? WHERE DO WE WANT TO GO?

Time: 20 minutes or more consideration time; open-ended if you decide to act on any of the ideas you have for where you want to go

Who this could be for: anyone who would like to consider what our collective wellbeing-learning future could or should look like

Resources needed: will depend on what ideas you generate

Why do this: consider what directions we might want to go in with our collective learning and wellbeing in light of our experiences during the COVID pandemic

This activity invites you and your co-learners to consider what you think the post-COVID learning-wellbeing world should look like and what values it should have. Do you think that we should be reconsidering our values, priorities and directions in response to the experience of the pandemic? Or do you think we should just forget it all as quickly as possible? It is also a chance to consider whether you yourself wish to think differently about your future in response to the experience. There is evidence emerging (see further reading) that the pandemic shifted expectations and priorities for people, including, for instance, our attitudes to work and its place in our lives, with people shifting to prioritising their health and wellbeing over work; the four-day week trials that are ongoing and proving popular are part of this (and may also link to de-escalating our "permanent growth" economic cycles; see Activity 51).

Use the following suggested structure to guide your discussion and capture your thoughts.

Values and priorities from before COVID that we want to keep
Values and priorities from before COVID that we want to change
SUMMARY: our selected post-pandemic values and priorities
How could we do this?   **Barriers to change, and opportunities for change**

FIGURE 5.3 Capture COVID thoughts

Going further

Read about the "pandemic amnesia" of a previous pandemic, the 1918 Influenza outbreak: https://pandemichistories.ca/reflections-on-pandemic-history-post-covid-19/ and related to this, read about memory consolidation, and in particular system consolidation. Start here: https://en.wikipedia.org/wiki/Memory_consolidation Are we still "too close" to the events of the pandemic for long-term memories to be fully consolidated – a process which can take from days, to years, and even decades? Might this, along with other factors, be a contributor to a feeling of forgetting or a wish to move on?

Further reading

How retrieval of memories from the long-term memory affects their retention over time: Inda, M. C., Muravieva, E. V., & Alberini, C. M. (2011 Feb 2). Memory retrieval and the passage of time: from reconsolidation and strengthening to extinction. *J Neurosci*,31(5): 1635–1643. https://doi.org/10.1523/JNEUROSCI.4736-10.2011. PMID: 21289172; PMCID: PMC3069643.

Microsoft 2022 work trend index annual report shows more people are likely to prioritise their health and wellbeing above paid employment than pre-COVID: https://www.microsoft.com/en-us/worklab/work-trend-index/great-expectations-making-hybrid-work-work

Pandemic amnesia or a new more ethical and equal post-pandemic social model? https://www.mdpi.com/2076-0760/11/8/340

System consolidation in our memory: https://www.sciencedirect.com/topics/psychology/systems-consolidation

The Great Resignation trend: https://en.wikipedia.org/wiki/Great_Resignation

The four-day workweek movement: https://en.wikipedia.org/wiki/Four-day_workweek

WHO expert describes risk that COVID pandemic amnesia could lead to not learning ready for a future pandemic: https://www.saltwire.com/nova-scotia/news/who-worried-covid-amnesia-will-lead-to-another-pandemic-525765/

Works well with

Activity 1, Chapter 7: Time for a learning-wellbeing rethink?
Activity 7, Chapter 7: Your future health and wellbeing

9. COPING WITH AND MANAGING CHANGE

Time: flexible depending on time available

Who this could be for: anyone who would like to consider ways of understanding the process of change and models of change

Resources needed: Internet access, writing materials physical or computer-based

Why do this: consider two models of change and use them to understand your own experience of coping with change in your life and your learning experiences; develop your own personal model of change to reflect how you experience change

Coping with change

As learners we are faced with change because change is fundamental to and inherent within the learning process. Learning changes us and this is the whole point of it; through learning, we change what we know, and what we think; we make new links between things we already know and our new learning; we change our understanding of our existing learning; and we may also change our understanding of the future through our learning activity. Learning has the potential to change who we are as people and to shift our understanding of the world around us. This is a lot of change! Managing change is therefore part of learning.

Change can also have impacts on our wellbeing. Change affects how we think and feel, and the effects can be both positive and negative. Positive responses to change might include feelings of excitement and opportunity, freshness and stimulation, enjoyment of challenge and the chance to find out or experience new things, and to make new connections. Negative responses to change might include stress, anxiety, defensiveness, withdrawal, feeling down or even (if the amount of change is excessive) feelings of being overwhelmed or out of control.

How we then respond to change can vary depending on how the change or changes affect us; either positively, negatively or a mixture of both. We might feel excited by the change but also a little overwhelmed; in which case, we might be more likely to feel able to cope with the change, and engage with making it work for us, whilst also feeling a bit stressed. Alternatively, we might feel anxious and stressed by change, and struggle with the uncertainty it brings; in which case, we might retreat into trying to either ignore change or avoid it altogether!

Managing change is therefore, in addition to being part of learning, also part of managing our wellbeing. This activity is a chance to consider some aspects of change and provides some ideas of how to manage the impact of change on you as a learner.

A map of change and how it might affect us: John Fisher's Personal Transition Curve

John Fisher developed a map (Fisher's Personal Transition Curve, 2012) of how we might react to change. Fisher's model is not a smooth progress with no hitches or setbacks – it is a rollercoaster ride of emotions and thoughts and has stages at which we might give up or withdraw from the change process. Fisher includes some of the difficult emotions we can experience as we cope with change. These can be enough to throw us off the change curve – unless we find ways of tolerating the challenge and sticking with the direction we want to go in. The curve moves from self-doubt and uncertainty at the outset of the change process, through the challenges of understanding the full impact of the change process, with the possibilities of giving up or disengaging, and then onwards through to sustained and embedded change and development as a learner.

As part of this activity, review this model and consider if you recognise any of the stages in your own experiences of change.

John Fisher's map of the process of transition is available at: https://www.r10.global/wp-content/uploads/2017/05/fisher-transition-curve-2012-1.pdf

Prochaska and DiClemente's Stages of Change Model (Prochaska & DiClemente, 1983)

Prochaska and DiClemente's stages of change model was based on studies of people who were able to give up smoking under their own initiative. It has gone on to be used as a model for understanding how we engage in changing our behaviour generally. The studies identified what factors helped people to make behavioural change and identified a cycle that is engaged in when we seek to deliberately make changes to what we do, our behaviours, or our habits. The model has five stages and there are entry and exit points within the cycle, where you might either disengage with the change process or rejoin it.

The five stages of change are described below and begin at a stage named "precontemplation." A sixth stage of "relapse" is sometimes included within the cycle, acknowledging that there are times when we might slip back into old habits despite our commitment to maintaining change. Relapse is a possible exit from the "maintenance" stage of the change cycle.

Precontemplation: at this stage, we might not be ready to change or even be thinking of it yet; if we were to think of change, at this stage we might be focused on the negative aspects of making change (even if it is needed or helpful).
Contemplation: at the next stage, "contemplation," we are beginning to think about making a change in the near future (within six months) and

we might be starting to realise that change could be helpful to us; we might also be more aware of the positive aspects of change, rather than just the negative aspects.
- **Determination:** at the "determination" stage, we're ready to make changes in the next month, and we might start taking steps towards making changes. We are now at a stage where we believe making a change is a positive thing for us.
- **Action:** at this stage, we have recently changed our behaviour and our intention and plan is to keep going with the change we've made. This is the stage of change at which we're closely involved in establishing the change we've made in our day-to-day life.
- **Maintenance:** at this stage of the cycle, we have kept with the change we've made for six months or more, and our intention is to continue with this change into the future. The maintenance stage is probably where we'll want to remain if the change we have made is working for us.

A diagram of the Prochaska and Diclemente model is available at: https://sphweb.bumc.bu.edu/otlt/mph-modules/sb/behavioralchangetheories/behavioralchangetheories6.html

Consider Prochaska and DiClemente's model of making behavioural change. Do you recognise any parts of this cycle? The model suggests it's easy to slip out of the change cycle even if the change you are working on is one you actively want to achieve. It also includes a stage at which we might see only the negative sides of making changes. So how you think about change make a difference to whether you are motivated to engage with change? What impact might the pre-contemplative stage of the model have on you as a learner if you are seeking to cope with change in a learning setting?

Creating your own personal model of change: what have you experienced?

Follow the steps below to create your own personal model of change and to reflect on your own experience of change.

Step one: draw your change experience model

Using the two examples from Fisher (2012) and Prochaska and DiClemente (1983), see if you can create a representation of your own experience of change. You might want to draw a change curve similar to the Fisher model, in relation to a specific situation of change that you have experienced. Or you might want to use a more circular structure like Prochaska and DiClemente's change cycle. Or you might have another model or representation in mind altogether. Draw or write it out and include details from what you experienced, thought, felt and how you behaved (if it's a specific situation), or how you typically think, feel and behave (if it's more of a representative cycle).

Step two: what do you notice? What do you want to add or alter?

Consider the personal model of change that you have produced. Are there any stages that you think could helpfully be different? You could add alternative directions off your change model with other ways of thinking or responding if you can see any alterations that might be interesting to try.

Step three: put your changes into practice

Try out any changed responses you have identified through step two. And then you could review what happened using a change model to analyse your findings.

Works well with

Activity 3, Chapter 7: Making a friend of uncertainty

Going further

To take this activity further, you could draw out one of your own personal experiences along the Fisher change curve (see main activity for link). Did you manage to stay on the curve, or did you leave it at some point? Does reflecting on a past experience of change you have experienced using this model reveal other responses or different coping that could have been useful if they had been available to you at the time? If so, how might you plan to bring these more useful responses into your life in the future when encountering change? What skills do you need to build to be able to stay on the curve? Don't forget to do this going further exercise in a self-compassionate way, if you try it – it's not an exercise in self-blame or self-attack but an exploration of possible different ways of being. See Activity 47: For more on self-compassion.

Reference

Prochaska, J. O. & DiClemente, C. C. (1983). Stages and processes of self-change of smoking: Toward an integrative model of change. *Journal of Consulting and Clinical Psychology*, 51, 390–95

Further reading

- 12 tips for coping with change: https://www.bhf.org.uk/informationsupport/heart-matters-magazine/wellbeing/mental-health/coping-with-change/tips-for-coping-with-change
- 15 ways that change can be good: https://www.minimalismmadesimple.com/home/change-is-good/

10. LETTER (OR TIME CAPSULE) TO THE FUTURE

Time: flexible; 20 minutes or longer, depending on how long you would like to spend writing a letter to the future (or capturing your ideas via another medium, for instance by creating a time capsule)

Who this could be for: anyone who would like to reflect on recent years and capture what they have learned and would like to let the future (either near or far) know about

Resources needed: something to capture thoughts with; a means of writing ideas down or relevant other materials if you select a different method of recording your ideas

Why do this: reflect on your recent experiences and gather them up into a letter (or other communication) to the future to both process and make sense of your recent experiences and to imagine how they might be usefully communicated to people in the near or far future

Although our present and recent past are very near to us right now, there will come a time when what we know about our experience of learning and maintaining our wellbeing during the pandemic will be quite distant from us. This activity is therefore a chance to consider what information you might send into the future about our present and our recent past. Creating a letter to the future, or creating a time capsule in addition to a letter (and then including the letter inside it), is a chance to both reflect on what you have experienced, and also a chance to consider what you would like to make people aware of in the future about what now was like, and what you (and we) learned.

You might already have some ideas of what you would like to write, and what you would like to include in your time capsule; the following prompts are therefore included to help your thinking if needed.

If you are writing a letter to the future:

- What have I learned about myself during the pandemic?
- What have I learned about other people during the pandemic?
- What is the most important thing I would like to tell people in the future about the last few years?
- What advice do I have for people in the future about how to keep hopeful even when things are difficult?
- What are your strongest memories of the last few years; both good and bad?

If you are creating a time capsule to put your letter to the future in:

- What three (or five, or more) objects would you include in the capsule to give people in the future an insight into your experience in the pandemic?
- What objects best represent this time?

- What images would give people a sense of what this time has been like?
- Do you want to send something helpful into the future? Or something puzzling that is going to make people who open the time capsule think?

Going further

To take this idea further, you could consider drafting a reply from someone in the future, back to you, having received your communication. What are they going to let you know about? If you have planned what you would put into a time capsule for the first part of this exercise, you could consider creating the time capsule that is sent back to you from the future (taking a leap that both-ways time capsule travel is possible, for the benefit of this activity!). When you open the time capsule from the future, what is in it? You could either create images of your ideas for what's in the time capsule from the future or make the objects if you prefer.

As a further stage to this, you could present your work to someone else, and ask them what they make of what you have been sent from the future. Can they work out what everything is and what is meant by it all?

Further reading

Ideas for creating a time capsule: https://www.wikihow.com/Create-a-Time-Capsule
Time capsules: https://en.wikipedia.org/wiki/Time_capsule

6
WELLBEING AND LEARNING ON YOUR OWN

This chapter considers how we can support and improve our wellbeing as learners when we are learning on our own. It may be that our learning is happening partly or even mainly in groups, with other co-learners, but there will still be times when we are learning in a more solitary setting. It may alternatively be that we find ourselves as either mainly or entirely solitary learners for a time. The activities and ideas in this chapter are relevant to both learning situations.

Whilst the focus in this chapter is on what we can do to self-support as learners managing our own wellbeing, it should always be kept in mind that maintaining good wellbeing is a collective responsibility and effort; the families, friendship networks, communities, employers and organisations around us and that we may be part of all have an important role to play in wellbeing. Even if the following activities suggest things we can do on our own, we are never truly alone in maintaining good wellbeing. With this in mind, the activities that follow include drawing on others around us to build a support team. An important part of wellbeing and learning on your own is to know that you are never alone with these challenges, and that there is always someone to reach out to for support, encouragement, help and hope.

ACTIVITIES

1. CHOOSING YOUR LEARNING PATH

Time: flexible, from 10–15 minutes to as long as required/helpful

Who this could be for: anyone who wants to consider how to develop as a learner and how to direct their learning efforts in self-directed study or learning

Resources needed: internet access; depending on what you're learning map reveals, ways of contacting relevant experts/accessing further resources (the resources this may involve will be highly dependent on your chosen area of learning focus)

Why do this: identify your own preferred learning structure to help yourself learn in a way that is supportive of your wellbeing and grows your confidence as a self-directed learner. Identify what other resources you need to grow and develop in your chosen area(s) of learning

Lev Vygotsky developed a helpful concept when thinking about how we learn and are supported to learn. This activity involves considering how Vygotsky's idea could help you to choose your own learning path and to support your own learning as you travel along it. And if you are already some way along a particular learning path, this is a chance to consider how you can go further in supporting yourself to continue with your learning development and progress.

Essentially, Vygotsky's idea is that there is zone of learning that an individual learner is able to manage without support; and around this, there is a zone of additional learning that an individual learner is able to reach with the right support (for instance, from another person who has relevant knowledge or experience). Further out beyond this zone that a learner can access with support (the zone of proximal development), there is a zone that the learner cannot (yet) access even with support. You can think of these zones as circles that move outwards, with the innermost circle being what a learner can learn themselves; a circle around that representing the zone of proximal development, with what a learner can learn with support; and a circle around that one of what is currently inaccessible to the learner. It's alternatively helpful to think of a path or road as your learning moves on over time rather than staying in the same place. And as your learning moves on, so the zone of proximal development around what you can learn yourself without support changes, and some of the previously inaccessible parts of learning may become accessible over time.

A visual representation of the Vygotsky model is available here: https://en.wikipedia.org/wiki/Zone_of_proximal_development

For this activity, take some time to read about Vygotsky's zone of proximal development as above and via the further reading and resources given below, and then consider:

- have you experienced this in relation to any of your past learning?
- is the concept relevant to any of your current learning experiences?
- does this concept seem a good reflection of the experience of learning to you, or would you add anything or express it differently?

Now take some time to map out a current learning experience you are involved with; perhaps a specific academic subject or theme, or a skill you are developing or pastime you are finding out about; using either the graph as shown in the link above or the concentric circle representation as you prefer. Add in what you have learned already yourself; what you have been able to learn with the support of relevant others (in the zone of proximal development); and (this might be difficult; if so, make your best guess) what you are not yet able to access or learn even with support.

When you have finished this, take some time to consider what your map reveals; what does your map tell you about the learning path you are on, and what does it suggest about how you should proceed further along your learning path related to the subject or theme you have worked on in this activity? Does it indicate what support you need to continue to build on your learning? Is there a way that you can access further learning that suggests itself, for example, are there other resources you need that will support you and your learning?

Going further

If you have identified ideas to try, seek ways to put them into place. For instance, if you have identified needing additional resources such as further information about a subject, make a plan for how to access this information. If you have identified that you need contact with experts in a field, find out how to make contact with relevant people and put your plan into place.

Further reading

Vygotsky's zone of proximal development: https://www.sciencedirect.com/topics/psychology/zone-of-proximal-development#:~:text=ZPD%20is%20defined%20by%20Vygotsky,86).

https://en.wikipedia.org/wiki/Zone_of_proximal_development

2. SELF-DIRECTED LEARNING – WHERE (AND HOW) DO I START?

Time: 30 minutes or longer if desired

Who this could be for: any learner who is involved in self-directed learning

Resources needed: writing materials

Why do this: understand what you can do to support yourself as a self-directed learner and identify helpful strategies for supporting your executive functions

Consider this description of self-directed learning:

> Self-directed learning describes a process in which individuals take the initiative, with or without the help of others, in diagnosing their learning needs, formulating learning goals, identifying human and material resources for learning, choosing and implementing appropriate learning strategies, and evaluating learning outcomes.
>
> *(Knowles, 1975)*

As a learner, you have probably had a lot of experience of learning that's led, directed, or initiated by others. This type of learning can be useful, engaging and relevant, and can include self-directed elements within it. Fully self-directed learning can feel very different. As the definition above sets out, self-directed learning is led by the individual at every stage of the process, from identifying what learning is needed to looking back on the process and considering how it went.

What do you need to set out on your self-directed learning journey?

You might already know what you want to learn, or you might be in a contemplative stage without a specific goal in mind. Whether you are all set to get started or just thinking that you might like to set out but are not sure where to, this activity is a chance to consider the role executive functions play in self-directed learning and to consider two particular skills you could build as part of supporting yourself on your learning journey; firstly knowing where to start (planning and prioritisation), and secondly knowing how to start (task initiation).

Executive functions: building your skills to support your self-directed learning journey

Executive functions are cognitive skills that we need when dealing with and successfully responding to the wide range of experiences that life presents us with. Particularly when we encounter a new or unknown situation, our executive functions are all potentially needed to help us make sense of and deal with the novel situation. Situations in which our executive functions are most likely to be needed have been defined as:

- Those that involve planning or decision-making
- Those that involve error correction or troubleshooting
- Situations where responses are not well-rehearsed or contain novel sequences of actions
- Dangerous or technically difficult situations
- Situations that require the overcoming of a strong habitual response or resisting temptation.

(Norman and Shallice, 1981)

It's clear that the types of situations you might encounter as a learner, and particularly as a self-directed learner, are very likely to include some or even all elements of the above.

Our executive functions are defined as:

1 Response inhibition (also defined as self-control)
2 Working memory
3 Emotional control
4 Sustained attention
5 Task initiation
6 Planning and prioritising
7 Organisation
8 Time management
9 Goal directed persistence
10 Flexibility
11 Metacognition (observing/awareness of own cognitive processes)
12 Stress tolerance

Executive functions develop over time, and some can take longer to develop than others, in line with the timescale over which our brains develop and mature. In fact, some of our executive functions don't fully develop until we are in our third decade!

The extended development of our executive functions shows that we are all truly lifelong learners. And it's worth bearing in mind that if you are frustrated with yourself for not making more progress in one or another area of your learning or your life, it might be that your executive skills relating to that area are still developing – knowing this might offer you a chance to be compassionate and supportive towards yourself and give yourself a break rather than criticising yourself or getting angry with yourself.

Where do I start? Planning and prioritisation in self-directed learning

A good first step in self-directed learning can be working out where to start. Setting learning goals you want to achieve is something that you might want to do alone, or in discussion with others. Here are some ideas for helping yourself to identify learning goals, and then plan and prioritise them:

- Set realistic time aside with minimal distractions to consider what you might want to learn about
- Notice what times of day and where you are most able to think forwards and to make links and connections between ideas and possibilities, and set time aside then – you'll be more likely to be able to plan and prioritise with ease
- Identify what you enjoy learning about, what engages you easily and what subjects or learning activities you are drawn to
- Ask others, part one; what do they enjoy learning about (academic subject, area of interest, creative activity, sport, game etc.)
- Ask others, part two; what do they think you might enjoy or value learning about? The insights that others can have into us can surprise us, and others may come up with ideas we wouldn't have thought of ourselves
- Find a way to capture your ideas and thoughts that works for you – write it down, record yourself speaking, make short videos or draw pictures – don't limit yourself to a bullet point list (like this one!) just because it's a common way of ordering information. These are your plans and priorities, and you can represent them however you want to
- Come up with a representation of possibilities; if you have a few possibilities and want to narrow your choices down, take some time to rate them (you can come up with your own rating scale for this) in order of, for example, value to you, or enjoyableness, or time and commitment required; whatever's relevant to help you choose
- Take a leap into the future and look back: if you imagine a future in which you've been able to engage with some, but not all, of the learning you might want to do, what do you feel is most important to have learned about, from your vantage point in your future – or thinking about it another way, what would you least regret not having learned about?
- Look at what you have identified so far, and consider if you can see any themes; if so, is there a way to fold these together into one learning

direction? For instance, would learning more about horticulture meet several of your learning priorities at once?
- Do not expect to complete this in one go! Planning and prioritising is something to come back to, probably several times. Give yourself some time to reflect on what you've identified before you get started
- Review your plans and priorities. Once you have started this process, find time to review what you've done, and feel free to make changes, add new ideas or take some away. Planning is a dynamic activity, and it should change and adapt as you make progress

How do I start? Task initiation

If the above ideas have helped you identify where to start with your self-directed learning, another executive function you may need to engage in is task initiation. Here are some ideas for helping yourself to get started with learning tasks and activities that you have selected:

Task initiation self-audit

Take some time to notice how good you are at task initiation currently. It might be that you find some tasks really easy to get started with and others either very difficult or nearly impossible! You will not be alone in this. Thinking about your day-to-day life, try to identify the types of tasks that you find easy, somewhat challenging, and impossible/nearly impossible to start in the table below. It's likely that you will experience different kinds of emotions relating to the ease or difficulty you feel in initiating the different tasks you have identified. You are also likely to notice different types of thoughts relating to each task. For instance, the thoughts relating to tasks you find easy to initiate may well be either quite positive, or there might not be many thoughts about the task at all and a mild emotional reaction – you're taking action and not stuck, so your focus is on what you're doing, not the difficulty in getting started. If there are any metacognitions (thoughts about and internal observations and critiques of your thinking processes), you might, for instance, be thinking "I'm really enjoying this task" or "it's great to get this task done" and you might notice feelings of interest, engagement, enjoyment or just a focused feeling.

For the more difficult tasks, you might notice more negative thoughts, perhaps including some self-critical metacognitive thoughts such as "why do I always find this so difficult?" or "can't believe I'm struggling with this again, why can't I just get on with it?" Accompanying these thoughts, there might be some negative emotions such as frustration and disappointment.

TABLE 6.1 Tasks (i)

Tasks I find it easy to get started on:	Tasks I find some difficulty in getting started on (but I can still get started)	Tasks I find next-to-impossible to get started on
Emotions I notice when doing the above tasks:	Emotions I notice when doing the above tasks:	Emotions I notice when doing the above tasks:
Thoughts I tend to have when doing the above tasks:	Thoughts I tend to have when doing the above tasks:	Thoughts I tend to have when doing the above tasks:

Once you've captured some tasks, thoughts and emotions, review what you've found and see if you can identify any themes in what you find easy, medium difficulty or very difficult/impossible. Are the tasks you find easy all similar? Do the tasks you find really difficult to initiate have anything in common? Is the way you think about the tasks contributing to whether you find them easy/not? For instance, do you tend to predict that you will not enjoy a difficult-to-start task, and this contributes to you avoiding making a start, and do you tend to predict you will enjoy (or feel neutral about) an easy-to-start task? Are there practical difficulties rather than inner thought processes getting in the way? This might lead you to the next step, adjusting your approach to make task initiation easier. Note any themes you have identified here:

TABLE 6.2 Tasks (ii)

THEMES with tasks I find it easy to get started on:	THEMES with tasks I find some difficulty in getting started on (but I can still get started)	THEMES with tasks I find next-to-impossible to get started on

Task initiation reset – practical changes

If the themes you have identified have revealed that any practical factors – such as time, access to necessary (or just helpful) resources, support from others – need to be addressed to make task initiation for the more difficult tasks easier, consider how this could be addressed.

Task initiation reset – build on the easy tasks (using cheat mode for the difficult tasks)

Look at what kinds of tasks you've identified that you find easy to initiate. Is there any way of taking what is easy in relation to those tasks and applying it to the difficult tasks? It might be you can use a cheat mode by thinking about the more difficult tasks in the way you tend to think about the easy tasks. Alternatively, can you bring anything from the way in which you initiate the easy tasks to how you initiate the difficult tasks? For instance, are the easier tasks always started quite spontaneously without lots of planning?

Task initiation reset – breaking it down into smaller tasks

You might have identified emotions around feeling overwhelmed and/or helpless or hopeless around the very difficult-to-initiate tasks. If so, consider if you are trying to bite off too big a task in one go. Can you break the difficult tasks down into sub-tasks and just tackle a part of it instead of everything in one go?

Task initiation reset – consider the role of avoiding in maintaining the difficulty

Sometimes tasks we are really struggling with initiating are things that we have avoided for some time. Bear in mind that this can sometimes skew our perception of how difficult the task in question is going to be, and we can start identifying even thinking about the task with some negative and overwhelming emotions. This then feeds itself in a bit of an avoidance loop – we don't like the emotions, we overestimate how difficult we will find the task, and we get more inclined to avoid starting the task. And we never get the chance to find out if it's as difficult as we are predicting. Avoidance tends to build the difficulty; if you can find a way to approach the task (or even just an element of it, see above), you might be surprised by what you find.

Task initiation reset – rewards

If a difficult-to-initiate task is particularly challenging and essential, can you build in any kind of reward or follow-up activity for yourself in order to have something on the other side of the task to look forward to?

Task initiation reset – get help or hand it over!

You might have identified some tasks you struggle with that in fact might be better done by others. If you can identify someone else who finds that task easy, or even enjoyable too, hand it over! Alternatively, sharing the task might be a better option if it's something you want to do but find some aspects of challenging.

Other ideas for improving task initiation

- Keep noticing your thoughts, emotions and themes around task initiation
- If you find something that helps you to initiate tasks, build the habit; practice what works
- Don't overload yourself
- Practice task initiation variation – make sure you have a range of activities to keep mentally and emotionally refreshed
- Be kind and supportive towards yourself
- If it didn't work, take a breath, note any changes you need to make, and go again
- Stay hopeful – you can do it! Making changes can be difficult. Note the progress, and don't dwell too long on the setbacks (unless there's something you can learn from them for next time)

A final thought: mindful task initiation

We can sometimes get very caught up in tasks, lists, actions, and the need to achieve. If you are feeling a bit overwhelmed or crushed by everything you want to do, take a step back and try thinking of what you are doing as a process or journey rather than a series of things to be done. We need to find value in and to enjoy the process of learning and developing rather than just work frantically to tick things off a task list. This last idea is supportive of developing two of your other executive functions: metacognition and stress tolerance.

Going further

You might want to find out more about your other executive functions and how they can help you with self-directed learning (see further reading). You might also want to select particular executive skills to develop further. These meta-learning skills will be helpful to you in your current self-directed learning, and in all the future self-directed learning you might engage in across your life.

You could also read about and consider David Kolb's Experiential Learning Cycle (1974). Kolb's cycle suggests a structure for experiential learning with four stages. In this model of experiential learning, the four stages are: 1) concrete experience (the learning experience itself); 2) reflective observation (reflecting on and reviewing the learning experience afterwards); 3) abstract conceptualisation (drawing the learning out of the experience) and 4) active experimentation (planning to put what you have reflected on and learned into practice, and then doing so). The experiential learning cycle then returns to the start again and you can run through the stages as many times as you wish. Particularly for self-directed learning, this cycle could be a useful concept to make use of if you wish to reflect on and direct your own learning.

Works well with

Activity 4, Chapter 2: Visualisation: your ideal learning supporter
Activity 9, Chapter 2: Thinking styles
Activity 9, Chapter 3: (in Building a positive self-image) Positive data log
Activity 8, Chapter 6: Positive learner data log

References

Kolb, D. A. (1984). *Experiential learning: Experience as the source of learning and development*. Prentice Hall.
Norman, D., Shallice, T., Lansman, M., & Hunt, E. (Eds.). (1986). *Attention to action: Willed and automatic control of behaviour*. Plenum Press. Full text available at: (2) (PDF) Attention to action: Willed and automatic control of behavior (researchgate.net)

Further reading

A burnout recovery kit for women with ADHD: https://www.additudemag.com/how-to-recover-from-burnout-women-adhd/
Recovering from ADHD burnout: https://neurodivergentinsights.com/adhd-infographics/adhd-burnout-recovery#:~:text=%E2%9C%A6%20There%20are%20various%20ways,enlivening%2C%20and%20supporting%20healthy%20rhythms.

3. INFORMATION OVERLOAD – FINDING YOUR FOCUS IN AN INFORMATION-RICH WORLD

Time: flexible, depending on time available

Who this could be for: anyone who would like to try some ideas for improving focus and concentration

Resources needed: no resources needed

Why do this: improve your focus and concentration to make learning more successful and reduce fatigue and overwhelm

Information overload – finding your focus in an information-rich world

If you look through this book, there is a huge amount of information. It's created by combining and re-combining just 26 letters and a few numbers and symbols. There are activities and facts and questions, links to further reading and information beyond the covers of this book, and those links can lead you on further to yet more information. And that's just a small corner of how much information there is in total available to you. It's overwhelming!

As a learner, you are always going to be faced with finding a way through this info-world and it's not always easy to focus in on what you need, or even to know what it is you need to know in the first place. Particularly for self-directed learning, it can be easy to lose your way in the quantity of information you can access. This activity includes some suggestions for dealing with information and finding your way through it to the learning you need, whilst minimising the risks of being overwhelmed with information.

- Set boundaries – time, quantity, subject

If the edges feel unknown for your information-finding or learning task, it will help to try to define some boundaries to what you are seeking. For instance, can you narrow your research to a particular time period, or to a particular area? Can you define how much time you have available to find out about or research a subject, and then set a time limit on how long you spend on this? Would it help to set a target for the number of different information sources you look at in one research or learning session?

- Understand expectations

If you are seeking information or researching something relating to an assignment or learning task that you have been set, understanding exactly what's required to complete it is an important part of avoiding getting overloaded with too much information, and also means you shouldn't find yourself researching non-relevant or unhelpful information. Get as much clarity as you can on what the assignment requirements and parameters are before you start.

- **Remember: your attention is being fought over!**

It is worth keeping in mind that the incredible range of information we can access online is often via platforms, sites and social media that are specifically designed to get and then to keep our attention. If you have ever fallen down a TikTok or YouTube rabbit hole (just two of many sites), you'll know that the information and diversion these sites offer are easy to engage with but can be very, very difficult to disengage with. This engagingness is intentional and part of the profit/business models that many sites run on. If a site that carries advertisements can catch and then keep the attention of a consumer of their information, their advertisers are going to be able to reach that individual for longer and with more detailed and persuasive advertising. Even if you know what information you are looking for on a site, you can call in, get the information and still find it difficult to leave again. If you are, as in a physical shop, "just browsing," often you are browsing for something that holds your attention; entertains or shocks you, engages you in some way. Then it's even harder to leave!

Consider setting yourself boundaries (as above) for either time spent or subjects engaged with as part of being in charge of where your attention goes. It's also worth thinking of your powers of attention as something valuable; and asking yourself, what do you want to expand your powers of attention on? If you find, on consideration, that you want to choose where this attention goes, this might result in you being more aware of when your attention is being taken up when you didn't fully choose it to be. You could consider keeping an attention-trap diary for a day, or longer, to monitor this; you might be surprised at what you find when you review it.

- **Ask for support with anything you know you find more difficult**

If you are aware that you have any weaker areas (i.e., time management) when it comes to dealing with information, seek out anyone who can help you – can you externalise some of those things to helpers? For instance, can you ask someone to remind you when you'll need to start a task or activity, and/or when you'll need to stop? Can you set an alarm or reminder on your phone? If you find it difficult to prioritise what you are looking for when seeking information, can you talk it through with anyone else to get their perspective or to help yourself find an answer?

- **Take breaks …**

It's helpful to take short breaks across an information-gathering session, to give your brain a breather from focusing and learning. Try to move and stretch, if possible, go outside for a short time, or if that's not possible, try to look outside into the middle distance. It helps to de-focus your eyes and reduces muscle strain which can make you feel fatigued, tense or induce a headache. A break can help you reset your attention so you can return refreshed to continue with what you're working on.

- ... including sleeping breaks!

Bear in mind that we can't fully assimilate information without a bit of time and space; pace your information-consumption so that if it's something you want to retain in the longer term, you have a chance to sleep on it, and return to it to embed the learning another day. Sleeping probably helps us to process the information we've taken in during our waking hours; just like you might need some time to digest a really big meal, your brain is going to need some time to process and store a lot of new information.

- **Acceptance: you can't know everything, and you will miss some things**

If you are thorough and don't like to miss anything, it can be very frustrating to feel you haven't found out everything there is to find out when you're seeking information. Sometimes we can feel if we just research a bit more, we'll get the full, complete picture – we'll know all there is to know about it! But there is a problem with this, especially in an information-overloaded world. It's virtually impossible to read, watch, access, consider all the information about any subject or area of interest; it is being added to constantly, so the available information is expanding, and some information is becoming obsolete as new information replaces it.

If you feel overloaded or overwhelmed by information, you could try a visualisation exercise. First, try visualising all the information available relating to the theme you are focusing on as a static, fixed, graspable quantity that, if you only try hard enough, you can assimilate all of. Then, try an alternative visualisation; try seeing it as more like a murmuration of birds; a shifting and altering thing comprised of interlinked things that change shape, with the relationships between each piece of information altering as the information shrinks, grows and moves. This image might make you feel more inclined to enjoy being able to observe the shapes and patterns of information as they change in front of you, rather than feeling overwhelmed.

- Be kind to yourself; the supportive coach

Try to be kind towards yourself if you find yourself struggling with information overload. You are not alone, and in many ways feeling overloaded with information is the rational response to our information-saturated world. If you notice that however much you try to take in, you have a gnawing feeling that it's never good enough, it might help to put in some perspective and ask yourself if it's realistic to try to get it exactly right, and to take in all the information that there is, or is it wiser to do the best you can and then know when to stop? Ask yourself what you'd like to hear from a wise, supportive, encouraging learning coach – and then say this to yourself.

Going further

Attention training is a helpful thing to practice to help build the ability to attend to something more fully. It involves focusing on particular aspects of sensory information, such as one type of sound, even though other types of sounds are also present (e.g., listening to birdsong whilst there are also noises of people talking, running water, cars going past). Especially when our attention is under pressure from so many directions, being able to attend is a difficult skill to retain and a useful skill to have.

Attention training resources and information:

https://mct-institute.co.uk/attention-training-technique/
https://www.youtube.com/watch?v=kbTkwMJExCc

Works well with

Activity 4, Chapter 2: Visualisation: your ideal learning supporter
Activity 6, Chapter 3: Keeping perspective
Activity 3, Chapter 2: Perfectionism and procrastination

Further reading and resources

A Teenager's Guide to ADHD, The ADHD Foundation: https://www.adhdfoundation.org.uk/wp-content/uploads/2022/05/ADHD_Found_Takeda_TeenagerBooklet_April2022_compressed.pdf

Wu, T. (2017). *The attention merchants: The epic struggle to get inside our heads.* Vintage.

Dawson, P., & Guare, R. (2016). *The smart but scattered guide to success: How to use your brain's executive skills to keep up, stay calm, and get organised at work and at home.* Guilford Press.

How sleeping on it helps learning: https://newsinhealth.nih.gov/2013/04/sleep-it#:~:text=When%20you%20learn%20something%20new,new%20ideas%20while%20you%20slumber

Knowles, M. S. (1975). *Self-directed learning.* Association Press.

Starling murmuration: https://www.rspb.org.uk/birds-and-wildlife/wildlife-guides/birda-z/starling/starling-murmurations/

4. LOOKING AFTER YOU: FROM SELF-CRITICISM TO BEING YOUR OWN SUPPORTIVE LEARNING COACH

Time: 10–15 minutes

Who this could be for: anyone who notices they tend to be quite self-critical or harsh with themselves and finds this can get in the way of getting on with things

Resources needed: No resources needed

Why do this: Try out a way to deal with your worst critic via giving them a short (or extended!) holiday

An important part of supporting your own learning and wellbeing is to find a balance between motivating yourself without being overly self-critical or self-attacking. This activity is something to try if you notice that you have a tendency to be really harsh on yourself if you make mistakes or get things wrong.

We can have a tendency to criticise ourselves very harshly for not getting things right, or not doing or being good enough. If you notice you have some really harsh ways of talking to yourself about your progress with something, for example, something you are learning about or working on, to the extent it's putting you off either getting on with it or even starting it in the first place, try this exercise.

1. Think of some examples of the kind of thing you say to yourself when you notice something you are doing (for instance, something you are trying to learn, research or practice) isn't good enough. It might be something like, "this work just isn't good enough!" or "what you are doing is completely useless, I don't know why you're bothering!" or "you're never going to be good enough at this, are you?" Your phrases will be personal to you, so examples here are given as a prompt but do not forget your own words are most relevant.
2. Close your eyes, and imagine these phrases are being pronounced in a courtroom by a very unforgiving judge. Notice how the judge looks, how they sound, what their courtroom looks like. Notice how it is making you feel to hear these phrases.
3. Now imagine yourself asking the judge if they would like to take a holiday somewhere nice (wherever suits them, it's completely their choice). Even if they don't want to at first, imagine talking them into it. Once they leave, imagine standing a sign on their bench that reads "On Holiday for Two Weeks."
4. Have a look around the empty courtroom and read the sign again and notice how you are feeling.

After you have tried this, the next time you notice some self-criticism and harsh self-talk that is getting in the way of you getting on and setting impossible standards that you can't seem to reach no matter how hard you try, visualise the empty judge's bench again. Read the sign you left there and remind yourself they've taken a holiday at the moment.

It might even be that when their two weeks' holiday is up, they don't want to come back to the courtroom at all, and in which case, you could ask them if they would like to take early retirement. You might want to update the sign on the bench in that case.

Going further

To go further with this activity, try the visualisation in Activity 4, Chapter 2: Visualisation: your ideal learning supporter. Will your alternative to the harsh self-critic be a more supportive and compassionate learning coach? Might this make a difference to your mood and your motivation levels as you learn?

Further reading

Research on benefits of using mental imagery in influencing mood states and wellbeing: https://pubmed.ncbi.nlm.nih.gov/26412097/

Works well with

Activity 7, Chapter 6: Self-compassion to support your learning and wellbeing

5. YOUR HEALTH AND WELLBEING WHEEL

Time: 20 minutes or longer

Who this could be for: anyone who would like to develop a holistic map of their own psychological, physical, emotional and other needs relating to their wellbeing and learning

Resources needed: health and wellbeing wheel structure to make notes on (you can draw this out yourself)

Why do this: create a straightforward structure to map out your needs for good wellbeing and learning – and use this to make sure you have the things you need in place in your life

The health and wellbeing wheel is a way to consider your health and wellbeing in a holistic way and to decide where you might like to make changes. It forms the starting point for this activity.

Creating your health and wellbeing wheel: stage 1

Read the description of the health and wellbeing wheel available via the links given in further reading and resources. Then, create your own wheel. Mark on the wheel how good things are in each segment, with the centre being the best things could be, and the further out you travel from the centre, the less good things are in that aspect of your life. To make this activity especially relevant to your experience as a learner, you can adapt the wheel to add in a segment for learning.

Creating your health and wellbeing wheel: stage 2

Now start a new wheel (or, if you prefer, just add your thoughts to the wheel you have started on). In each segment, make a note or draw an image of what you need to improve your health and wellbeing in this area of your life. What moves you more towards the centre of your wheel?

Going further

To go further with this activity, you could adapt the structure of the health and wellbeing wheel you have created in stage 2 of this activity, to reflect important areas for you. You could also consider creating some further outlying wheels, giving more detail about each of the segments of the central wheel; like cogs in a mechanism that turns to support your wellbeing. The next stage of going further is of course to use what you create as a reference to help you ensure you get the right things into your life for optimising your health, wellbeing and learning.

Further reading and resources

Health and wellbeing wheel: https://www.england.nhs.uk/south/wp-content/uploads/sites/6/2018/10/Health-and-Wellbeing-Wheel-1.pdf

Health and wellbeing wheel, alternative source: https://www.nuffieldhealth.com/article/rate-your-wellbeing-using-this-wellbeing-wheel

Works well with

Activity 9, Chapter 6: Values Based Living

6. WHO IS ON YOUR LEARNING AND WELLBEING SUPPORT TEAM?

Time: 15 minutes or longer

Who this could be for: anyone who wants to identify and build their learning and wellbeing support network

Resources needed: time to identify and add to your learning and wellbeing support team

Why do this: identify who is on your learning and wellbeing support team already, and who you might like to add to this network

As a learner, you may sometimes feel a little alone. This exercise is a chance to reflect on who is on your support team – who you can turn to and draw on for support, encouragement, suggestions or just some learning company on your journey. At times when you might be struggling to make sense of something new, or not able to see a way forward to build on what you know, learning can be a challenging business. These are times when you might want to draw on your support team. As we have suggested throughout this book, learning and wellbeing are closely wrapped together, and so when you think of your support team for this exercise, you are identifying who supports you with both your wellbeing and your learning journey, as both are really the same journey.

This exercise is not just about thinking of who is on your support team when things are challenging; the support team you identify is also who you celebrate your successes with, and who you enjoy time with, whether it's co-learning, or just relaxing and unwinding.

Identify your learning and wellbeing support team:

Take some time to reflect on who is on your learning and wellbeing support team. Who is in your life who you can turn to for encouragement when you need it? Who will be understanding if you need to vent your frustrations if you are struggling? Who has information, knowledge, skills or experience that you could draw on? You might want to identify different sources of help for distinct aspects of what you want to learn more about. And it might not just be humans who are on your support team; are companion animals/pets part of it, or a particular place where you feel especially good or find interesting? Are you on your own learning and wellbeing support team? If not, it might be interesting to think about why not ...

Your support team list might look like this (but this is just a suggestion, your own team will be unique to you):

- Friends
- Family members
- Tutors/teachers
- Myself
- Other members of a group/club/team you belong to
- Social network with a shared interest area
- Companion animal(s)/pet(s)
- Local nature reserve

What to do next with your learning and wellbeing support team:

If you want, you can let the members of this team know they are on it! You don't have to, but if you do, you can let them know you appreciate them and their support.

- Keep your team in mind, you might want to make a contact list and save it somewhere you can refer to it easily when needed.
- The next time you feel the need for some support with your learning and wellbeing, take a look at your team list and see if there is someone you can call on.
- Keep your team up to date; you might want to add new members as you go.

Going further

If doing this exercise has shown you that there are gaps in your team, or that you do not have enough sources of learning and wellbeing support, spend some time working out how you could identify others who can offer you the support that would be most useful to you. Who else do you need on your team?

If doing this exercise has made you realise you are not being a good team member for yourself; for instance, because you are sabotaging yourself, or not supporting your own efforts or believing in yourself and your abilities, it might be worth having a look at some of the other activities in this book, for instance, chapter 1, activities 3 and 4, or chapter 2, activity 9.

Further reading

The Circles of Support model: https://www.hse.ie/eng/services/list/4/disability/newdirections/a%20guide%20to%20circles%20of%20support.pdf

7. SELF-COMPASSION TO SUPPORT YOUR LEARNING AND WELLBEING

Time: flexible, from a few minutes to as long as you want to spend exploring ideas of self-compassion

Who this could be for: any learner who would like to understand how self-compassion can benefit wellbeing and help us learn more effectively

Resources needed: writing materials or ways to record your thoughts

Why do this: understand how self-compassion can help our wellbeing and support us to feel safe to learn

Kristin Neff defines three core elements of self-compassion; practicing self-kindness instead of self-judgement; seeing common humanity in our suffering rather than feeling isolated and alone in it; and being mindful of our experience without becoming too caught up in our distress. Some self-compassion ideas include treating yourself as you would a good friend, altering your self-critical thought patterns, and working with your parasympathetic nervous system to increase feelings of calm and safety.

Consider how the idea of self-compassion could help your overall wellbeing and support you in your learning too. If you think it could be helpful to you, see going further for putting some of these ideas into practice.

Going further

Explore the resources on the self-compassion website self-compassion.org (see further reading and resources). There are a range of activities and ideas for building on self-compassion practice. Try any of these that you think could be helpful to you.

References

Neff, K. D. (2009 Jun). The role of self-compassion in development: A healthier way to relate to oneself. *Human Developement*, 52(4): 211–214. https://doi.org/10.1159/000215071. PMID: 22479080; PMCID: PMC2790748.

Further reading and resources

Neff, K. D. (2009 Jun). The role of self-compassion in development: A healthier way to relate to oneself. *Human Development*, 52(4): 211–214. https://doi.org/10.1159/000215071. PMID: 22479080; PMCID: PMC2790748.
Self-compassion resources: https://self-compassion.org/
Self-compassion benefits to wellbeing across our lives: https://www.ncbi.nlm.nih.gov/pmc/articles/PMC2790748

Works well with

Activity 7, Chapter 3: Rest

Activity 4, Chapter 6: Looking after you: from self-criticism to being your own supportive learning coach

8. POSITIVE LEARNER DATA LOG

Time: flexible

Who this could be for: anyone who would like to build a habit of noticing positive aspects of their learning

Resources needed: a method of recording the information you notice

Why do this: build your habit of noticing your learning successes, determination, and general good qualities, to boost your wellbeing and support your learning development

This activity involves and focuses on gathering positive information about yourself as a learner and using this information to build a positive data log. Getting into the habit of noticing when you've done well, tried hard and been determined, received positive feedback from others, and other examples of positive data is supportive of your overall wellbeing, and can help to keep you motivated to learn.

The first step is to gather evidence and information from your daily life of your learning successes, when you showed tenacity to keep trying with learning even when it was tough, when you received positive feedback about your work, and anything you feel proud of relating to your learning experience. Don't wait for something big to come along; even a small thing is relevant. There will be something to capture in this exercise every day, even if at first you find it really difficult to notice anything. It's all part of building a habit of noticing positive things about yourself as a learner.

TABLE 6.3 Positive learner data log: reflect on the evidence and information

When I've succeeded in learning something	*When I stuck with learning even though it was challenging*	*When I received some positive feedback about my learning or my work*	*Something I feel proud about*

Identify a time when you can read through what you have captured in the table above, and set aside, for example, ten minutes to reflect on and remember each situation the evidence you have gathered relates to. It can help to visualise the scene as you remember it, as visual images are more powerful in affecting our thinking and emotions than just words. Try to hold the good feelings in your awareness that you felt at the time, and also notice the good feelings that arise whilst you are reflecting on the evidence.

Set some time aside every day to practice this for a week, and see how you feel at the end of this process. Is there a change in how easy you find it to reflect on your learning in a positive manner or to identify positive evidence and information about yourself as a learner?

Going further

To take this activity further, you could consider if the information you have gathered reveals anything to you about your learning progress, how you learn, or if it suggests anything that you could focus on in the future to support yourself as a learner. If it reveals anything you could do, make a plan and put it into place.

Further reading

Open University: learning how to become a reflective learner: https://www.open.edu/openlearn/education-development/learning-how-learn/content-section-9.1

9. VALUES BASED LIVING – AND VALUES BASED LEARNING

Time: 15–30 minutes or longer if you wish

Who this could be for: anyone who would like to consider what they value in their life and what they'd like to work on bringing into their life more to better reflect their values

Resources needed: no resources required initially; to go further, resources will vary depending on what is chosen to work on

Why do this: identify your values and make a plan for bringing more into your life that reflects your values

As part of supporting your own wellbeing and identifying learning directions you may wish to go in, either now or in the future, the concept of values based living can be a helpful tool. Values based living, contained within Acceptance and Commitment Therapy (ACT), is a chance to reflect on what you hold as values in your life, and also to consider your experience as about travelling with your values in mind, rather than a series of goals to be achieved.

Values based living – find out what you value

To try this idea out for yourself, firstly identify your values in life. What's important to you? There are some prompt questions to help your thinking here: https://www.therapistaid.com/worksheets/values-discussion-questions

You can break your consideration of values down into different areas of life. Use the suggested areas available on this worksheet:

https://www.therapistaid.com/worksheets/values-self-exploration

An alternative structure is included in this worksheet, where a bullseye diagram can be used to indicate how near (or far!) you are from living in line with your values in different areas of your life:

https://drexel.edu/~/media/files/studentlife/counseling/bulls%20eye%20values%20exercise.ashx?la=en

(See also Activity 5, Chapter 6: Your health and wellbeing wheel, for a similar visual tool.)

Next, identify what needs to change to bring you more towards living in line with the values you have identified. For instance, have you noticed that being able to spend time with others is really important to you, but your life rarely gives you the chance to do this? Consider what needs to change, and make a plan. You could make an all-encompassing plan for values based living, or take smaller steps and do some things now, with more in mind for later.

The next step is of course to put your plan into place, whether wide-ranging or smaller scale, and start making your life align more with your values as you have found them to be in completing this exercise.

Values based learning – what do you value in learning?

To develop this idea further, you might like to consider the values based living idea with specific reference to your own learning. Are you learning in line with your identified values? What (especially if you have identified any thoughts about what we will need in the future via other activities in this book) do you think you need to learn in order to benefit your family, friends, community, the wider world or yourself (or all of those)? How do we move what and how we learn to be in line with identified values that we might hold as individuals and communities?

Going further

Read about ACT, see further reading and resources. Values based living is a concept used in ACT and it offers other interesting ideas for how to approach life too.

Further reading and resources

Acceptance and Commitment Therapy: https://www.psychologytoday.com/gb/therapy-types/acceptance-and-commitment-therapy

Dr Russ Harris on the values-focused v. the goals-focused life: https://www.youtube.com/watch?v=eiPxLpYlw4I

10. ... AND BREATHE

Time: 5 minutes to try two breathing exercises

Who this could be for: anyone who would like to try breathing as a way to relax and help themselves learn

Resources needed: lungs

Why do this: try out two breathing techniques to support your general wellbeing and learning

This chapter has covered a lot – time for a breather to close on. There is a close link between our emotional state and our breathing. One of the things that can happen when we're feeling tense and anxious is that we tense and tighten up our muscles, including in our torso and chest, and as a result we can take quite shallow breaths. Another way that our emotional state can affect our breathing is if we're acutely anxious or frightened (as we can be in the midst of a panic attack), or even angry; we can breathe quite rapidly and end up "over-breathing" or hyperventilating. Hyperventilation changes the correct balance of gases (oxygen and carbon dioxide) in our lungs, and this can make us feel faint, dizzy, sweaty and really uncomfortable physically. Breathing differently can, in both of these examples, help to change both our physical and our emotional states and we are able to return to a more equitable state; homeostasis.

Square breathing, or box breathing

A simple and useful breathing technique is known as square breathing, or box breathing. This breathing technique is one to try for helping yourself let go of tension and anxiety, and also manage feelings of acute anxiety and other strong emotions. As a learner, being able to use this technique will help you manage physical and emotional responses that might get in the way of your learning. It might also be useful before a very anxiety-provoking learning situation such as a test, presentation or examination.

How to practice square breathing, or box breathing

As you are breathing, visualise going around a square or box. Inhale slowly and deeply, as you visualise going up the first side of the square. By the time you've travelled up the first side, you will have filled your lungs. Turn the first corner of the square, and hold your breath for up to five seconds, as you visualise heading along the top side of the square. When you get to the end of the second side, visualise heading down the third side of the square as you breathe out slowly. Pause as you head along the final, fourth side of the square, taking up to five seconds to return to where you started, ready to start breathing in again as you go around each side of the square in turn. Take a few breaths using this visualisation.

Belly breathing, or diaphragmatic breathing

A related breathing technique is belly breathing, or diaphragmatic breathing. This can have a similar effect to the first breathing technique; slowing and calming your breathing and helping you to let go of tension and strong emotions. This technique helps you use your diaphragm, the large muscle just beneath our lungs that helps us respire (breathe in and out).

How to practice belly breathing, or diaphragmatic breathing

Make yourself comfortable either sitting or lying down. Take a deep slow breath in through your nose; expand your stomach muscles to draw air into your lungs (rather than using your upper chest). Imagine as you breathe in that there is a balloon in your stomach expanding; if it helps you, put a hand on the top of your stomach to help yourself feel the expansion. Hold your breath for a count or two, then breathe out slowly through your mouth. Keep doing this for a few minutes or until you feel calm and relaxed.

Going further

There is an interesting link between the breath and ideas as far as ancient Greece was concerned; the ancient Greeks (and other ancient cultures too) considered that ideas and inspiration came from outside the self, and a human could be the conduit for a gods-given creative outburst. From Greek to Latin, and our modern word "inspiration" means both the process of breathing in, and the experience of being struck by a great idea (indeed the expression "being struck by" an idea shows we might still think of ideas as things that arrive in us from somewhere outside us). See further reading and resources to read more about the ancient conceptualisation of inspiration. To go further with this activity, in addition to practicing the breathing technique as and when useful, consider if you see any links between the physical process of breathing in, and the conceptual process of generating ideas and learning. And if, in particular, you find using this breath technique of any help in your learning.

Further reading and resources

Diaphragmatic breathing, or belly breathing: https://www.nhs.uk/mental-health/self-help/guides-tools-and-activities/breathing-exercises-for-stress/

Inspiration: https://en.wikipedia.org/wiki/Artistic_inspiration

Over-breathing or hyperventilation: https://www.nhsborders.scot.nhs.uk/media/213548/Hyperventilation.pdf

Video guide to square breathing or box breathing: https://www.youtube.com/watch?v=tEmt1Znux58

Read more about types of breathing in different living creatures: https://bio.libretexts.org/Bookshelves/Introductory_and_General_Biology/Book%3A_General_Biology_(Boundless)/39%3A_The_Respiratory_System/39.10%3A_Breathing_-_Types_of_Breathing#:~:text=Types%20of%20breathing%20in%20humans,each%20requires%20slightly%20different%20processes.

Read more about another breathing technique: https://www.buteykobreathing.org/

7
THE FUTURE OF WELLBEING AND LEARNING – YOUR IMPACT ON THE WORLD

The future of learning and the future of wellbeing are intertwined, just as the present of learning and wellbeing are. This chapter is a consideration of some potential directions we may need to move in, both individually and collectively, if we are to continue to learn and thrive in an increasingly environmentally, economically and socially pressured world. Profound changes in multiple aspects of how we live have happened and are happening, with attendant profound impacts on our collective wellbeing and on our opportunities to learn effectively and beneficially. Both what we learn in the future, and how we learn it, are going to need to change, and change radically, in order for us to be able to build a liveable future.

Three key themes relating to the future of learning and wellbeing are considered below: climate change and climate collapse; the information-rich hyperconnected world; and finally, the need for finding ways to foster hope in the face of these challenges. The activities that follow this consideration are a start in perhaps offering some ways to prepare for our shared wellbeing-learning future.

Learning and wellbeing in a world impacted by climate change and climate collapse

One of the most significant factors impacting on the future wellbeing of us all will be climate change, or as it is now often described, climate breakdown. It would be a mistake to understand the types of harm and damage that climate change is and will cause as hierarchical, or to see some types of harm as located in one place and other types of harm located elsewhere. The immediate risk to life and damage to physical infrastructure, and the loss of liveable

DOI: 10.4324/9781003326786-8

places, due, for instance, to increased and more severe flooding or fires related to heatwaves, may indeed be geographically located, but the impacts of these harms in our interconnected world flow out from their locations and impact the wider world. Nor does the psychological impact of climate change locate itself only in those who live in areas not physically impacted by, for instance, extreme weather events; the psychological impacts of directly experiencing such events are obviously traumatic and significant. It may be more helpful to consider how to manage and respond to both the physical and the psychological impacts of climate change holistically; we cannot address one aspect without addressing the other.

Quite apart from the physical effects as they will impact our lives, the wellbeing effects of climate change are already significant and without question will become more so in the coming years. For those at the start of their lives today, this wellbeing impact is already significant. As Wendy Brown describes in *Nihilistic Times: Thinking with Max Weber*, "No generation has ever stared so directly into its own lack of collective future while managing such intense, complex requirements for building its personal and immediate one." Solastalgia is a word suggested by Glenn Albrecht in 2003 to describe the emotional and existential distress caused by an awareness of environmental change, destruction and degradation. In "This Changes Everything: Capitalism vs. The Climate," Naomi Klein writes of how her distress when reading about unexplained and climate-change linked species loss whilst researching her book was contrasted with reading children's stories to her young son about animals, and rock pooling with her niece. She describes speculating about her son's chances of seeing the animals she is reading to him about and fears he may not get to see some of the species under threat. In October 2021, William Shatner became the oldest human to go into space and described the experience as one that released strong emotions. "It was among the strongest feelings of grief I have ever encountered. The contrast between the vicious coldness of space and the warm nurturing of Earth below filled me with overwhelming sadness. Every day, we are confronted with the knowledge of further destruction of Earth at our hands: the extinction of animal species, of flora and fauna … things that took five billion years to evolve, and suddenly we will never see them again because of the interference of mankind. It filled me with dread. My trip to space was supposed to be a celebration; instead, it felt like a funeral" (Shatner 2022). There are many similar examples of psychological distress in the face of climate breakdown and ecological threats. The emotional impact of being conscious of the ongoing and potential further future loss of environmental richness, species and habitats, and the feeling of powerlessness attendant with knowing one's own individual actions may make little difference to this process, is fundamentally challenging to live with and is a significant consideration in managing our wellbeing. Having a name for the experience is one step, but the wider challenge we face is: how do we find ways to manage the impact of climate change on our collective wellbeing? We will need to consider how we manage and mitigate the significant impact on collective wellbeing of our new ecological and climate realities. This is already happening within, for instance, the scientific community and will need to be more broadly acknowledged and addressed in our societies in the years ahead.

Considering how to maintain wellbeing at an individual, community and wider society level is important. The changes already being experienced in our lives and in our social structures connected to climate change, and the associated disruptions that are likely to accelerate in the near future, are already creating, and will continue to create, distress and are already affecting, and will continue to affect, wellbeing. Managing these issues is becoming relevant for all of us. As elsewhere, this section considers the interlinked nature of learning and wellbeing. The activities in this chapter are some ideas for finding ways forward in supporting our own and our collective wellbeing and for facilitating our progress as learners both individually and collectively as we live with the consequences of human impacts on our global climate.

Learning and wellbeing in a world experiencing significant change in how information is created, shared, valued and learned

In recent years, the arrival and development of the Internet, and particularly social media, have profoundly changed the ways in which we share, access, store, value and understand, create and interact with information. There are difficulties along with opportunities in this ongoing fragmentation and pluralism of our representations of reality to ourselves.

David Bowie, speaking in an interview in 1999, said of the Internet (emergent at the time), "I don't think we've even seen the tip of the iceberg. I think the potential of what the Internet is going to do to society, both good and bad, is unimaginable. I think we are actually on the cusp of something exhilarating and terrifying!" He added, "I am talking about the actual context and the state of content is going to be so different to anything that we can really envisage at the moment, where the interplay between the user and the provider will be so in simpatico it's going to crush our ideas of what mediums are all about." Linking the emergent Internet with the developments in early twentieth-century art, he stated artists such as Duchamp advanced "the idea that the piece of work is not finished until the audience come to it and add their own interpretation, and what the piece of art is about is the grey space in the middle. That grey space in the middle is what the twenty-first century is going to be about." See further reading and resources to watch the full interview. This profound change to how information is shared and how art is created is with us now; as is a profound change to how our understanding of the world is shared and built, and this is all in the process of impacting on our wellbeing and on what and how we learn in wide-ranging ways.

More recently, the development of generative AI technology is beginning to have and will continue to have significant impacts on the nature of information: how we generate it, how we explore and access it, the sense we make of it, and on the ethical boundaries of authorship, creativity and understandings of origin in relation to what will be a very broad range of information sources. As AI chatbots become more prevalent, we are also about to face challenges to our understanding of what it means to have an interaction with another sentient being.

The changes and challenges to, and the impacts on, both how we learn, and on our collective wellbeing, are myriad. There have clearly been significant impacts from the above factors already and as these developments continue there are highly likely to be more. What we learn, how we learn it, and the value and validity of information itself are being shifted by these changes. There are potential beneficial developments; for instance, new forms of co-creating and collaborative work are enabled by social media-based interactions between user and provider in the "grey area" Bowie describes and these creations are already interesting and new. There are also more ambivalent, or even actively negative, developments, such as the spread of misinformation and the potential for manipulating democratic processes and societies. Navigating through the years of profound change ahead will be, as Bowie described, both exhilarating and terrifying.

Are we living in a blip culture?

Alvin Toffler describes a potential future of "blip culture" in his 1980 book *The Third Wave*. The extract below was published 24 years before the establishment of Facebook (established in 2004), 26 years before Twitter (2006), 30 years before Instagram (2010) and 36 years before TikTok (2016). In reading the extract, consider to what extent Toffler's description fits your experience of news, information and social media today. Toffler uses the First Wave as a term to describe the agricultural revolution, a wave of development and change spanning thousands of years; the Second Wave as a term to describe the industrial revolution, a wave of development and change spanning hundreds of years; and the Third Wave as a new wave of development and change commencing in the mid-twentieth century and continuing forward into the present time.

> The de-massification of the media de-massifies our minds as well. During the Second Wave era the continual pounding of standardized imagery pumped out by the media created what critics call a "mass mind." Today, instead of masses of people all receiving the same messages, smaller de-massified groups receive and send large amounts of their own imagery to one another. As the entire society shifts toward Third Wave diversity, the new media reflect and accelerate the process.

> This, in part, explains why opinions on everything from pop music to politics are becoming less uniform. Consensus shatters. On a personal level, we are all besieged and blitzed by fragments of imagery, contradictory or unrelated, that shake up our old ideas and come shooting at us in the form of broken or disembodied "blips." We live, in fact, in a blip culture.
>
> (Toffler, 1980)

Toffler goes on to argue that this rising blip culture creates different responses; one response, from anyone happier in the Second Wave world of more structured media and information-sharing, will be one of anger and disorientation, yearning for more easy certainties expressed as nostalgia for earlier forms of media, and feelings of isolation and withdrawal from engaging in this blip culture. The other response, Toffler argues, will be from those who feel at ease with these random, disconnected, blips of information. He writes, "Third Wave people…are more at ease in the midst of this bombardment of blips…they gulp huge amounts of information in short takes. But they also keep an eye out for those new concepts or metaphors that sum up or organise blips into larger wholes. Rather than trying to stuff the new modular data into the standard Second Wave categories or frameworks, they learn to make their own, to form their own "strings" out of the blipped material shot at them by the new media."

Aside from perfectly describing a Twitter thread a quarter of a century before the first one was to be posted, Toffler depicts a Third Wave world in which fragmented and disconnected information is something that may either overwhelm or hyper-engage its occupants. It also offers the opportunity, Toffler argues, to shape our sense of reality; "Instead of merely receiving our mental model of reality, we are now compelled to invent it and continually reinvent it." Finally, he argues that this Third Wave world, with its highly diverse culture, requires much higher levels of information to flow between all its constituent parts, to enable one part to predict how and what other parts may do in response to change. He writes, "As the people around us grow more individuated or de-massified, we need more information – signals and cues – to predict, even roughly, how they are going to behave towards us." These much higher requirements for informational flows and exchanges will result in the requirement for a completely different framework for what he terms "the info-sphere."

Toffler's descriptions of a possible future in 1980 seem to describe the informational, media and social media landscapes of the present with a great deal of acuity. If we are in any way concerned with learning; whether we are a learner, a co-learner or supporting client-learners whilst learning ourselves; then we need to be interested in what this Third Wave world means for learning. It is clear that it has already fundamentally altered both how we learn, and what we learn.

So what might living in a blip culture, with changed ways of creating and sharing and valuing information, mean for our collective wellbeing, and for learning? The prevalence of mental health difficulties may indicate that there are problems with our current cultures in terms of the effect on our wellbeing of living within them and participating in their methods of interaction and exchange. The negative impacts on mental health of, for example, social media have been prominent in public debate for some time; however, the opportunity to form networks of direct contact with other people, with geography and physical characteristics mattering, or mediating, less, is a benefit we might want to keep and build on. How to do so whilst lessening the potential for disbenefits? We are still all collectively working on that. And in terms of learning, the situation is equally complex. How we understand information and facts and truth, and how we know what to learn are changing, and indeed, as is considered throughout this book, may well need to change much more to meet our current and future needs.

How might our new modes of interacting and sharing information be affecting our wellbeing?

Use of social media platforms involves enormous numbers. Twitter is estimated to have over 350 million active monthly users; Instagram around 2.35 billion active monthly users; TikTok over a billion and Facebook over 2 billion. In a sense, we are in the process of externalising our internal mental functions to external locations; we share our ephemeral, passing thoughts online, as we have them, and they are broadcast to an audience without edges. They are also held on servers, like insects dropped into amber, and can be re-considered over and over again, and certainly long after the thought has passed across our minds. This is both fascinating and revealing, and also completely contrary to the way that we have lived until this point in our development.

If we see our current social media platforms as reflections of how we think, and if we see the technologies we develop as reflective of the ways our brains work, we can consider that what we've so far developed, has externalised only some parts of our brain structures. The ways in which our social media platforms currently work, with heightened emotions, lowered rationality, a sensory focus, high reactivity and a quick response particularly to ideas of threat and danger, as well as to pleasure, seem to fit with the here-and-now, limbic system, amygdala-influenced parts of our brains. This can be what makes them fun and exciting to engage with, and quite addictive too, but also explains why these platforms can be poor or even malevolent learning environments and can stoke problematic rather than strong learning.

So, have we managed to externalise some parts of our brains, but haven't yet managed to externalise the other parts that we need to use too? Are we living with our lids permanently flipped, as psychologist Dan Siegel's hand model of the brain demonstration might put it (see further resources)? Our current social media platforms definitely seem to lack the processing, timestamping and long-term memory formation elements that our hippocampi help us with. It's always now; Twitter, for instance, asks, "What's happening?" to prompt the tweeter, not "What happened?" And if it's always now, we're not creating any retained long-term memories. Additionally, being stuck in an always-now prevents us from being able to process and make sense of our distress; dealing with trauma (very frightening or terrible experiences) requires us to move even distressing experiences into our long-term memories. Given the prevalence of distressing content that we can encounter online, and given its tendency to hold us in an always-now state, preventing us from processing our distress, whilst continuing to serve up more distress (algorithms bringing us more of what we focus on), the environment can work as a kind of trauma machine.

Do we need to find ways of externalising our hippocampi and our prefrontal cortexes now too? And, for the sake of our collective wellbeing, do we need to consider how our current social media platforms could develop to bring more of these important brain functions into their operation, so that when we interact in those spaces, we can benefit from the many good ideas within them, without getting stuck inside an always-now trauma machine?

Holding hope for a learning-wellbeing future

Consider the following perspectives on the possibility of hope:

> Your actions matter. No action or voice is too small to make a difference.
> *(Nakate, 2021)*

> We can no longer let the people in power decide what hope is. Hope is not passive. Hope is not blah blah blah. Hope is telling the truth. Hope is taking action.
> *(Thunberg, 2021)*

> One of the tasks of the progressive educator is to unveil opportunities for hope, no matter what the obstacles may be.
> *(Friere, 1994)*

> We succumb to fatalism, and then it becomes impossible to muster the strength we absolutely need for a fierce struggle that will re-create the world. I am hopeful, not out of mere stubbornness, but out of an existential concrete imperative.
> *(Friere, 1994)*

Any act of learning is fundamentally an act of hope. In seeking to acquire new information, to incorporate it with what we already know, and to apply it to new situations, we express, by and in the act of so doing, whether consciously or not, a belief in the possibility of a future in which we will need and will be able to make use of this new learning. As hope is foundational to our wellbeing, we must ask ourselves, faced with the uncertain and challenging present, and the uncertain and challenging future, how do we keep learning, and maintain hope? The answers to these questions are likely to be as various and idiosyncratic as those who consider them and will depend profoundly on the life context of, and the opportunities available to, anyone seeking answers to them. The following activities are therefore not so much an attempt to provide easy answers (which there may not be) as an invitation to consider possible options and to identify possible directions, whether on an individual, personal level, within small learning and/or community groups, or within wider societal contexts. It may be that considering the questions will set us on the road towards both further, more helpful questions, and towards hope.

References: Learning and wellbeing in a world impacted by climate change and climate collapse

Shatner, W. (2022). *Boldly go: Reflections on a life of awe and wonder*. Simon & Schuster.

Further reading: Learning and wellbeing in a world impacted by climate change and climate collapse

11,000 Scientists warn the world faces a clear climate emergency: https://academic.oup.com/bioscience/article/70/1/8/5610806

Albrecht, G. (2005). Solastalgia: A new concept in human health and identity. *Philosophy, Activism, Nature*, 3: 41–55.

Brown, W. (2023). *Nihilistic Times: Thinking with Max Weber*. Harvard University Press.

Climate breakdown and wellbeing:

What is climate grief: https://www.climateandmind.org/what-is-climate-grief

Could feelings of climate grief catalyse change and action? https://www.abc.net.au/religion/rupert-read-climate-grief-could-be-the-making-of-us/14076522

Diagnosing "climate disorder": https://theecologist.org/2021/sep/27/diagnosing-climate-disorder

https://theecologist.org/2021/sep/27/diagnosing-climate-disorder

https://en.wikipedia.org/wiki/Ecological_grief

https://en.wikipedia.org/wiki/Solastalgia

Degrowth and eco-economic decoupling:

https://en.wikipedia.org/wiki/Degrowth

https://en.wikipedia.org/wiki/Eco-economic_decoupling#Lack_of_evidence_for_decoupling

Distress of scientists witnessing glacier loss:
https://www.theguardian.com/world/video/2023/apr/01/its-going-so-fast-the-decline-of-new-zealands-glaciers-video
https://www.theguardian.com/world/2023/apr/01/slipping-through-our-fingers-new-zealand-scientists-distraught-at-scale-of-glacier-loss

Donald, P. F. (2023). *Traffication: How the car killed the countryside*. Pelagic Publishing.

Ecological grief as a mental health response to climate change-related loss: https://www.nature.com/articles/s41558-018-0092-2

How climate breakdown and ecological crisis is impacting wellbeing: https://www.climateandmind.org/about

Intergovernmental Panel on Climate Change sixth assessment report: https://www.ipcc.ch/assessment-report/ar6/

Klein, N. This Changes Everything: Capitalism vs. the Climate. New York: Simon & Schuster, 2014

Reporting the impact on mental health of local population in a severe flooding event, British Columbia, November 2021:
https://bc.ctvnews.ca/it-s-overwhelming-one-missing-desperation-setting-in-for-b-c-residents-displaced-by-shattered-highway-8-1.5679872?cid=sm%3Atrueanthem%3Actvvancouver%3Atwitterpost&taid=619ee04ea5e4bc0001bd0ccd&utm_campaign=trueAnthem%3A+Trending+Content&utm_medium=trueAnthem&utm_source=twitter

Rupert Read. 2022. Why Climate Breakdown Matters: https://www.bloomsbury.com/au/why-climate-breakdown-matters-9781350212039/

Some ideas for managing eco-grief: https://ucalgary.ca/news/eco-grief-how-cope-emotional-impacts-climate-change

Study of the Permian-Triassic mass extinction indicates that rapid ecosystem collapse can follow biodiversity loss: http://bristol.ac.uk/news/2023/february/great-dying-biodiversity-loss.html

The economics of climate change: https://en.wikipedia.org/wiki/Economics_of_climate_change

The impact of climate breakdown on mental health: https://theecologist.org/2021/dec/21/climate-and-mental-breakdown

Vince, G. (2016). *Nomad century: How to survive the climate upheaval*. Penguin.

References: Learning and wellbeing in a world experiencing significant change in how information is created, shared, valued, and learned

Watch psychologist Dan Siegel demonstrating a "hand model" of the brain: https://www.youtube.com/watch?v=gm9CIJ74Oxw

Further reading: Learning and wellbeing in a world experiencing significant change in how information is created, shared, valued, and learned

Interview with David Bowie including description of how changes to the media landscape will bring about profoundly new forms of creating: https://www.youtube.com/watch?v=FiK7s_0tGsg

Toffler, A. (1980). *The third wave*. Collins.

References: Holding hope for a learning-wellbeing future

Friere, P. (2021). *Pedagogy of hope*. Bloomsbury Academic.

Nakate, V. (2021). COP26 Climate Summit, 2021: https://www.theglobeandmail.com/world/article-powerful-voice-of-ugandan-vanessa-nakate-helps-reframe-climate/#:~:text=Climate%20activist%20Vanessa%20Nakate%20attends%20a%20meeting%20at,year%20when%20Vanessa%20Nakate%20found%20her%20true%20voice.

Thunberg, G. (2021). TCOP26 Climate Summit, 2021: https://www.cnbc.com/2021/11/05/greta-thunberg-says-cop26-climate-summit-is-a-failure-and-a-pr-event.html

Further reading: Holding hope for a learning-wellbeing future

Freire, P. (1992). *Pedagogy of hope: Reliving pedagogy of the oppressed*. Continuum.

Oettingen, G., Sevincer, A. T., & Gollwitzer, P. (Eds.). (2018). *The psychology of thinking about the future*. The Guilford Press.

Pedagogy of hope: global learning and the future of education: https://uclpress.scienceopen.com/hosted-document?doi=10.14324/IJDEGL.13.2.01

ACTIVITIES

1. TIME FOR A LEARNING-WELLBEING RETHINK?

Time: 10 minutes or longer for reading and consideration time

Who this could be for: Anyone who would like to consider an alternative way of thinking about both personal and national/societal growth, beyond typical models

Resources needed: (optional) Internet access

Why do this: consider the potential parallels between the concepts of economic and personal growth, and identify what alternative conceptual models of both we might be able to develop

Considering the changes and challenges we are all facing, both in the present and that are likely to arise in the near future, is it time for us to reconsider our approach to both learning and wellbeing? This activity is a consideration of how our economic and individual ways of thinking might coincide and relate to each other; and how they might both, in synchronicity, be due for some changes.

From Gross Domestic Product to new ways of understanding national and international development

The modern concept of Gross Domestic Product was developed by economist Simon Kuznets in the 1930s as a measure of an economy's activity. A country's GDP is the total value in money of all goods and services produced inside a country's borders over a set period of time. Some possible limitations of GDP as a measure of activity were acknowledged, including by Kuznets himself; for instance, the potential for the over-simplification of the concept to result in a reductive or narrow application when measuring "success" for a national economy. Nevertheless, GDP has been widely used as an economic measurement since its creation. More recently, a series of developments and extensions of the idea have been proposed; see below, and further reading and resources for some examples.

Degrowth: beyond the concept of permanent economic growth

First named in the 1970s, degrowth has gone on to develop as a concept that offers a counterpoint to the idea that continued economic growth is always good. Degrowth seeks to reposition human health and happiness at the centre of how we understand the economic systems we live within. Instead of pursuing economic growth, degrowth focuses on directly improving human health and happiness. Degrowth also asks us to consider if focusing on economic growth in fact directly and indirectly impacts on and reduces human health and happiness, and also negatively impacts the environment; the world we share and live in together. It proposes an alternative way to develop, linked to reducing inequality; the least wealthy nations develop to move into line with wealthier nations; the wealthiest nations, already having enough wealth and resources for their needs, de-escalate growth. To read more about the concept of degrowth, see further reading and resources.

Personal development: a parallel with economic development?

Concepts of personal development, personal growth and personal improvement, developed from the early twentieth century onwards as the field of psychology progressed from analysis to concepts of active attempts to make personal change. The idea of self-improvement, whilst not wholly new, can be considered in relation to the idea of economic development. In fact, one of the earliest "self-help" works is closely aligned with economic growth; Wallace Wattles' 1910 *The Science of Getting Rich* offers ways to use changes to your thinking to attract wealth. Any perusal of the books for sale in airport departure lounges today will reveal how the intertwining of psychological change and self-work with getting richer is still very much active, as will any reading of social media accounts that promise psychological insights into the successful (i.e., wealth-generating) mind and how to make your mind more successful (i.e., wealth-generating).

A very widely known example of the interlinking of personal development and improvement with wealth–improvement is "the American dream;" a phrase first used in 1931 by American writer and historian James Truslow Adams in his book *The Epic of America*, where he defined it as meaning "that dream of a land in which life should be better and richer and fuller for everyone, with opportunity for each according to ability or achievement." Richer is the key word to keep in mind here. The economic development approaches of the twentieth century have certainly paid attention to the first section of the concept as Adams describes it; perhaps what Adams goes on to write is less well-known, but worth consideration in the light of this activity. He goes on to write, of "the American dream," that it "is a difficult dream for the European upper classes to interpret adequately, and too many of us ourselves have grown weary and mistrustful of it. It is not a dream of motor cars and high wages merely, but a dream of social order in which each man and each woman shall be able to attain to the fullest stature of which they are innately capable, and be recognized by others for what they are, regardless of the fortuitous circumstances of birth or position" (James Truslow Adams, *The Epic of America*, 1931, pp. 214–215). It may seem, in retrospect, that the "richer" part of the definition has won out over the statement that it is "not a dream of motor cars and high wages merely."

In short, the concept of personal wellbeing has often been linked to wealth increase, and the promise of improving one leading to improving the other has sold a countless number of self-help books. The language itself reinforces the idea that a "perpetual growth" model is appropriate, desirable and in fact beneficial in relation to individual character and experience. Perhaps the way we think about ourselves has mirrored the way that we have considered and conceptualised economic developments in the twentieth and early twenty-first centuries. If so, at what cost to our true wellbeing needs?

It may be that we are starting to reappraise the validity of connecting economic growth and personal satisfaction and wellbeing; potential new ways of supporting wellbeing, such as the four-day workweek movement (see further reading and resources), may indicate that we are beginning to consider ways of fostering wellbeing outside our previously held economic-societal norms. Additionally, the growth in popularity of secular meditation and mindfulness may also indicate a growing awareness that wellbeing is not about achievement but can be about just being and noticing, just as we are right now. Could moving away from concepts of personal development, and towards less work and more mindful noticing, be part of a recipe for a post-perpetual economic growth, learning-wellbeing rethink?

Learning

The politics of learning; who learns, who learners are educated for, what is learned, and what the purpose of mass education is, is such a vast subject as to be almost impossible to summarise briefly. In relation to the possible parallels between economic and personal growth, we can consider whether our ideas around learning are also reflective of this perpetual growth approach. Seeing learning as a perpetual linear movement from ignorance to knowledge would echo the concept of growth; is this however the best way of understanding learning? Running parallel to this concept of learning, however, are variations of the statement "the more I know, the less I know," attributed in varying forms to Aristotle, Socrates, Einstein, Percy Bysshe Shelly and Tony Bennet. If we acknowledge this venerable description of learning and gaining knowledge, we are thinking of a very non-linear journey; less a progression from ignorance to knowledge, and more a circular journey that might lead you back to not merely where you started out, but some way further back than that.

Would a rethinking of how we see learning be relevant in light of a potential change to how we see wellbeing? Particularly if we consider that the politics of what learners learn, and who they learn it for, in a perpetual growth-aligned society is likely to reflect the needs of perpetual growth; learners need to be educated into being participants in the perpetual growth model. What is learned will have to relate to what goods and services are produced; both in the sense of providing future workers within those goods and services-producing fields, future researchers, engineers, product developers etc., and in the sense of providing consumers of those goods and services. If our current systems of learning serve this end, we will need to reconsider them to reflect moving away from perpetual growth economic models.

A wellbeing and learning rethink: some ideas and questions to reflect on …

Having read the above, here are some questions for consideration. In twentieth- and early twenty-first-century culture, the concept of perpetual economic growth has been accompanied by concepts relating to character or personality growth on an individual level. Phrases such as "personal growth," "personal development" and "personal improvement" have all been used to describe the process of self-improvement. What if we've internalised the perpetual economic growth-oriented mindset and it's influenced how we see and understand ourselves? The concepts of personal development and self-improvement have a similar linear, developmental trajectory to the concept of economic growth; from less developed to more developed; from not good to better. What if we took another view in relation to ourselves and our state of "personal development?" What if, for example, we were to say, instead of that we are on a linear path of progression towards an improved self, that we are enough, and good enough, just as we are, and right now?

With the increasing prominence of alternative ways of understanding and conceptualising the development of our cultures, and a potential move away from the idea of perpetual economic growth, do we need to consider an aligned alteration in how we think about the support of our wellbeing? What would a non-linear, cyclical concept of wellbeing look like? Are there alternative models of wellbeing and personal development that we could draw on to help us move away from the growth-oriented model of individual wellbeing through personal development? Other models the world may offer us for understanding wellbeing both individual and collective may include models that are agricultural, cyclical or oceanic; can you identify other options?

In many senses, centring the self and reinforcing individuality is important and helpful in a consumer/capitalist economic culture; "because I'm worth it." Would the use of different models to conceptualise wellbeing de-centre the individual self and ground each individual self more within cycles of other selves who are equally important, or within communities?

What if we also developed alternative ways of understanding and conceptualising the experience of learning, both its nature and the reasons for it, in light of our rethinking about economic growth and personal wellbeing? Does this idea lead us to question and perhaps understand differently the process and purpose of learning; what exactly it is we are doing when we learn, and why exactly we do it? If we thought of the process of learning in this different way, would we also need to consider what it is that we need to learn, to be part of this changed development-wellbeing-learning society?

Going further

Read the World Happiness Report's chapter on wellbeing and state effectiveness (see further resources and reading). What does the chapter have to say about what attributes and qualities a state needs to have to support the wellbeing of its citizens? You could also consider the nine domains of Bhutan's Gross National Happiness Index to inform your thinking:

1 Psychological wellbeing
2 Health
3 Education
4 Time use
5 Cultural diversity and resilience
6 Good governance
7 Community vitality
8 Ecological diversity and resilience
9 Living standards

(Gross National Happiness Index, 2023)

When you have considered what qualities are needed for a state to support and foster wellbeing according to the World Happiness Report, and also considered the nine domains that the Bhutan GNH Index uses in its measurement of happiness, take some time to come up with a plan for how a country of your choice (or a country you might like to make up for the purposes of this extended activity) can either enhance and protect these building blocks of wellbeing if they are already present, or introduce and develop them if they are not. You could also come up with some domains to measure success against drawing on what you have read for this activity.

References

Gross Domestic Product: https://en.wikipedia.org/wiki/Gross_domestic_product

Further resources

A history of the degrowth concept: https://degrowth.info/en/history
Beyond GDP, World Economic Forum: https://www.weforum.org/focus/beyond-gdp
Degrowth: https://www.weforum.org/agenda/2022/06/what-is-degrowth-economics-climate-change

GDP and beyond: measuring progress in a changing world, EU: https://eur-lex.europa.eu/LexUriServ/LexUriServ.do?uri=COM:2009:0433:FIN:EN:PDF
Gross Domestic Product: https://en.wikipedia.org/wiki/Gross_domestic_product
Gross national happiness index:
https://www.grossnationalhappiness.com/
https://ophi.org.uk/policy/gross-national-happiness-index/
Meadows, D. H., Meadows, D. L., Randers, J., Behrens, III., & William, W. (1972). The limits to growth; A report for the club of Rome's project on the predicament of mankind. *Demography*, 10: 289–299. https://doi.org/10.2307/2060819
Open letter advocating for degrowth, 2020: https://degrowth.info/en/open-letter
The four-day work week movement: https://en.wikipedia.org/wiki/Four-day_workweek
The Limits to Growth, fifty years on: https://www.clubofrome.org/ltg50/ https://ophi.org.uk/policy/gross-national-happiness-index/
World Happiness Report 2023: https://worldhappiness.report/
World Happiness Report: Wellbeing and State Effectiveness: https://happiness-report.s3.amazonaws.com/2023/WHR+23_Ch3.pdf

2. MODELLING AND PASSING IT ON

Time: flexible; depending on which aspects of the activity you select to try

Who this could be for: anyone who wants to boost their learning by taking advantage of the protégé effect

Resources needed: depending on the activity elements selected; potential resources needed may be research materials, Internet access, teaching aids such as presentations or visual aids

Why do this: boost your learning by sharing your learning with others; gain an additional benefit in supporting your own wellbeing by gaining a sense of achievement, reinforcing your self-efficacy and giving to others

Having an impact on the world is something you might want to do; it might be that you would like to positively impact the world via improving your own wellbeing, and supporting the wellbeing of others. It may be that you enjoy learning and sharing what you have learned with others. This activity offers a way to bring both of these together; in the main activity, by finding out about the protégé effect, and using it to boost your own learning; in the going further section, by finding out about social learning theory and considering how it could be relevant to having a positive impact on the wellbeing of others now and into the future, considering the challenges we will face and are already facing. If, as social learning theory proposes, we learn by observing others, then to influence the world in positive ways, modelling the behaviour that you want to encourage around you is important. Writer Annie Dillard goes further, asserting that not sharing what we know with others results in us losing what we try to keep for ourselves; "… the impulse to keep to yourself what you have learned is not only shameful, it is destructive. Anything you do not give freely and abundantly becomes lost to you. You open your safe and find ashes" (Dillard, 1989).

The protégé effect, or the learning-by-teaching effect, is worth knowing about. You can boost your own learning by using this effect to your advantage, as well as benefiting others too. Essentially, if you spend time teaching others what you have learned, you will understand it better, and retain your new knowledge about what you have studied better, than if you simply go over it again for yourself. One possible way this effect helps and boosts your learning is by making you retrieve the information you have learned in order to share it with others; repeated retrieval seems to help embed learning. There may be other mechanisms at work too, for instance, being motivated to learn something more thoroughly due to the social expectation of others; if you are presenting your learning to a group, you might feel negatively motivated to do it well (or not to do it badly!) in order to avoid looking silly or embarrassing yourself; or you might be somewhat more positively motivated to do a good job so that your learning colleagues can get the best learning experience they can.

For this activity, select an aspect of something you are currently learning about. You are going to share your knowledge with others, how you do this is your choice and may depend on the type of knowledge you are going to share; you might, for example, prepare a brief presentation of your knowledge, or set up an experiment that you are going to demonstrate, or build a model, or have one or more physical examples of what you are going to be sharing. You might have chosen to demonstrate a dance move you have learned, or how to play a musical instrument. You might consider giving a demonstration and making it participative; are you going to give your attendees a chance to join in and have a go? When you are ready, invite at least one other person (ideally more, if possible) along to hear and see what you have to share.

Take some time to reflect on what you have learned from this activity afterwards, and also notice what effect it has had on your understanding of the learning that you have shared with others. Do you notice that you have a different grasp on the subject now than you had before you completed this activity?

Going further

If you have completed the first part of this activity and shared your learning with others, ask for their feedback. How did they find it? What went well, what could have gone better? Do they have any suggestions for improving or changing how you share your learning with them? You can use this further step to inform your own learning even more. Seeking responses also has the added benefit of giving you experience of handling feedback, including negative feedback; this is a skill that actually a lot of people can struggle with, but something that is of huge benefit to you if you want to learn from others and improve what you do. If you can learn to stay with the feeling of being criticised legitimately, rather than getting away from it as quickly as possible if you find it aversive, you can learn that it's not fatal and actually is potentially one of the best presents you can be given!

Some tips on handling feedback and benefiting from it can be found here:

https://www.ausmed.co.uk/cpd/articles/how-to-handle-feedback-in-10-steps
https://www.themuse.com/advice/taking-constructive-criticism-like-a-champ
https://www.creativeboom.com/tips/how-to-deal-with-feedback-and-criticism-positively/

An additional going further is to read about Albert Bandura's Social Learning Theory (see further reading and resources). Bandura's theory proposes that we learn via observing and then making sense of the behaviours of others that we see around us; if this is the case, take some time to consider how you might use this to positively influence others around you. Could you draw on this to influence littering behaviours in shared outdoor areas, for example?

Works well with

Activity 8, Chapter 2: Approach/avoid awareness: goal orientation theory and your learning

References

Dillard, A. (2013). The writing life. Harper Collins Publishers.

Further reading

Brown, T., Ham, S., & Hughes, M. (2010). Picking up litter: An application of theory-based communication to influence tourist behaviour in protected areas. *Journal of Sustainable Tourism*, 18: 2010/08/2010. https://www.researchgate.net/publication/45192938_Picking_up_Litter_An_Application_of_Theory-based_Communication_to_Influence_Tourist_Behaviour_in_Protected_Areas

Logan, F., & Mayer, R. E. (2013). The relative benefits of learning by teaching and teaching expectancy. *Contemporary Educational Psychology*, 38(4): 281–288.

Lun, K., Aloysius, W., Lee, Sze Chi, & Lim, S. W. H. L. (May/June 2018). The learning benefits of teaching: A retrieval practice hypothesis. *Applied Cognitive Psychology*, 32(3).

Social Learning Theory: https://www.simplypsychology.org/bandura.html

3. MAKING A FRIEND OF UNCERTAINTY

Time: 15 minutes or longer depending on the activity or activities selected

Who this could be for: anyone who would like to find out more about how their response to uncertainty influences their wellbeing and their learning

Resources needed: Internet access; then resources depending on which, if any, uncertainty-befriending activities you try

Why do this: make a friend of uncertainty to boost your overall wellbeing and benefit your learning

The future is going to contain a lot of uncertainty. As we have explored in this book, the intersecting crises, and challenges we face from economic, environmental, conflict, displacement and community health perspectives are interacting, and are going to continue to interact, in unpredictable and disruptive ways for many years. Being able to cope with the uncertain future and thrive is going to be a key part of maintaining our wellbeing as learners and as members of our communities. In short, uncertainty is something to make a friend of now to be a current, and near-future successful learner.

Uncertainty is also of course a core element within the experience of learning; if we see learning as a process of taking on new information, making new links, and building new understandings, uncertainty is a fundamental part of learning. As we learn, we are often moving from a situation of uncertainty; there are things we don't know; to certainty; we gain knowledge. The opposite is also an important part of learning; we can move from being certain of something to becoming uncertain of it when our previously held understandings are challenged by new information and learning. We might have thought we knew how something worked, for example, and we learn something that makes us realise we didn't understand how it works at all. Being able to manage uncertainty is clearly relevant to us as learners.

If you are aware that uncertainty is something you either dislike, or seek to minimise, or if you notice you put a lot of effort into acquiring certainty, this activity offers some ideas for playing with uncertainty and in doing so building more of a toleration for it, and even, maybe, an enjoyment of it.

If you dislike uncertainty or find it difficult to tolerate, one of the things you might find yourself doing is trying to reduce, minimise or even eliminate it completely from your experience. This can be a little like trying to grasp flowing water; the more you try to grasp it, the more it runs through your hands! An alternative, somewhat counter-intuitive approach is to stop trying to get rid of uncertainty because that's an impossible task, and instead build a toleration of uncertainty and even perhaps make friend of it.

You can test your levels of toleration of uncertainty by completing the Intolerance of Uncertainty Scale – see further reading and resources. If uncertainty does seem to be something you dislike, and if you notice that you do make efforts to lessen or remove it that either backfire or make some kind of negative impact on your life, without being successful, you could go on to try some of the ideas below for building up a tolerance of uncertainty and even potentially finding some positive attributes in it. Here are just a few suggestions for making a friend of uncertainty. If you can think of other, better ideas, then go ahead – this activity is likely to be most beneficial to you if it involves ideas you have chosen yourself, and which activate the most unenjoyable elements of uncertainty for you.

Uncertainty befriending idea 1: the chicken of uncertainty

This idea involves drawing a chicken. Select something to draw on, and some drawing materials, in different colours. Set your work area up so you have what you are going to draw with (pens, pencils, pastels etc.) laid out in easy reach. For each part of the chicken you draw (beak, wing, neck, feet etc.), select a different colour, but do it with your eyes closed. You can open your eyes once you've selected the colour, but when you've completed that bit of the chicken, close your eyes to select a colour for the next bit. By the time you have finished drawing your chicken, it should be looking quite colourful!

If you enjoyed drawing the chicken of uncertainty, you might like to try the same technique with some other animals and draw a whole wildlife reserve, jungle, forest, ocean or ecosystem of uncertainty.

Uncertainty befriending idea 2: surprise supper (or breakfast, lunch, tea, midnight snack, etc.)

Meal planning can give us some certainty; this idea is bringing in the opposite of this in relation to what you are going to have for a meal of your choice. This will probably work best with tinned food, but any food you can remove identifying information from for use in this activity could also be used. Select some tinned items, between three and five tins would be enough, and remove their labels. Try not to keep track of what is in what tin! Now randomly choose two or three tins. This is your surprise meal; open the tins and decide what you're going to make. You can incorporate other ingredients in if you want. If you have any tins left over, keep them to one side ready for a further surprise meal.

For consideration if you want to try this activity: if you are not responsible for buying your household's food, check with whoever buys the food before trying this activity. If your food budget is tight, don't undertake this activity if it would reduce the amount of nutrition you can get; an alternative activity might be more helpful. If you are preparing food for others using this activity idea, make sure you are aware of any food allergies those you are preparing food for have and select your ingredients accordingly, at the stage prior to removal of labels!

Uncertainty befriending idea 3: visualisation: from trying to hold running water in your hands, to ...?

Take some time to visualise uncertainty as water running from a tap, or a spring. Visualise trying to grasp and stop it all as it flows; notice the feelings as you find you can't capture it all. Now imagine an alternative visual image for uncertainty; what can you visualise it as, that changes the feeling of trying and failing to grasp and stop it? If you keep with the water theme, do you want to visualise giving up grasping, and instead diving into the water and letting yourself swim and float in it? Try to identify an alternative visual image that makes interacting with uncertainty a more pleasant and less stressful experience. What this might be is entirely dependent on you.

Uncertainty befriending idea 4: odd socks experiment

If you wear socks, when you are next getting dressed, select the socks you are going to wear either 1) without looking or 2) by mixing up your pairs of socks and taking a lucky dip approach, so you might end up with matching socks, or not. Notice how it makes you feel to try this. To really increase the uncertainty exposure in this idea, if it's safe to do so, keep your eyes closed while you put your socks on and don't look at what you're wearing until you have put them on. See how long you can hold off taking a peek to see what you've ended up with on your feet. You can take this idea even further by purchasing some socks that are already odd! You can select another item of clothing to try this idea with if you would prefer.

Going further

The above ideas are just four of very many possibilities for generating a feeling of uncertainty in order to build up a toleration for, and even an enjoyment of it. Feel free to come up with more of your own ideas; you could also ask others to suggest some ideas for you to try. If you keep practicing this kind of activity you may notice that you start to feel differently towards uncertainty over time. It's worth re-reading the Intolerance of Uncertainty Scale (see further reading and resources) after a while of practicing these ideas to see what and how your feelings towards uncertainty have shifted. Have you learned anything about uncertainty, and about yourself, in doing these activities? What would you say now about uncertainty compared to what you might have said before?

Further reading

Buhr, K., & Dugas, M. J. (2002). The intolerance of uncertainty scale: Psychometric properties of the English version. *Behaviour Research and Therapy*, 40: 931–945.

Dugas, M. J., Gagnon, F., Ladouceur, R., & Fabien, M. H. (1998). Generalized anxiety disorder: A preliminary test of a conceptual model. *Behaviour Research and Therapy*, 36(2): 215–226. https://doi.org/10.1016/S0005-7967(97)00070-3.

Dugas, M. J., Sexton, K. A., Elizabeth, A., Hebert, E. A., Bouchard, S., Gouin, J.-P., & Shafran R. (November 2022). Behavioral experiments for intolerance of uncertainty: A randomized clinical trial for adults with generalized anxiety disorder. *Behavior Therapy*, 53(6): 1147–1160.

How the brain reacts to uncertainty: https://nesslabs.com/uncertain-mind

Intolerance of Uncertainty Scale: https://www.phenxtoolkit.org/protocols/view/650701

4. GOING BEYOND PROBLEM-SOLVING

Time: 15–30 minutes or longer as you wish

Who this could be for: anyone who would like to explore some ways of thinking that might be beyond, or beside, the problem/solution framework

Resources needed: for some of the activities, you will need someone else to work with, paper, and writing materials

Why do this: go beyond problem-solving to find different ways of considering things and of thinking about things. Find out if taking a different perspective on structuring what to think about and what to learn gives you a different perspective on what to ask in the first place

Problem-solving is a learning approach that is embedded into the way many subjects are taught and is frequently part of learning situations. It can be particularly useful, but is there something beyond or beside the problem-solving approach that might become relevant and helpful in the future? This activity asks whether there is an approach to learning beyond the problem/solution dichotomy and makes some suggestions for you to build on as to what that beyond problem-solving approach might comprise.

Going beyond problem-solving: is there a way of thinking about things beyond the problem/solution dichotomy?

A way of thinking known as the law of instrument, or Maslow's hammer, was defined by Abraham Maslow as "If the only tool you have is a hammer, it is tempting to treat everything as if it were a nail." The idea seeks to encapsulate the way that we might rely too much on a familiar option; perhaps to the extent of failing to notice that the option we are so well-used to using isn't actually all that good a fit for the situation we are using it in. Essentially, not everything needs hitting with a hammer! In consideration of what may lie beyond problem-solving, we might extend Maslow's hammer concept to "if the only way you make sense of the world is as a series of problems, it is tempting to believe you need to find solutions to everything."

There are of course benefits to a problem-solving mindset and there are many times when we need to work on changing how something is done or organised to make things better, more efficient, fairer, or to make some other relevant gain. What happens, however, if we decide to frame the world differently? Do we miss noticing the non-problematic elements of a situation once we define it as a problem that needs fixing? Is there a way of making sense of the world that doesn't set up the problem/solution dichotomy? What if this binary approach, in short, isn't as helpful as it can seem? At the risk of falling into the problem/solution dichotomy-thinking that we are discussing, and seeing "problem/solution thinking" as the problem that we're seeking solutions to, the following ideas are for your consideration; do they take us beyond a problem-solving mindset to a more helpful approach? If they don't, what might do so?

Can we use the attributes of the problem to help – does the problem contain its own solution?

What if the problem that we have noticed has already solved itself; or already contains the solution to what seems to be a problem within itself? If you want to try this idea, identify something you consider to be problematic; either directly within your own life or a situation you are aware of in the wider world. Firstly, express the problem as a statement or sentence. Next, take the view that either 1) this problem I have defined has already been solved or 2) the solution to this problem I have defined is already contained within itself. Now, work backwards from there; what do you notice? Does this way of thinking unlock anything helpful to you? If the problem has already been solved, see if you can identify what's happened for this to be the case. If it contains its own solution, what aspects of it are part of that?

This style of thinking might lead you on to seeing problematic situations in a different way and possibly help to identify resources and opportunities that wouldn't be as apparent if you were seeing a problem/solution dichotomy. Two examples:

- If, for instance, we were to consider malaria and other diseases spread by mosquitoes as a problem, if we see the problem as containing its own solution, could we use mosquitoes to deliver malaria vaccines, or medicine? (yes: https://www.npr.org/sections/goatsandsoda/2022/09/21/1112727841/a-box-of-200-mosquitoes-did-the-vaccinating-in-this-malaria-trial-thats-not-a-jo)
- If we were to see hay fever as a problem, if we see the problem as containing its own solution, could we use tree-like structures to disseminate pollen-like antidotes to hay fever that could be released and breathed in by hay fever sufferers at the same time trees are releasing their pollen?

The inventor's paradox

Read about the inventor's paradox. Does this idea align or complement the above approach?

The inventor's paradox: https://en.wikipedia.org/wiki/Inventor%27s_paradox

Yes, No or Mu: the concept of unasking the question rather than solving the problem that the question frames

We often find ourselves working within a problem-solving mindset and within problem-based frameworks when we learn. This is often encouraged or facilitated by the way that the information we are learning or studying is framed and it definitely has a lot of value as a learning approach. However, is there another way of learning, beyond (or alongside) this? The concept of "mu" provides the opportunity to consider, have we framed what we are seeking to understand or explore correctly? Or, do we need to take a step or two back, and ask ourselves different questions altogether?

This activity is relevant to both learning and personal wellbeing too; it might be that you can identify ways that the response of "mu" is more helpful than either "yes" or "no," when it comes to dealing with questions about your own life choices and how to look after your own wellbeing.

For this activity, work with one or more others to generate an asking/unasking game. There are four stages:

1 Choose a subject you are learning about or studying (or that is of interest to participants) and generate a list of closed questions that you might ask about it. The questions can have any theme or content relevant to the subject you have selected. The questions you generate should be potentially possible to answer with either a yes or a no. For example, if your theme is geography, a closed question might be "is it possible to identify the source of a river?"
2 Once you have generated a reasonable number of closed questions, write each one on a separate piece of paper ready to deal out like playing cards.
3 Take it in turns to deal out each question; the dealer asks the other player or players, who can respond with either "yes," "no" or "mu." Anyone who says "mu" should be prepared to explain why they are proposing that this question is "unasked."
4 If you want to, any questions that resulted in a "mu," can be considered further; do you want to come up with new or reframed questions? Do those questions point you to further learning or send you in a different direction with the subject or an aspect of the subject you chose?

Going further with the yes, no or mu game: wellbeing

Using the same structure as outlined above, generate an asking/unasking game with the theme of personal wellbeing. As an example, one of your question cards could be, "should I work harder to achieve happiness?" with the players choosing to respond, either "yes," "no" or "mu," and prepared to explain and elaborate on their choices.

Finally: if after all that you still really like problem-solving …

Hungarian mathematician George Pólya provided an interesting guide to problem-solving in his 1945 book, *How to Solve It: a system of thinking which can help you solve any problem*. Along with suggestions for a sequential approach to considering any problem, he also offers a range of heuristics (methods or techniques for resolving issues that aren't exactly perfect but offer a "good enough" answer or approximate answer; for example, taking your best guess) to help with solving tricky problems. The heuristics are as follows:

TABLE 7.1 How to solve it

Heuristic	Informal description	Formal analogue
Analogy	Can you find a problem analogous to your problem and solve that?	Map
Auxiliary Elements	Can you add some new elements to your problem to get closer to a solution?	Extension
Generalisation	Can you find a problem more general than your problem?	Generalisation
Induction	Can you solve your problem by deriving a generalisation from some examples?	Induction
Variation of the Problem	Can you vary or change your problem to create a new problem (or set of problems) whose solution(s) will help you solve your original problem?	Search
Auxiliary Problem	Can you find a subproblem or side problem whose solution will help you solve your problem?	Subgoal
Here is a problem related to yours and solved before	Can you find a problem related to yours that has already been solved and use that to solve your problem?	Pattern recognition Pattern matching Reduction
Specialisation	Can you find a problem more specialised?	Specialisation
Decomposing and Recombining	Can you decompose the problem and "recombine its elements in some new manner"?	Divide and conquer
Working backward	Can you start with the goal and work backwards to something you already know?	Backward chaining
Draw a Figure	Can you draw a picture of the problem?	Diagrammatic reasoning

Source: Polya (1946)

Consider Polya's ideas for problem-solving as given in the table above and see if they lead you beyond problem-solving in relation to anything you are working on or learning about.

Works well with

Activity 6, Chapter 3: Helicopter view: getting some perspective
Activity 7, Chapter 5: Building new ways of learning

Further reading

Closed questions: https://en.wikipedia.org/wiki/Closed-ended_question
Heuristics: https://en.wikipedia.org/wiki/Heuristic
Koans: https://www.britannica.com/topic/koan
Maslow, A. H. (1966). *The psychology of science: A reconnaissance.* Harper & Row.
Mu, or unask the question: beyond yes/no answers: https://www.awakin.org/v2/read/view.php?tid=583
https://en.wikipedia.org/wiki/Mu_(negative)#:~:text=The%20Japanese%20and%20Korean%20term,in%20Buddhism%2C%20especially%20Zen%20traditions
Open questions: https://en.wikipedia.org/wiki/Open-ended_question
Polya, G. (1990). *How to Solve It: A system of thinking which can help you solve any problem.* Penguin.

5. WELLBEING AND LEARNING ONLINE: FROM TRAUMA MACHINE TO A MORE WELLBEING-SUPPORTIVE SOCIAL MEDIA ENVIRONMENT?

Time: 15 minutes or more

Who this could be for: anyone who would like to consider how we could change the online world and social media platforms to make them more human-friendly and less damaging to our wellbeing

Resources needed: Internet access if looking at examples/researching

Why do this: come up with some ways to make the online world less trauma-generating, without losing the good aspects of our connected information sphere

If we see our current social media platforms as reflections of how we think, and if we see the technologies we develop as reflective of the ways our brains work, we can consider that what we've so far developed, has externalised only some parts of our brain structures. The ways in which our social media platforms currently work, with heightened emotions, lowered rationality, a sensory focus, high reactivity and a quick response particularly to ideas of threat and danger, as well as to pleasure, seem to fit with the here-and-now, limbic system, amygdala-influenced parts of our brains.

This can be what makes them fun and exciting to engage with, and quite addictive too, but also explains why these platforms can be poor or even malevolent learning environments and can stoke problematic rather than strong learning.

So, have we managed to externalise some parts of our brains, but haven't yet managed to externalise the other parts that we need to use too? Are we living with our lids permanently flipped, as psychologist Dan Siegel's hand model of the brain demonstration might put it (see further resources)? Our current social media platforms definitely seem to lack the processing, timestamping and long-term memory formation elements that our hippocampi help us with. It's always now; Twitter, for instance, asks, "What's happening?" to prompt the tweeter, not "What happened?" And if it's always now, we're not creating any retained long-term memories. Additionally, being stuck in an always-now prevents us from being able to process and make sense of our distress; dealing with trauma (very frightening or terrible experiences) requires us to move even distressing experiences into our long-term memories. Given the prevalence of distressing content that we can encounter online, and given its tendency to hold us in an always-now state, preventing us from processing our distress, whilst continuing to serve up more distress (algorithms bringing us more of what we focus on), the environment can work as a kind of trauma machine.

Do we need to find ways of externalising our hippocampi and our prefrontal cortexes now too? And, for the sake of our collective wellbeing, do we need to consider how our current social media platforms could develop to bring more of these important brain functions into their operation, so that when we interact in that space, we can benefit from the many good ideas of them, it without getting stuck inside an always-now trauma machine? Consider the above. Do you find this a helpful way of thinking about social media? If so, what parts of our brains do you equate with what types of social media platforms?

For the final part of this activity, if you found some parts and functions of our brains that aren't really replicated in any type of online platform, identify which parts and processes you consider to be missing from our online environments. As a further step, give some thought to what type of online environment you would design that would mimic or complement the brain activity and process of the part or parts you identified as missing.

Going further

If you come up with any good ideas to extend and support wellbeing working with learners, you could consider developing a new social media platform to test out your plans.

References

'To better explain how the barking dog and wise owl work, Dr. Dan Siegel developed a simple hand signal to explain to young children. This easy-to-teach hand model helps kids better understand what is happening in their brain and why they feel the way they do in a given moment.'
www.thebehaviorhub.com/podcast/2022/8/26/the-brain-in-the-palm-of-your-hand-dan-siegels-hand-model
The Brain in the Palm of your Hand: Dan Siegel's Hand Model

Further reading and resources

How Mastodon works: https://en.wikipedia.org/wiki/Mastodon_(social_network)
How the brain works: https://www.hopkinsmedicine.org/health/conditions-and-diseases/anatomy-of-the-brain
How trauma affects us: https://www.psychologytoday.com/gb/blog/the-addiction-connection/202103/how-trauma-affects-the-body
Mastodon's description of itself: https://joinmastodon.org/
Vicarious trauma: https://www.bma.org.uk/advice-and-support/your-wellbeing/vicarious-trauma/vicarious-trauma-signs-and-strategies-for-coping
Watch psychologist Dan Siegel demonstrating a "hand model" of the brain: https://www.youtube.com/watch?v=gm9CIJ74Oxw

6. HOW CAN WE MANAGE ECO-GRIEF AND ECO-ANXIETY?

Time: 15 minutes or longer

Who this could be for: anyone who would like to consider how climate breakdown is impacting our wellbeing and how we might manage that

Resources needed: Internet access

Why do this: understand the impacts on wellbeing of climate breakdown and come up with some ideas for managing these

Solastalgia is a word suggested by Glenn Albrecht in 2003 to describe the emotional and existential distress caused by an awareness of environmental change, destruction and degradation. Anxiety, grief and distress are reasonable and increasingly common psychological responses to the combination of climate breakdown, extreme weather and the perceived difficulties in making changes to the way that we live in and use our world. Other descriptive terms for these feelings include ecological grief or eco-grief, and eco-anxiety.

The emotional impact of being conscious of the ongoing and potential further future loss of environmental richness, species and habitats, and the feeling of powerlessness attendant with knowing one's own individual actions may make little difference to this process, is fundamentally challenging to live with and is a significant consideration in managing our wellbeing. It has a significant impact on the physical safety as well as the psychological wellbeing of anyone directly impacted by climate breakdown and extreme weather events, of course; even those in relatively privileged positions where they are not at risk of immediate severe harm themselves from climate breakdown-related events are negatively impacted; for instance, scientists studying the decline of the Great Barrier Reef describe negative responses including hopelessness and fear (Conroy, 2019).

Both now, and increasingly in future years, we will need to consider how we manage and mitigate the significant impact on collective wellbeing of our new ecological and climate realities. This activity asks you to consider, either with others in a learning group or on your own, how do we find ways to manage the impact of climate change on our collective wellbeing?

Spend some time considering these questions, and research and find out more using the further reading and resources section to start you off. You can use the following prompt questions to help your thinking; don't limit yourself to these if you would rather consider other questions.

- How does what's happening with our global climate affect my wellbeing?
- How does what's happening with our global climate affect the wellbeing of others; the wellbeing of scientists who are involved in researching it; our collective wellbeing?
- What might help us maintain good wellbeing despite these realities?

Going further

To go further with this activity, if you, and/or others whom you have worked with, have come up with any ideas for wellbeing management in response to climate breakdown, consider putting your ideas into practice. Have you identified a project or projects that will engage others around you in an activity that supports wellbeing and benefits your local environment, or the wider environment? Do you have a proposal for increasing hope and therefore increasing motivation to engage with making change? If you try anything out, and it has a positive impact – share it! Let others know about what you've done; perhaps via social media, other media, word of mouth, or any other relevant options.

References

Conroy, G. (2019). 'Ecological grief' grips scientists witnessing Great Barrier Reef's decline. *Nature*, 573 (7774): 318–319.

Further reading

Could feelings of climate grief catalyse change and action? https://www.abc.net.au/religion/rupert-read-climate-grief-could-be-the-making-of-us/14076522
Eco-grief: https://en.wikipedia.org/wiki/Ecological_grief
Ecological grief as a mental health response to climate change-related loss: https://www.nature.com/articles/s41558-018-0092-2
How climate breakdown and ecological crisis is impacting wellbeing: https://www.climateandmind.org/about
How scientists are coping with ecological grief: https://www.theguardian.com/science/2020/jan/12/how-scientists-are-coping-with-environmental-grief
Solastalgia: https://en.wikipedia.org/wiki/Solastalgia
Some ideas for managing eco-grief: https://ucalgary.ca/news/eco-grief-how-cope-emotional-impacts-climate-change
What is climate grief: https://www.climateandmind.org/what-is-climate-grief

7. YOUR FUTURE MENTAL HEALTH AND WELLBEING: WHAT WOULD YOU LIKE THE FUTURE TO HOLD FOR YOU?

Time: Flexible; depending on the amount of time you wish to spend considering the questions and prompts this activity includes

Who this could be for: If you are considering what the future holds for your own wellbeing and if you want to consider what you can do now to positively impact your future mental health and wellbeing.

Resources needed: Access to the Internet if you wish to read further or research ideas and options

Why do this: this activity offers a chance to future-proof your wellbeing and to consider what you may wish to bring into your life now to benefit your medium- and longer-term wellbeing

If you have tried some of the other activities in this book, you may well have quite a lot of thoughts by now about what you might want for your own wellbeing in the future. There are some more ideas to read about in further reading to help you identify what you might want. This activity invites you to summarise your thoughts and ideas and to make some plans. You can treat it as a summary exercise to reflect on other parts of this book, or as a stand-alone exercise, as you find most useful to you. It offers some brief suggestions for generating ideas. There are other models and structures for reflecting on similar matters in this book, and you could adapt one of those to this activity if you wish.

Four suggested structures for considering your ideas for your wellbeing future:

- **Stepping stones or bridge to the future structure**
  Draw a series of stepping stones, or a bridge, that takes you from your present into your wellbeing future. What's on each stepping stone that will get you there? Or, what's the bridge made of that reaches into your future?
- **Take a leap and then look back**
  Close your eyes, and imagine taking a jump into your future. Where might you like to be and how you might like to feel in the future? Can you see yourself in a particular situation? What is the feeling associated with where and what has come to your mind? Are you sitting peacefully with, or without, others around you? Are you in a frantically exciting and busy setting? Now, look back to your present (where you've just leaped from). What steps do you need to take to get from one place to the other – with your eyes open this time?
- **Values based model**
  Identify a direction of travel for your wellbeing rather than a destination (and then enjoy the journey!)

- **Lego model**
  Can you see the components of good wellbeing for you as Lego bricks that click together to build a wellbeing-positive future for you? What is each of the bricks made of? What other component parts do you need to build the model you'd like for your future wellbeing? And are there any parts you need to unclick that will, over time, potentially reduce your psychological and/or physical health?

The structure you use to capture your ideas will depend on the type of model you use; either one of the models suggested above, or another model from elsewhere in this book or your own model. Make sure you record your ideas and check back with them to start moving towards your desired wellbeing future.

Going further

Invite others that you know to get involved in building their own wellbeing futures; can you share any ideas that you have and build on any successes?

Further reading

Exercise and satisfying relationships are the secrets to good health in later life: https://www.theguardian.com/science/2023/feb/22/exercise-and-satisfying-relationships-are-the-secrets-to-good-health-in-later-life#:~:text=Exercise%20and%20satisfying%20relationships%20are%20the%20secrets%20to%20good%20health%20in%20later%20life,-New%20research%20finds&text=Enjoying%20satisfying%20relationships%20with%20partners,old%20age%2C%20two%20studies%20suggest

Health and wellbeing across life: a preventative approach: https://www.gov.uk/government/publications/health-matters-life-course-approach-to-prevention/health-matters-prevention-a-life-course-approach

Self-compassion benefits to wellbeing across our lives: https://www.ncbi.nlm.nih.gov/pmc/articles/PMC2790748

Social relationship satisfaction and accumulation of chronic conditions and multimorbidity: a national cohort of Australian women: https://gpsych.bmj.com/lookup/doi/10.1136/gpsych-2022-100925

What effects wellbeing across our lives: https://whatworkswellbeing.org/blog/wellbeing-across-the-lifecourse-the-big-picture/

Further viewing

Byrne, D. (Talking Heads). https://www.youtube.com/watch?v=5IsSpAOD6K8

Works well with

Activity 8, Chapter 5: Where do you want to go? Where do we want to go?
Activity 9, Chapter 6: Values based living – and values based learning

8. THE WELLBEING OF THE NATURAL WORLD

Time: from 30 minutes to an extended activity over days, months, or even longer if undertaking the going further idea.

Who this could be for: Anyone who would like to think beyond human wellbeing and consider what an inclusive and holistic wellbeing plan would look like for an area of the world.

Resources needed: Depending on the extent to which the activity and going further is undertaken; from no resources (if discussing ideas with others) to any resources decided upon for the holistic wellbeing plan.

Why do this: think beyond the standard concepts of human-centric wellbeing and learning and consider a new perspective on what wellbeing means for interconnected communities and places; not just people but also animals, insects, plants, natural features in any area you choose to consider for this activity.

We may find it reasonably easy, or, if not easy, at least possible, to define what general wellbeing means for humans. What if, instead of just considering what these concepts mean for and from a human perspective, we broaden them out further? This activity and the going further ideas may raise some interesting questions, and challenge some of our assumptions about who, what and where our concept of wellbeing reaches to.

This activity asks you to consider the concept of wellbeing from a beyond-human perspective. You can either consider this idea on your own, discuss with others, or do both, and/or also work up your discussions and thoughts into a plan. Consider, discuss, and then create a wellbeing plan for one, or all (or nominate your own non-human subject) of the following subjects, from their (or its) own perspective:

- A tree
- A colony of bees
- A river
- A shoreline
- A flock of migrating birds
- An artificial neural network
- A building

Some questions to prompt your thinking (or that may arise naturally as you consider this idea):

- How would these subjects understand and describe the concept of wellbeing?
- What are they entitled to in terms of rights to good wellbeing?
- What is our role as humans in facilitating that?

- If on discussion you consider they are entitled to rights relating to wellbeing, do they currently have these? If not, why not? How could this change – what would need to happen to bring about this change (or changes)?
- What rebounds back to our own human wellbeing, if we attend to the concept of wellbeing as other, non-human subjects may experience that concept?
- How do we think beyond our own cognitive structures and assumptions to imagine what other non-human subjects may experience or require?

Our means of expressing our ideas on non-human wellbeing may need to use the languages and means of expressing used by the non-human subjects we have thought about the wellbeing of. In creating your wellbeing plan for, as an example, a colony of bees (a wellbeeing plan, of course), you may feel this would not be expressed only in words or pictures, but in sounds and movements; even dance steps.

Going further

1 If you have developed a wellbeing plan for a non-human subject, you could begin to set this up, if you have access to appropriate space; windowsill; garden; allotment; community hall; station platform; office roof.
2 Develop and implement a holistic wellbeing plan for every human, animal, bird, reptile, amphibian, fish, invertebrate, natural feature, and human-made structure in a specific area. A shared wellbeing plan underlines the position that wellbeing isn't individualistic, nor isolationist, nor merely human, but interlinked, holistic and symbiotic.
3 Consider: what difference does it make to how we live, if we hold the following to be true, and expand it beyond humans to the entirely of the world around us; "if some of us aren't OK, none of us are OK?"
4 If this activity has identified some rights the nun-human subjects you have considered should, yet currently don't, have, you could consider starting an awareness-raising activity to bring your thinking to others and encourage the rights you have identified to come into being.

Further reading

An international foundation dedicated to the wellbeing of bees: https://wellbeeing.org/

Buchmann, S. L. (2023). *What a bee knows: Exploring the thoughts, memories, and personalities of bees*. Island Press.

Chittka, L. (2022). *The mind of a bee*. Princeton University Press.

Law in the Emerging Bio Age; Law Society report that argues non-human entities need to be granted legal status, rights, and protections: https://www.lawsociety.org.uk/topics/research/law-in-the-emerging-bio-age

Lawyers for Nature: https://www.lawyersfornature.com/

Plants communicate with each other about environmental stressors above ground, through their root systems: https://journals.plos.org/plosone/article?id=10.1371/journal.pone.0195646

Rights for rivers: https://www.researchgate.net/publication/352368570_Rights_for_rivers

https://www.sciencedirect.com/science/article/pii/S2590332220300920

Stefano, M. (2023). *Tree stories: How trees plant our world and connect our lives*. Profile Books.

Why bees are essential, the UN environment programme: https://www.unep.org/news-and-stories/story/why-bees-are-essential-people-and-planet

9. MEASURING PROGRESS – AND TAKING THE PRESSURE OFF

Time: 10–15 minutes reading time

Who this could be for: anyone who has had a think about the future of wellbeing and learning and is feeling a bit overwhelmed or down as a result!

Resources needed: Internet access

Why do this: get some perspective on what future changes might or might not happen for our collective wellbeing and learning futures; reflect on whether we can really know for sure what's progress and what isn't

If thinking about the future of wellbeing and of learning in the activities in this chapter has been either overwhelming or a little depressing, then this activity offers a counterpoint to those feelings and offers a chance to reflect on whether we will be able to measure progress for our collective wellbeing and learning. Read the quotes below, which all offer different descriptions of, and ideas for managing, the pressure we might feel for answers, progress, narratives and conclusions in our lives. The writers ask us to consider that perhaps these things are less knowable, indeed even less desirable, than we might think.

Here are three different perspectives to consider on how to live in the here-and-now, and how to move into your future:

> I'm not telling you to make the world better, because I don't think that progress is necessarily part of the package. I'm just telling you to live in it. Not just to endure it, not just to suffer it, not just to pass through it, but to live in it. To look at it. To try to get the picture. To live recklessly. To take chances. To make your own work and take pride in it. To seize the moment.
> *(Didion, 1975)*

> I want to beg you, as much as I can, dear sir, to be patient toward all that is unsolved in your heart and to try to love the *questions themselves* like locked rooms and like books that are written in a very foreign tongue. Do not now seek the answers, which cannot be given you because you would not be able to live them. And the point is, to live everything. *Live* the questions now. Perhaps you will then gradually, without noticing it, live along some distant day into the answer.
> *Rainer Maria Rilke, letter to Franz Xaver Kappus, July 16th 1903*

> There's my life, why not, it is one, if you like, if you must, I don't say no, this evening. There has to be one, it seems, once there is speech, no need of a story, a story is not compulsory, just a life, that's the mistake I made, one of the mistakes, to have wanted a story for myself whereas life alone is enough.
> *(Becket, 1967)*

To aid your consideration of these ideas, watch the Kurt Vonnegut talk on the structure of stories (see further reading and resources), and read the "good luck, bad luck, who knows?" parable. What do you think of these different perspectives on our need for answers, progress, narratives and conclusions?

Going further

Consider the idea that different living beings might have different perceptions of time; creatures with a faster metabolic rate such as flies, for example, experience time more slowly (which is why they can get out of the way of a swatter so easily!) (Healey et al., 2013). Considering the potential differences in time perception, how do you think the following would measure progress in the areas of concern to them: a fruit fly; a five-year-old human; a 95-year-old human; a *Sequoia sempervirens* California Redwood tree; an octopus?

Does considering the idea of progress as it might be measured from the perspective of these other living things, change anything about your own understanding of and perspective on progress?

References

Beckett, S. (1967). Stories and texts for nothing. Grove Press.
Didion, J. (1975). University of California Riverside commencement address. Joan Didion at University of California, Riverside, 1975: The Best Commencement Speeches, Ever: NPR.
Healey, K., McNally, L., Ruxton, G. D., Cooper, N., & Jackson, A. L. (2013). Metabolic rate and body size are linked with perception of temporal information. *Animal Behaviour*, 86 (4): 685–696. https://doi.org/10.1016/j.anbehav.2013.06.018.

Further reading

Fischer, D. H. (1999). *The great wave: Price revolutions and the rhythm of history.* Oxford University Press.
Fisher, R. (2023). *The long view: Why we need to transform how the world sees time.* Wildfire.
Good luck, bad luck, who knows? https://theunitycodex.wordpress.com/2015/04/04/good-luck-bad-luck-who-knows/
Kurt Vonnegut on the shape of stories:
https://www.youtube.com/watch?v=GOGru_4z1Vc
Time perception (in human and non-human beings): https://en.wikipedia.org/wiki/Time_perception
Time perspective: https://en.wikiversity.org/wiki/Time_perspective

Works well with

Activity 8, Chapter 7: The wellbeing of the natural world

10. REFLECTIONS OF IMPACT: MAKING SENSE OF RIPPLES

Time: 10 minutes for reading the activity; potentially further time if taking the ideas within the activity further

Who this could be for: anyone who wants to reflect on how we can effect change in the world and influence both ourselves and each other in positive directions

Resources needed: no initial resources required; depending on how this activity is used, resources may become relevant, but these will be idiosyncratic to each use of the ideas in this activity

Why do this: if you want change to ripple through your world, how might you go about it? Weigh up some ideas and then have a try (if you want to)

It's a tricky thing to understand how we can impact the world in a positive way. Our collective wellbeing-learning future may however require us to understand how we can do this. Two similar starting points are described in the quotes below; firstly, by changing ourselves, our own inner world, in some way, we change how the world around us addresses us; secondly, changing ourselves is what we are left with when changing a situation is impossible.

> We but mirror the world. All the tendencies present in the outer world are to be found in the world of our body. If we could change ourselves, the tendencies in the world would also change. As a man changes his own nature, so does the attitude of the world change towards him. This is the divine mystery supreme. A wonderful thing it is and the source of our happiness. We need not wait to see what others do.
>
> *(Gandhi, 1913)*

> When we are no longer able to change a situation, we are challenged to change ourselves.
>
> *(Frankl, 2004)*

In the complicated mesh of connections and interconnections – within us between aspects of ourselves, between us and other people, and between groups of us and other groups of us – perhaps the picture becomes more complex and richer. By changing ourselves, we are also changing our collective selves; a change dropped into the interactions of us and our world may ripple out in unexpected ways.

Here is some information on some different theories relating to how to effect change in human systems. They may give you some ideas to consider for going about making change in the world around you.

The United Nations Development Group: theory of change

The UN Development Group offers a theory of change as a way of explaining how a particular intervention is expected to lead to developmental changes. It outlines important elements of a theory of change, such as consultation, basing the proposed change in evidence and continuously learning. This theory of change encourages thorough planning and consideration of the change and the identification of those who will be involved in attempting the change. It suggests approaches for analysing what change is needed, for example, via creating a "problem tree" and an accompanying "solution tree." See further reading for more on the UNDG theory of change.

Choice architecture: nudging and behavioural insights to encourage change

In 2010, the UK government set up what became known as the "Nudge Unit," a department focused on using insights into human behaviour to design policies. Using behavioural insights into how people make decisions (not always in a visibly rational manner, the theory behind the unit's work suggested), it was considered possible to create, for example, more effective policies that worked with how people tend to behave. The unit, now partly privatised and co-owned by the Cabinet Office, NESTA, and its staff, The Behavioural Insights Team describe their work as to "create and apply behavioural insights to drive positive change and help people, communities and organisations thrive" to develop "better systems, policies, products and services" by applying "an evidence-based understanding of human behaviour."

You can read more about the concepts involved; see further reading and resources. The concept of nudging raises some ethical dilemmas; how is nudging reconciled with allowing people to make their own choices, even if they are bad ones? Can this approach be fully reconciled with freedom of choice? Does the idea of addressing human behaviour unfairly return the responsibility (and blame) back to the individual, when the behaviour may have been engineered or made inevitable by poor planning and governance decisions? Who decides what direction to nudge in?

Another way of thinking about change: change through chaos

A notable feature of the two theories for effecting change considered so far is the assumption that change can be planned and considered and then proceed in a rather orderly, intentional fashion. Chaos theory has other views about this! Chaos theory does not theorise complete chaos in systems, but rather that the patterns and interactions within a system (including one under change conditions) are so intricate and dynamic that they may appear chaotic and completely random. In counterpoint to the carefully considered and planned change implementation of the first two change theories above, chaos theory in relation to change might prompt us to keep the Yiddish proverb "der mensch tracht, un Gott lacht" (man plans, and God laughs) in mind. The upside of being aware of the potential for chaos when making change is that although we might hope to be good at predicting the outcomes of our actions, in fact very often, systems are so dynamic and complex that our predictions might be wildly off course. Perhaps chaos theory might encourage us to remain flexible and responsive as we attempt to effect change, and open to the developing outcomes as they arise, rather than fighting to stick to our planned outcomes in an inflexible manner.

Going further

Having read about and considered the theories and ideas above on how change can be encouraged, take some time to consider if there is a change you would like to encourage in your life. The scale is up to you; either within your own home, or local area; within a community or institution you are part of (educational, employment, other); or on a wide scale. If you have thought of something that you would like to see change, make a plan for how you are going to go about encouraging the change. Or if you are favouring a more chaos-theory-oriented approach, perhaps ease off on the detailed planning! Is there anything in the ideas as above that you are going to draw on to help your idea for change take off? Put your plan into action and see what happens; watch the ripples!

References

Frankl, V. E. (2004). *Man's search for meaning*. Rider.

Further reading

Chaos theory: https://en.wikipedia.org/wiki/Chaos_theory
Gandhi, M. (1913). Accidents Snake-Bite, Indian Opinion. (Translated from Gujarati). The Collected Works of Mahatma Gandhi, Volumes I–XII (1884–1914). Ed. By Indian Ministry of Information and Broadcasting. (Delhi, India: [Government] Publications Division, 1958–1964). Published online by Cambridge University Press.
How to change the world: https://www.htctw.org/
Nudging and Choice Architecture: Perspectives and Challenges
Revista de Administração Contemporânea, vol. 26, no. 5, e220098, 2022
Associação Nacional de Pós-Graduação e Pesquisa em Administração
Podcast: ways to change the world https://www.channel4.com/news/ways-to-change-the-world

Thaler, R. H., & Sunstein, C. R. (November 2010). Nudge: Improving decisions about health, wealth and happiness. Cambridge University Press. UK. *Economics & Philosophy*, 26(3): 369–376. https://doi.org/10.1017/S0266267110000301

The Behavioural Insights Team: https://www.bi.team/about-us-2/

The science of chaos: https://www.popularmechanics.com/science/a41334070/what-is-chaos-theory/

The United Nations Development Group: Theory of Change https://unsdg.un.org/sites/default/files/UNDG-UNDAF-Companion-Pieces-7-Theory-of-Change.pdf

8
LEARNING TO BE WELL

Attending to the learner's physical and mental wellbeing needs to be our priority. Without the basic needs of a learner-client being met, little else towards developing a learner-client's wellbeing will happen. Physical safety, food security, nurturing sleep and exercise are, as we have seen when discussing the views of Abraham Maslow essential to good wellbeing. Maslow emphasised the importance of meeting physiological needs before the learner-client can focus on other higher level needs associated with complete wellbeing.

As a key part of promoting wellbeing, we need to remember that when a learner-client is given "permission" to address their bodily experience, they may become aware of tensions, aches and pains which will need care and attention. They may also require "catch-up" sleep. We should not be too critical and just acknowledge the body may be asking you to rest more often and to address your sleep behaviour. (Mair, 2019).

The complete learner

What worries me is that we have lost the "joy" and "awe" in learning in many cases. We need to nourish the body, mind and soul of our children and youth and one another in these trying times (Sisk, 2021).

Global infrastructure is under severe pressure and the increasing anxiety of existence encouraged by repressive governments concerned with the survival of structures that favour themselves makes humane and decent behaviour challenging. Humanity is vulnerable. As conflict increases, as the perception of reduced resources grips the wealthy and powerful, we are all in different ways and degrees traumatised, anxious as to our condition, and we may sense the light of life as a frail thing.

Who suffers most in climates such as the one we are in and the developing one we appear to be entering? Those who seek hope and those who are delighted by knowing more, inventing a positive future and expressing love and kindness through their honest and ethical actions. Within this group of frustrated decency are young people and challenged older learners who deserve better. It is not because young learners are often loaded with the burden of being "our future" which compromises their existence and sees them as a tool of others that younger learners deserve better, but because they are, they exist, they need to learn.

The standard answer is to make children attend schools, and if they are not in a school, they know nothing and are worthless. Why and by what right do we make this judgement? Why and by what right do we make children go to school and be endlessly tested? Are children cattle? Is learning a commodity? John Ruskin wrote, You do not learn that you may live – you live that you may learn (Ruskin, 1904)

1. Collectively we need to make it safe to be a child learner and to be an adult learner – to ask questions – help people understand the power of questioning and listening critically to answers when answers are available. Not every question has a clear answer. We need to learn to live with and respect ambiguity.
2. Focusing on developing, nurturing and supporting emotional resilience – wellbeing, mindfulness and emotional intelligence should be our mission. Wellbeing is our friend and healing companion.
3. Focus on nourishment – food for the hungry body – food for the hungry mind.
4. Embrace and resolve the issue of the forgotten and hidden learner – how do we embrace them and allow them to embrace learning without fear, without ethical compromise and above all without identifying them as a group that threatens existing power and/or social structures, how do we identify without making hidden learners targets for those with malign intent, who would respond by seeking to reject those identified as otherwise intelligent?
5. Create a wave of global desire to be an able continuous learner who recognises that to truly be alive is to be a constant – perpetually – resilient creature of curiosity and explorer without prejudice or jealously.
6. What do you hear yourself wanting to know – wanting to do? In addition to the considerations we have discussed in this book, we must also give attention to managing a range of predictable risks. The key principles behind "Well Learning" support, guidance and readiness to be a well-learner are not simply about the setting learning is proposed to take place in, nor the physical and psychological environment surrounding

the learner and their wellbeing. As we have discussed earlier, many factors affect how a learner and their wellbeing is supported, or is not supported sufficiently, for them become a well learner. The learner will not learn if they are hungry or if they are in fear of harm or if they are cold. Of paramount importance is the learner's demonstration of what is described as mental competence, which is generally accepted to mean that mental competency is demonstrated by an individual having the ability to understand the nature and effect of the act in which the individual is engaged.

John Holt is the first to admit that in his writing he cannot expect to speak for everyone and that he addresses a minority who recognise that children (learners) like all of us can expect to:

> ... live better, learn more, and grow more, to be able to cope with the world if they are not constantly bribed, wheedled, bullied, threatened, humiliated and hurt; if they are not set endlessly against each other in a race which all but a few lose; if they are not constantly made to feel incompetent, stupid, untrustworthy, guilty, fearful and ashamed; if their interests, concerns, and enthusiasm are not ignored or scorned; and if instead they are allowed, encouraged, and (if they wish) helped to work with and help each other, to learn from each other, and to think, talk, write, and read about the things that most excite and interest them.
> *(Holt, 1977)*

Mental competency

Here, we are specifically addressing the needs and care required affecting a young learner of 16 years and less. A child's safety and wellbeing are always paramount.

Medical definition of mental capacity

1. Sufficient understanding and memory to comprehend in a general way the situation in which one finds oneself and the nature, purpose and consequence of any act or transaction into which one proposes to enter
2. The degree of understanding and memory the law requires to uphold the validity of or to charge one with responsibility for a particular act or transaction (Merriam-Webster, 2020)
    - Teaching and Learning, Therapy and Counselling, Mindfulness and Wellbeing all have associated risks attached to them which can affect one or all who are involved in sensitive activities

- Our duty of care should address competency, liability, health and safety considerations and both individual and collective responsibility to enable the learner to be a safe and well learner

Competence is the ability to undertake responsibilities and perform activities to a recognised standard on a regular basis. It combines practical and thinking skills, knowledge and experience. The competence of individuals is vital whether as in our area of interest we are working with learner-client's risks have to be considered and addressed (Health and Safety Executive, 2022).

Gillick competency and Fraser guidelines

The Mental Capacity Act (2005) currently applies to adults aged 18 years and above. The Gillick competency and the Fraser Gillick competence were established in 1983 following a challenge to the Department of Health Guidance to allow girls under the age of 16 to access medical advice and treatment without parental consent. The original question answered by the Gillick competency and Fraser guidelines was around the use of contraception; the full ruling covers a child's own medical treatment without their parents knowing or giving permission.

In order to assess an under-16's capacity to provide informed consent, they must pass the Gillick test.

Medical professionals are required by law to consider Gillick competency if a young person under the age of 16 wishes to receive treatment without their parents' or carers' consent or, in some cases, knowledge.

Gillick competency applies mainly to medical advice, but it is also used by practitioners in other settings if for example:

- A child or young person: would like to have therapeutic support but doesn't want their parents or carers to know about it
- The child is seeking confidential support for substance misuse
- A child has strong wishes about their future living arrangements which may conflict with their parents' or carers' views (NSPCC, 2022)

Child protection concerns

There is no set of defined questions to assess Gillick competency. The child's age, maturity and mental capacity and their understanding of the issue and what it involves – including advantages, disadvantages and potential long term as listed by the WSCP in 2022 – are a clear basis to build upon determining any intervention or support when assessing a child's capacity to consent. Illustrated below are some of the questions and circumstances that need to be considered when assessing whether a child is Gillick competent or not including. Further things to consider:

- Their ability to explain their reasoning and decision making
- The levels of stress they may be experiencing
- Mental health conditions they may be experiencing
- The advantages and disadvantages of the issue they face
- Can they articulate a rationale around their reasoning and decision making? (WSCP, 2022)

    - Remember that if a young person is being pressured or influenced by someone else, consent will not be regarded as valid
    - A child may be considered Gillick competent to make one decision but not competent to make a different decision
    - When assessing Gillick competency if there are concerns about the safety of the young person, checks should be made as to whether previous child protection concerns have been raised and any factors that could put them at risk of abuse explored
    - Child protection concerns must always be shared with the relevant agencies, even if this may go against a child's wishes

Personal and institutional liability

- Providing support for learner-wellbeing clients of any age and in varied circumstances is attached to a degree of risk. The risks may be related to negligence, differing views with regard to the support and guidance produced for a learner-client. Consideration should be given to seeking advice as to appropriate insurance products that give you professional protection against claims that may be made against you.

Collective responsibility for well learning

- Effective health and safety management requires competency across every facet of an organisation and through every level of the workforce. The Management of Health and Safety at Work Regulations requires an employer to appoint one or more competent people to help them implement the measures they need to take to comply with the legal requirements (MHSWR, 1999).
- Under the Safeguarding of Children Act, all associated staff in schools must have an Enhanced DBS Check and those who are in regulated activity with children will be subject to a check of the Sex Offenders Register as part of their DBS check.

Additional factors to consider

- Learning to be well is a complex business, a challenging journey which involves the safety of all individuals involved in the journey to feel safe and secure. In your relationship with a fellow learner be sure you all have the appropriate legal protections you need for yourself as a learner, for your learner-client and for your institution.

Going further

Chapter 8 has reviewed some essentials in relation to learning to be well; there are many directions you and your co-learners could take things in from here. This is one idea to consider as part of learning to be well.

Shinrin-yoku
   Forest bathing: a natural form of nature wellbeing therapy.

Shinrin-yoku translates literally as "Forest shower" or "Forest Bathing" and is an invitation to totally immerse ourselves in the embrace of the woods. Shinrin-yoku originated in Japan in the 1980s as a response to mass urbanisation, disconnection from the land and the results of unhealthy lifestyles in large, overcrowded cities. First documented in 800 BC, the practice was carried out by Shinto practitioners.

In Japan, "therapy roads" are an essential ingredient within the philosophy of Shinrin-yoku. The original therapy roads established themselves within the profound response in Japan to the natural world. This feeling may be accessible through a response to your own particular landscape, a natural landscape with ancient woods, managed forests and working landscapes and what can only be described as magical walks.

Shinrin-yoku is a rich and meaningful response to healing and bringing a person to a state of wellbeing. Shinrin-yoku is about living in the moment, allowing your own response to the sounds and sites as you walk – becoming in tune with your natural environment and in particular trees.

Shinrin-yoku offers many benefits in increasing our sense of wellbeing:

- A perfect place for Wellbeing and Mindfulness exercises
- Improving our sleep and providing restfulness
- A wellbeing natural connection of ecological belonging
- Reduce blood pressure and stress levels
- Boosting our immune system
- Sensory attunement with our environment
- Communicating with the "other than human" world around us in plain sight
- Meeting mental and spiritual needs – a state of renewable wellbeing
- Releasing natural antidepressants
- Boosts creativity and our ability to deal with stress and trauma.

Shinrin-yoku is not simply a matter of just going for a walk – although this too is good for fitness. Physical health and mental health are both boosted after spending time in the forests.[1]

Identify the nearest forest or group of trees near to you.

Plan your walk, and consider the duration, your safety and what your main focus will be:

Smells
Sounds
Sights
Tastes
Textures

It will be challenging at first – many people suffer a disconnect from the natural word. It takes time to engage in concentration as a rewarding event.

If you do not have a forest or even a copse to enjoy being in and practicing Shinrin-yoku then create one.

Draw a forest and all the details you know make up a forest environment, and find a quiet place and imagine your walk developing a deeper sense of wellbeing and relaxation.

Remember

Pick a safe place. Be sure to let someone know where you will be and when you expect to be back from your forest bathing.
Choose a quiet time of day.
Be still and quiet.
Use all of your senses.
Calm your breathing.
Relax and enjoy your forest bathing for as long as you have available.

References

Colin, C. (2022). What is 'forest bathing' – and can it make you healthier? *The Guardian*. https://www.theguardian.com/us-news/2018/aug/22/forest-bathing-california-shinrin-yoku-nature-therapy
Health and Safety Executive. (2022). https://www.hse.gov.uk/competence/index.htm
Holt, J. (1977). *Instead of education*. Penguin Books.
Mair, D. (2019). *The student guide to mindfulness*. SAGE.
Mental Capacity Act 2005, c. 9. Available at: https://www.legislation.gov.uk/ukpga/2005/9/contents/enacted (Accessed: 4 April 2023)
Merriam-Webster. (2020). https://www.merriam-webster.com/medical/mental%20capacity
Ruskin, John (1904) Selections from the writings of John Ruskin, George Allen.
Sisk, D. (2021). Private correspondence with John Senior.
Wirral Safeguarding Children Partnership. (2022). Gillick competence and Fraser guidelines. https://www.wirralsafeguarding.co.uk/gillick-competence-and-fraser-guidelines/

Note

1 When considering the nature and value of Shinrin-yoku, it is interesting to compare it with the intent and benefits for those who undertake Pilgrimages.

Further reading

Benefits of walking on wellbeing and mental health

Appendix D. Overview of 26 Studies on Long-DistanceWalking and … 2021.
www.ncbi.nlm.nih.gov/pmc/articles/PMC8345809/Overview of 26 studies on Long-Distance Walking. 2021. www.ncbi.nlm.nih.gov/pmc/articles/PMC8345809/
Guzik, H. (2022). Pilgrimage. http://natureandtherapy.co.uk/shinrin-yoku/

Health, safety, and wellbeing in schools

https://www.gov.uk/government/publications/keeping-children-safe-in-education--2
https://www.nationaltrust.org.uk/features/what-is-a-pilgrimage
Meighan, R. (2002). John Holt: Personalised learning instead of 'uninvited teaching'. Educational Heretics Press.
Mental Capacity. (2022). Gillick competence and the Fraser guidelines. https://mental-capacity.co.uk/gillick-competence-fraser-guidelines/
Miller, J. (2019). *International handbook of holistic education*. Routledge.
National Trust. (2022). https://www.nationaltrust.org.uk/lists/a-beginners-guide-to-forest-bathing
Research on benefits of using mental imagery in influencing mood states and wellbeing: https://pubmed.ncbi.nlm.nih.gov/26412097/
Research on relaxation techniques including PGMR: https://www.ncbi.nlm.nih.gov/pmc/articles/PMC8272667/
Sherwood, H. https://www.theguardian.com/environment/2019/jun/08/forest-bathing-japanese-practice-in-west-wellbeing
Shinrin Yoku – Nature and Therapy UK. natureandtherapy.co.uk/shinrin-yoku/
Sisk, D. (2008). *Making great kids greater*. Corwin.
Statutory guidance: Keeping children safe in education. https://www.gov.uk/education/health-safety-and-wellbeing-in-schools
The Management of Health and Safety at Work Regulations 1999. UK Statutory Instruments (legislation.gov.uk)
Tolan, S. (2000). *Welcome to the Ark*. Harper Teen.

Further viewing

Sometimes overlooked as a form of exercise, walking briskly can help you build stamina, burn excess calories and make your heart healthier. You do not have to walk for hours.
University of Oxford. Wellbeing Walks
Walking for health - NHS. www.nhs.uk › live-well › exercise

APPENDIX

A guide to online mental health, wellbeing and learning provision

The world of internet provision and support for the key areas addressed in this book is huge and increases almost by the hour. At the time of writing, search results for the three main areas of interest are:

- Mental Health: 189,000,000 internet search results
- Wellbeing: 258,000,000 internet search results
- Learning: 925,032,704 internet search results

It is clearly difficult to compile a definitive list of websites that will meet precise needs and address precise situations. Only your specific searching will yield the help you are seeking. Here below are a selection of broad "starting points" for aiding your searches.

If a learner wants to learn, they should always address their basic needs. The central need in becoming a successful learner is wellbeing. The internet can provide as much information as you – a learner, therapist or teacher – require, while at the same time keeping in your thoughts and acting upon the fundamental guidance to help you succeed in achieving your goals.

Five steps to mental wellbeing

Evidence suggests there are five steps you can take to improve your mental health and wellbeing. Trying these things could help you feel more positive and able to get the most out of life.

1 Connect with other people
2 Be physically active
3 Learn new skills

4 Give to others
5 Pay attention to the present moment (mindfulness)

Mental health

Online community information resources for sharing ideas, resources and guidance:

- Anxiety UK: https://www.anxietyuk.org.uk/get-help/compassion-focused-therapy/
- Children's mental health – Every Mind Matters – NHS. https://www.nhs.uk/every-mind-matters/supporting-others/childrens-mental-health/

If you're concerned about a child or young person's mental health, you can get free, confidential advice via phone, email or webchat from the Young Minds Parents Helpline.

- Early Prevention Programmes for Mental Health – Guide for Schools. https://www.worthit.org.uk/guides-resources/intervention-prevention-school-mental-health
- Eye Movement Desensitisation and Reprocessing (EMDR): https://emdrassociation.org.uk/
- Mental Health Act. https://www.nhs.uk/mental-health/social-care-and-your-rights/mental-health-and-the-law/mental-health-act/
- Mental Health UK. https://mentalhealth-uk.org/
- Mind: Mind Infoline: 0300 123 3393
- Mind: https://www.mind.org.uk/information-support/types-of-mental-health-problems/suicidal-feelings/useful-contacts/
- Mind: https://www.mind.org.uk/information-support/tips-for-everyday-living/wellbeing/wellbeing/
- National service framework: mental health – https://www.gov.uk/government/publications/quality-standards-for-mental-health-services
- National Improvement Hub. Creativity and Wellbeing: https://education.gov.scot/improvement/practice-exemplars/creativity-and-wellbeing
- World Health Organization. https://www.who.int/westernpacific/health-topics/mental-health#tab=tab_1
- World Health Organization: Mental health: https://www.who.int/health-topics/mental-health#tab=tab_1

Wellbeing

Online community information resources for sharing ideas, resources, and guidance:

- Community Wellbeing Service
  https://www.ccp.org.uk/communitywellbeing

- Wellbeing Support | Activities & ideas | British Red Cross
  https://www.redcross.org.uk/get-help/get-help-with-loneliness/wellbeing-support
- Community Wellbeing – Inspire Wellbeing
  www.inspirewellbeing.org
- Health and wellbeing: a guide to community-centred approaches https://www.gov.uk/government/publications/health-and-wellbeing-a-guide-to-community-centred-approaches
- The King's Fund
  https://www.kingsfund.org.uk/
- Community mental health and wellbeing supports and services: framework
  www.gov.scot/publications/community-mental-health-wellbeing-supports-services-framework/pages/4/
- Services & Support | Community Wellbeing NI
  communitywellbeing.infoIsle of Man Government – Community Wellbeing Service
  https://www.gov.im/categories/caring-and-support/mental-health-service/community-wellbeing-service/Center for Wellbeing & Happiness: Center for Wellbeing
  www.centerforwellbeing.nyc
- NHS Gloucestershire ICB
  https://www.nhsglos.nhs.uk/your-health-services/healthy-communities/community-wellbeing-service/Community Wellbeing Service | Independence Trust
  www.independencetrust.co.uk Network of Wellbeing
  https://networkofwellbeing.org/improve-wellbeing-in-your-community/

Learning

Online community information resources for sharing ideas, resources and guidance:

- What Is Learning? – Verywell Mind
  https://www.verywellmind.com/what-is-learning-2795332Learning_styles
  https://en.wikipedia.org/wiki/Learning_styles
- Kolb's Learning Styles and Experiential Learning Cycle
  https://www.simplypsychology.org/learning-kolb.html
- Adult Learning Styles Explained | Dean College
- https://www.dean.edu/news-events/dean-college-blog/story/adult-learning-styles-getting-most-out-continuing-education-experienceOvercoming Adult Learning Anxiety
- https://www.ool.co.uk/blog/overcoming-adult-learning-anxiety/Ways To Manage Anxiety For Adults With Learning ... – ECL

- https://www.ecl.org/about/latest-news/blog/ways-to-manage-anxiety-for-adults-with-learning-disabilities35 Anxiety Coping Skills: A List of Effective Remedies thedawnrehab.com/blog/anxiety-coping-skills-list/
- Learning Styles & Autism – Autism Research Institute https://autism.org/learning-styles-autism/

AFTERWORD

The very purpose of life is to be happy. From the very core of our being, we desire contentment. In my own limited experience, I have found that the more we care for the happiness of others, the greater is our own sense of well-being. Cultivating a close, warm-hearted feeling for others automatically puts the mind at ease. It helps remove whatever fears or insecurities we may have and gives us the strength to cope with any obstacles we encounter. It is the principal source of success in life. Since we are not solely material creatures, it is a mistake to place all our hopes for happiness on external development alone. The key is to develop inner peace. (Dalai Lama, 2008)

We can reduce our anxiety by resolving our curiosity about ourselves and others, our past and our future. Through a focus on learning to learn, we are also happier.

> When listening is educative, teachers learn how to guide learners – not simply toward predefined answers, but toward figuring out what questions to ask, or more generally, how to productively engage with the struggle of learning. If learners are to engage in discussion in classroom learning and not become passive listeners, then teachers must learn how to differentiate what they hear. They must seek to understand how a student's response relates to how that particular student is thinking about the subject matter. This idea of educative listening in teaching thus relates to what William Hare calls "being a good listener". Hare points out that being a good listener involves judgment of what is heard and knowledge of "how to take things and what to listen for."
>
> *(English, 2013)*

According to Hare (1975), a good listener is one who is open-minded and willing to listen to the ideas and thoughts of the other person in such a way that allows those heard ideas to potentially change what the listener thinks.

Our happiness and wellbeing and the happiness and wellbeing of others are connected. Everything has a wellbeing connection. We benefit when we do things to benefit others. Our thoughts, words and actions are reflected back to us, and with a focus on resilient wellbeing, we can become emotionally and intellectually confident. We can recognise that our awareness of happiness and emotional equity for ourselves can be shared with others.

> Next to the right to life itself, the most fundamental of all human rights is the right to control our own minds and thoughts. That means, the right to decide for ourselves how we will explore the world around us, think about our own and other persons' experiences, and find and make the meaning of our own lives.
>
> *(Holt, 2004)*

We hope this book is helpful in contributing in a practical way to your learning-wellbeing effectiveness, the wellbeing and learning of those around you, and to shared emotional peace.

An afterthought

Using the activities and ideas in this book, you will have many successes and perhaps one or two challenges to resolve. With a blog, you and others could share your successes, inspiration and lessons learned about wellbeing and learning.

Share what you learn

What is a blog and why should you create one. https://blog.hubspot.com/marketing/what-is-a-blog

What makes deep listening?
https://twitter.com/CFigueres/status/1615037803167125505

What makes good eLearning?
https://timslade.com/blog/good-elearning/

References

Dalai Lama XIV. 2008. *In My Own Words: An Introduction to My Teachings and Philosophy*. Carlsbad, CA: Hay House.

English, Andrea R. 2013. *Discontinuity in Learning. Dewey, Herbart, and Education as Transformation*. Cambridge, NY: Cambridge University Press.

Hare, William. 1975. "Has Listening Had a Fair Hearing." *Agora* 3, no. 1-2: 5–13,9.

Holt, John. 2004. Instead of Education: Ways to Help People Do Things Better. Boulder, CO: Sentient Publications.
Ingvaldsen, Siri. 2017. Media and Information Literacy in Higher Education. Chandos Publishing.
Medical News Today. 2018. https://www.medicalnewstoday.com/articles/320875
Oxford Dictionaries. 2022. https://languages.oup.com/dictionaries/

GLOSSARY

ADHD   attention deficit hyperactivity disorder (ADHD) is a condition that affects people's behaviour. People with ADHD can seem restless and may have trouble concentrating and may act on impulse. NHS: Attention deficit hyperactivity disorder (ADHD) - NHS (www.nhs.uk).

Advanced Achievement Goal Therapy

- Goal Setting in Counseling and Therapy (Incl. Examples) (positive psychology.com)
- Goals Worksheets | Therapist Aid

Affective blunting   the loss of the ability to express emotions.
Alogia   the loss of the ability to think and speak fluently.
Amygdala   one of the four basal ganglia in each cerebral hemisphere that is part of the limbic system which governs our fight-flight-freeze response.
Anhedonia   loss of the ability to experience emotions.
ASMR   Autonomous Sensory Meridian Response.
Avolition   loss of the ability to initiate goal-directed activity.
Biopsychosocial model   the biopsychosocial model was first conceptualised by George Engel in 1977, suggesting that to understand a person's medical condition, it is not simply the biological factors to consider but also the psychological and social factors:

- Bio (physiological pathology)
- Psycho (thoughts emotions and behaviours such as psychological distress, fear/avoidance beliefs, current coping methods and attribution)
- Social (socio-economical, socio-environmental and cultural factors such as work issues, family circumstances and benefits/economics)

Biopsychosocial Model – Physiopedia (physio-pedia.com)

Bipolar disorder   people with bipolar disorder have episodes of depression – feeling extremely low and lethargic and mania – feeling extremely high and overactive.

Blog   a website that contains online personal reflections, comments and often hyperlinks, videos and photographs provided by the writer.

COVID   coronavirus disease (COVID-19) is an infectious disease caused by the SARS-CoV-2 virus.

Depression   depression is a low mood that can last a long time or keep returning, affecting your everyday life.

Dyadism   Noun (usually uncountable; pl. dyadisms) the tendency to categorise things into dyads or pairs; binary classification.

EMDR therapy   EMDR stands for Eye Movement Desensitisation and Reprocessing. It is a therapy used to help people recover from distressing events and the problems they have caused, like flashbacks, upsetting thoughts or images, depression or anxiety. https://emdrassociation.org.uk/

Gross Domestic Product   GDP is a monetary measure of the market value of all goods and services produced and sold in a specific time by a country or countries. https://en.wikipedia.org/wiki/Gross_domestic_product

Memory   the ability to remember information, experiences and people: https://dictionary.cambridge.org/dictionary/english/memory

- STM: short-term memory
- LTM: long-term memory

Mitochondria   Mitochondria are often referred to as the powerhouses of the cell. They help turn the energy we take from food into energy that the cell can use. But there is more to mitochondria than energy production. Present in nearly all types of human cell, mitochondria are vital to our survival. They generate most of our adenosine triphosphate (ATP), the energy currency of the cell.

Molluscs   an invertebrate of a large phylum which includes snails, slugs, mussels and octopuses. They have a soft unsegmented body and live in aquatic or damp habitats, and most kinds have an external calcareous shell.

OCD   obsessive compulsive disorder (OCD) is a mental health condition where a person has obsessive thoughts and compulsive behaviours.

Personality   personality in usage in the discipline of psychology has a specific meaning. A personality trait is an aspect of behaviour or thought that is largely unchanging over a prolonged period.

PTSD   post-traumatic stress disorder (PTSD) is an anxiety disorder caused by very stressful, frightening or distressing events. https://www.nhs.uk/mental-health/conditions/post-traumatic-stress-disorder-ptsd/overview/

Zone of Proximal Development is "the distance between the actual developmental level as determined by independent problem solving and the level of potential development as determined through problem-solving under adult guidance, or in collaboration with more capable peers" (Vygotsky, 1978, p. 86).

INDEX

active listening 137–139
active partnerships 141
activities 82
Adams, James Truslow 233
ADHD 27, 41, 202, 280
adolescents 6, 36
Advanced Achievement Goal Therapy 280
affective blunting 34, 280
afterthought 278
AI (Artificial Intelligence) 1, 11, 23, 29
Albrecht, G. 223, 229, 252
Alogia 34, 250, 280
Alvarez, A. 88
amygdala 30, 227, 250, 280
Andreasen, N. J. C. 27, 34, 35, 36
anhedonia 34, 280
anxiety 2, 10, 14, 21, 23, 27, 31–32, 42–45, 73; anxiety disorders in children 32, 36
APA, Dictionary of Psychology 24, 35
approaches to learning 14
aspects of anxiety 103
assertiveness 65–68; communication style 65, 67–68
aural (auditory) 17
Autonomous Sensory Meridian Response (ASMR) 57, 59, 280
avolition 34, 280

baby learners 10–12
baby centre 11, 35

Bach-Mortensen, A.M. 158
ball and box grief analogy 162, 164
barriers and blocks to learning 30–31
Barton, J. 143
Beck, Aaron T. 3
Beckett, Samuel 260
bees 256–257
behavioural 183–187, 262
behaviourist 13
Betthäuser, B.A. 158
Bhutan 236
Biden, J. 1, 7
biological 26, 280
biopsychosocial 4, 6; Biopsychosocial Model of Mental Health 6
bipolar disorder 27, 281
Bloom, Benjamin 21; Bloom's Taxonomy 21, 36
Bowie, D. 224–225, 231
brain fog 158, 170–173
Bringuier, J. C. 26, 35
Brown, K.W. 126
Brown, T. 240
Brown, W. 223, 229
butterfly hug 54–59
Byrne, D. 255

carers 11, 268
Carnie, F. 29, 30, 35
CBT 2–7, 21, 25, 165–167
CFT 5–7
Chambers, Bette 25, 35

Champion 4–5, 33
chaos theory 262–263
Cheung, Alan 35
child protection 268–269
children 21, 25–30, 32, 266, 268
China 33–34
client-centred approach 22
cognitive behavioural therapy 4, 7, 24
Colin, C. 271
Collins 2
compassion 5, 7, 52, 77; compassion formulation (CFT) 5,7
competency 268; mental competency 267–269
computers 10
Conroy, Gemma 252–253
Counsellors 22–23
COVID 6, 19, 64, 119, 141, 156–158; COVID-brain fog 170, 172; COVID-impacted world 158, 165; long COVID 156–158, 170–173, 179–180
creativity 27, 34; creativity and mental health 27; creative writing 28

Dalai, Llama 277–278
dark learning 145, 150–153
DBS 269; disclosure and barring service 269; enhanced 269
degrowth 229, 232, 236–237
Delphis 6–7
depression 21, 30, 91, 94, 281, 131
developing ideas 28
Didion, Joan 259–260
Dillard, Annie 238
Donaghy, Michael 142
Donald, Paul F. 230
Dryden, W. 7
Duffell, N. 34–35
Dyadism 36, 281

eco-anxiety 252
emergence 24, 26, 130–131
empathy 148–149, 168
English, A. 277
Ericsson, K. Anders 13
EMDR 59, 274, 281
emotional barriers 30
empathic understanding 22
Engzell, P. 158
environment 30
executive functions 195–202

Fadel, C. 28, 35
Feltham, C. 7
Fisher, John 187; Fisher's Personal Transition Curve 187
forest bathing 270–271
forest shower 270
Frankl, Viktor E. 261, 263
Freud, S. 19
Friere, P. 228, 231
fusion 28, 34

GAD (generalised anxiety disorder) 32
Gandhi, M. 261, 263
genuineness and congruence 22
Gestalt 24
Gilbert, P. 7, 52, 116
Gilbert Model 3 systems 5, 114, 116
Gillick competency and Fraser guidelines 268–269
glacier loss 230
Gladwell, M. 13,35
Glazzard, J. 36
Gogh, Van 27
Gollwitzer, P. 231
Gopnik, A. 10, 13, 35
GOV.UK 3, 7, 90, 94
Greenberg, J. 7, 35
Greenberger, D. 6
Griffin 21
Gross Domestic Product 232, 236
Gross National Happiness Index 236–237
Growth Mindset for Teacher 36
gut-brain 91, 94
Guzik, Helena 272
Gyarmathy, E. 9, 19, 29, 31, 36

Hattie, J. 26, 35
Health and safety Executive 268, 271
Hepple, S. 6, 7
Herschel, Lauren 162
Hippocampus 40–41
Hogarth 27
Holt, John 5, 9, 35, 267–279
Holy See 33
Hoskins, S. 36
How Babies Think 35
humanistic 14, 21, 61
humans 33, 62, 148

IAPT 141
imitation 12, 232
Ingvaldsen, Siri 279

Innerarity, D. 33, 35
insomnia 87–88
inventor's paradox 246
invisible learner 18
Ireland 141
Izzy, Garbutt 183

Jaehnig, J. 19, 35
James, W. 80, 81
Japan 142, 270, 272
Japanese 164
Jones, Jonathan 36
Juskalian, R. 32, 35

Kaufman, S. B. 15–16, 29, 35
Kaylin, Haught 142
Kierkegaard, Søren 103, 106
Kinaesthetic 17–18
Kintsugi 49, 164–165
Klein, Naomi 223
Knowles, E. 195
Knowles, Malcolm S. 221
Kolb, D. 202, 275
Kuznets, Simon 232
Kuzujanakis, Marianne 21, 32, 35

learning: behaviours 69–72; effectiveness 16; map 176–177, 193; about patterns 12; styles 14–18, 28, 35, 37
Lincoln, Abraham 150
listening 137, 149
Logan, Fiorella 240
love and intimacy 20

magical thinking 76
Mahon Derek 142
Mair, D. 20, 35, 126, 265, 271
Maslow, A. H. 19–21, 249
Maslow's hierarchy of needs 19–20
Mayer, Richard E. 240
Mcleod, S. 26, 35, 64
Meadows, Donella 237
memory 171; LTM (long term memory) 41; STM (short term memory) 41
mental capacity 25, 267–270
mental health 27–29, 251; Mental Capacity Act 268, 271; mental health and self-efficacy 1, 38–45
Merikangas, K. R. 32, 36
Merriam-Webster 267

MHSWR (Management of Health and Safety at Work Regulations) 269
microbiota 92–94
Miller, J. 272
mindfulness 123–124, 126, 267, 270
mirages 109
mitochondrial dysfunction 31
modelling 119, 238
molluscs 9, 34, 281
murmuration, of birds 205, 221
muscle relaxation, progressive 87, 99, 101, 108

Nakate, V. 228, 231
National Trust 272; National Trust for Ireland 141; National Trust for Scotland on walks 141; The National Trust on walks 141
nature (environmental) 17
Neff, K. D. 213
neuromyth of learning styles 28
New Economics Foundation wellbeing research 83
New Economics Foundation Five Ways to Wellbeing report 83, 117, 158
New Zealand Teaching Council PWPs 7
NHS: NHS advice and information for better sleep 88; NHS Digital's report, Mental Health of Children and Young People 2022 128; NHS 5 steps to mental wellbeing 117
Nin, Anais 109
Norman, Donald 196, 202
NSPCC 268
Nudging 262–263

OCD (obsessive-compulsive disorder) 281
Oettingen, G. Sevincer, A. T., & Gollwitzer, P. 231
Oliver, Mary 142
Orgasms 13

Padesky, C. 7, 122, 147, 167
Palestine, State of 33
pandemic amnesia 185
parents 268, 274
Peake, Mervyn 27
pedagogic 3, 12, 26, 182
perfectionism 31, 46–47
performance 1, 31, 43, 70–71, 92, 115
Perls, F. 24, 36

personality 19, 22, 33, 35, 126–137, 164, 235, 281
Philo, S. 19
photography 28
Piaget, Jean 24–26, 34–37
Polya, G. 247–248, 249
positive data log 122, 202, 215
Porter, Katherine Anne 36
posttraumatic growth inventory 164
pottery 28
Pound, Ezra 27
Pringle, Z. 28, 36
precontemplation 187
Pretty, J. 143
Prochaska and DiClemente's Stages of Change Model 145, 187
progressive muscle relaxation 87, 99
psychodynamic 14
psychologists 13, 26–27, 70
PTSD 32, 170

questions: closed questions 247, 249; closed-ended question 249; open questions 68, 249

Ramblers Association 141
Red Cross 147, 275
Reiss, Sally 37
relaxation techniques 95, 102, 272; Relaxation techniques from Harvard Health 102
Richter, J. P. 16, 18
Rilke, Rainer Maria 53, 259
Robinson, K. 27, 36
rock pooling 223
Rogers, Carl. 21–24, 36, 61, 137–138
Rollo, May. 105
Roosevelt, Eleanor 69, 73, 74
Roozenbeek, Saleh N. 153
Read, Rupert 229–230
Ryan, R.M. 126

Schein, E. 14, 37; organizational culture and leadership 37; Schein's model of transformative change 37
schema change processes in cognitive therapy 24, 122
schizophrenia 27
self-actualization 18, 21, 26
self-directed learning 73, 195–197, 206
self-educators 9
self-efficacy 38

Seligman, L. 7
Senior, J. 29, 31, 36
Serotonin 30, 92
Sevincer, A. T. 231
sex 13, 20, 269
Shakespeare 88
Shallice, Tim 196, 221
Shatner, William 223
Shen, Wangbing 36
Sherwood, Harriet 272
Shinrin Yoku – Nature and Therapy UK Shinrin-yoku 272
Simpson, A. 7
Sisk, D. 10, 36, 265, 271
Skinner B. F. 19, 35
Slavin, Robert E. 35
sleep 81; Sleep Charity 88; sleep hygiene 84, 88
smartphones 154
smells 271
social (interpersonal) 17
social anxiety disorder (SAD) 32
Socrates 17, 19, 36, 234
Solastalgia 223, 229, 252, 253
soul 265
spiritual intelligence 10
Spoons theory 179–180
starling murmuration 206
Sternberg, R. 8, 36
Stott, R 165
suicide 6
Switzerland 33

Taiwan 34
Tang, Zhiwen 36
TASC 144–145, 153
task initiation 198, 202
tastes 58, 108, 271
teacher wellbeing 1, 7
teenagers 159
textures 57, 108, 271
Thaler, Richard H. 264
therapists 1, 5, 8–9, 11, 15, 21, 31
thinking styles 75
Third Wave 225–226
three-systems model of emotional regulation 116
Thunberg, Greta 228, 231
time capsules 191
Toffler, A. 225–226, 231
Tolan, S. 272
traffication 230
transition curve, Fisher's 187

uncertainty 187, 243–244
unconditional positive regard 22, 61, 64
UNESCO 152, 158–159, 181–183
United Nations 33, 119, 152, 262, 264
Uscinski, Joseph E. 153–154

VARK 18, 37; VARK learning styles 18
Verbal (linguistic) 17
Vince, Gaia 230
Vinci, Leonardo da 18
Visualisation 41, 50, 99, 125, 205, 208, 220, 243
Voluntary Service Overseas 120
Vygotsky, L. S. 193–194
Vygotsky's zone of proximal development 193–194

Wadsworth, B. J. 37
Walker, Matthew 88
walking and wellbeing 141, 272

Wallace, Belle 61, 64, 144, 233
Wei Lun Koh, Aloysius 240
wellbeing and learning 92, 157
Wilde, Oscar 19, 36
Wolters, Christopher 70, 73
Woolf, Virginia 27
World Health Organization 15, 274
WSCP (Wirral Safeguarding Children Partnership) 269
Wu, Tim 154, 206

Xing, Qiang 36

Yoku 141, 270–272

Zhao, Rongium 28, 36
Zone of Proximal Development (ZPD) 193–194, 281

For Product Safety Concerns and Information please contact our EU representative GPSR@taylorandfrancis.com
Taylor & Francis Verlag GmbH, Kaufingerstraße 24, 80331 München, Germany

www.ingramcontent.com/pod-product-compliance
Lightning Source LLC
Chambersburg PA
CBHW070301240426
43661CB00057B/2610